cG

Catherine Paton was born in Hamilton, Lanarkshire in 1946, and married Doug Black when she was nineteen. After a series of jobs, Doug became a coal miner in 1974 and worked at Bevercotes pit for the next decade. After becoming a mum to five children, Catherine joined Bevercotes colliery herself, working in the canteen to serve miners breakfast, lunch and dinner. During the great strike in 1984, Catherine was one of the few female official picketers when she joined her husband in the fight to stop the pit closing under the Tory Government.

Catherine now lives with Doug and their two Westie dogs in Ollerton, another former pit village, where a giant Tesco now stands where the Ollerton pit once was. The couple have twelve grandchildren, and one great grandchild on the way. Catherine hopes this book will keep the pit spirit alive.

At the Coalface

CATHERINE PATON BLACK

headline

First published in 2012
by HEADLINE PUBLISHING GROUP

1

Cataloguing in Publication Data is available from the British Library

ISBN 978 0 7553 6325 4

Typeset in Adobe Garamond by Palimpsest Book Production Limited,
Falkirk, Stirlingshire

Printed and bound in Great Britain by
Clays Ltd, St Ives plc

Headline's policy is to use papers that are natural, renewable and recyclable
products and made from wood grown in sustainable forests. The logging and
manufacturing processes are expected to conform to the environmental regulations
of the country of origin.

HEADLINE PUBLISHING GROUP
An Hachette UK Company
338 Euston Road
London NW1 3BH

www.headline.co.uk
www.hachette.co.uk

This book is dedicated to all the miners and their wives who went on strike.

Acknowledgements

With many thanks to my ghostwriter Shannon Kyle, my agent Diane Banks, and my children Susan, Lorraine, Carrie and Allan for all their help.

Chapter One

My first memory, aged two, was shrieking at my mum, Mary. The poor woman was only trying to get a styrene suit on me, an old-fashioned all-in-one to keep out the harsh Scottish winter, but I wasn't having any of it. My baby sister, also Mary, had just arrived and my tantrums were born out of jealousy. Mum bonded with her in ways I never had. But in many ways I didn't care. After all, I lived with my beloved paternal grandparents, Kate and Jock, who were like a surrogate mum and dad to me.

Born in their cosy house in Burnbank, Hamilton, near Glasgow in Scotland, Grandma and Grandad always said I felt like their own from the start. Their son, my father, George, was a drunk gambler, always looking for a quick buck to pour down his throat, and my mum suffered a heart condition all her life and struggled to cope. Luckily my grandparents stepped into the breach and became my heroes.

Grandma was a lovely woman with a knot of grey hair tied at the back of her head. She was always smiling and teaching me things. Thanks to her I became a dab hand at making pastries, delicious warming soups and any cake you can think of. Her kind, patient voice filled the kitchen as she explained how to knock up something out of nothing, always letting me lick the spoon or bowl. It was a good job she did love cooking too, as Grandad could certainly put it away. After she'd make an apple pie he'd sit down and cut a slice – then take the rest for his own plate, making us laugh out loud.

Grandad's appetite was as big as his character. Standing at 6' 4" in his socks, he towered over me, and made me feel warm and protected with his big bear hugs. And didn't my poor mum know it. After spending my formative years in my grandparents' spare room, I was devastated when Mum moved us out to a house down the road, begging for visits with them as often as possible. Every weekend, Dad would sit me on a cushion on the handlebars of his bike and cycle me there. Once I was dropped off, I didn't give him a backward glance as I ran full pelt towards the familiar green door. Quickly it was opened and into Grandad's open arms I'd dive.

'I'm home!' I'd yell. 'What we having for tea?'

Although I shared the same mop of dark hair and bluey-green eyes as my mum and sister, it was my grandparents' house where I felt I belonged. This must have been hard on my mum. One day, as Friday evening finally arrived and I bounced up and down with excitement at the prospect of another visit, Mum's face darkened.

'You love your grandparents more than you love me,' she said, sadly.

'Yes I do!' I giggled, with no understanding or care for the pain my words caused.

Looking back, my heart goes out to my poor mum. She had a lot to put up with, what with Dad's drinking and her own medical complaints. Over the years she had several pioneering open-heart operations at Glasgow Hospital to stretch her heart valves, including having them replaced with pig valves, then tin and then plastic. She also volunteered to be examined by other young doctors to help with their training. After her many ops she'd come home looking exhausted and drained. Often she'd return to a cold house with little food in it, as Dad was hopeless managing without her.

'He can't even keep coal in the grate,' Mum moaned. And she was right. We were always running out, and Dad could rarely afford to restock it.

Living on the other side of us was a bachelor called Hugh, who worked down in Cardowan pit. A busy miner, he'd get free coal on a weekly basis. We'd watch out the window as a coal truck pulled up like clockwork to deliver a load to Hugh, whereas we would be sitting in the cold, thanks to 'your useless father', as Mum would call him. In desperation she'd send us out with Dad and a wheelbarrow to pinch the 'gum' – the leftover slack from the heap in the old pit. Back home we'd take the powder into the kitchen and fashion egg-shaped pellets out of it with our hands to burn in the grate.

For all the difficulties Mum never complained. Whenever she could she'd play with us kids. Taking down the washing line, she loop it high into the air so Mary and I could skip to our hearts' content. We never had any inkling of how serious Mum's heart problems were and how she should have been resting. All we knew was Mum disappeared to hospital every now and then and I was quite content to be staying overnight at my grandparents'.

My wee sister Mary took great delight in teasing me when Mum got home, chanting: 'You don't belong here, Cathy.' And she was right. Although whenever Mum wanted anything doing, she never hesitated calling for me. If she was laid up in bed, I'd end up rushing home, to do the washing, cooking and cleaning, while Mary got to play outside the window. Mum relied on me but I didn't feel she treated me the same. She was always leaning on me and didn't let me get away with just being a kid like Mary was.

'Why don't you ask Mary?' I would complain.

The lazy minx would be skipping outside without a care in the world or nattering with her school friends while I was up to my elbows in soapsuds or changing the beds.

'It's not fair!' I'd shout at my mum.

'But you're the eldest,' she'd sigh.

There were other inequalities in the family, too. Even at a very young age, I registered the stark difference between Grandad and Dad, despite the fact they were father and son. While Grandad went to work every day, Dad never had any money and his hot breath would constantly stink of beer. Grandad was always immaculate in his suits and ties and shiny shoes, whereas Dad seemed to roll out of bed and pull on the first thing he found, whether it matched or not. Grandad even helped the rest of the street stay smart, by offering to cut the local lads' hair for a shilling every Sunday and cobbling people's shoes. Dad always looked like he'd been dragged through a hedge backwards.

Dad was still my dad though and I loved him all the same. I was his favourite, as he knew he could get to my grandparents through me.

'Go and ask Grandma for ten bob for us, Cathy,' he would wheedle.

'No!' I'd cry, refusing to be blackmailed. I was a tough

nut compared to my petite baby sister. I was the son Dad never had. He taught me how to fight and held my head away with his hand while I tried to punch him. I loved the rough and tumble.

Unlike my dad, Grandad was a grafter, and worked his whole life. Among his many jobs he collected the money from the gas meters. He'd come home clinking, carrying bags heavy with pennies. We'd sit for ages at the kitchen table, counting and scooping the coins into bags. Eventually he got copper poisoning in his hands from handling the money all day long.

As a family it was the cinema that occasionally brought us together. Mum sometimes worked as an usherette and got cheap tickets. Dad loved any films about boxing and of course all the old favourites featuring stars like Cary Grant and Clark Gable. It was only in the silence, watching the screen, that we sat contently as a family for a few hours.

But the celluloid lives of the Hollywood stars were a world away from my own. Although I was a bright child who knew how to count, read and cook very quickly, I didn't care for school and lessons. I found it boring. Besides, from a young age, us girls knew our fates. We'd grow to be wives and mothers like our mums and maybe get a job in a factory if we had to. That was our lot in life and we didn't know any different. No one sat down and talked about other 'options'. It never occurred to me there might be any.

When I was eleven, I came down with a terrible bout of Asian flu. As ever, my grandma welcomed me into her home with open arms to care for me in their spare bedroom upstairs while Mum worked. She'd sit and hold a cold flannel to my head to reduce the temperature and do anything to try and tempt me to eat. On her fingers she'd go through every single item in her cupboard to try and find something to keep my strength up. As soon as I showed any interest, she'd shoot off to make it for me.

'Have some just for Grandma,' she'd say, trying to spoon a little something in.

Some nights I was delirious and saw balloons bursting in front of my eyes. She'd hold me as I shivered one moment and impatiently threw my bedclothes off, drenched in sweat, in another.

'My poor Cathy,' she'd soothe, holding me close. I loved her smell of soap. As much as my grandad's smell of tobacco.

Even though I was so unwell, I could sense my grandma was also struggling. She looked tired, and unsteady on her feet. Grandad told her she was doing too much, and tried to take over looking after me too. However ill I felt, having those two around gave me the most incredible feeling of safety and comfort. I knew I'd be OK.

A few weeks later, as I was now feeling a bit better, Grandad carried me downstairs and Grandma made up a bed on the settee for me to convalesce. As Grandma plumped up the cushions for me we heard the 'ting-ting' of the ice-cream van's bell.

'Ooh, let me get you one of those, it'll soothe your throat,' Grandma said.

My appetite slowly returning, I agreed that a vanilla cone with raspberry ripple might go down a treat. Grandma flashed me a smile as she made her way out of the living room, wobbling a little as she went. A few minutes later, Grandma still wasn't back but a neighbour was banging on the door. I could hear Grandad's concerned voice, and heavy footsteps on the stairs.

Struggling up, I tried to see what was happening but the room was spinning.

'Go back and lie down Cathy,' Grandad ordered, his tone hushed. 'There's nothing to see.'

Out of the window I saw him half-carrying Grandma, her eyes rolling in her head, her face blackened with bruising. I heard him telling someone that Grandma had fallen outside, hitting her head on the gate-post.

'She'll be right as rain in the morning,' Grandad was saying. 'Thank you for helping.'

The next day, though, Grandma wasn't up making breakfast. Instead Grandad creaked up and down the stairs to her bedroom, taking trays of uneaten plates of toast back down. His face looked pinched with worry. The house felt so empty and quiet.

Finally I managed to get upstairs myself, my head still light and empty with a mild fever. 'Grandma,' I whispered, scared. She looked so small and sunken in the pillow. 'It's Cathy.'

Her eyes opened into two slits, her pupils barely focused. 'Do you need anything?' I said.

'Nae,' she replied, her eyes drooping back shut.

As I was growing stronger, Grandma seemed to grow weaker, her bruised face now almost black, her breathing quiet. Grandad just kept saying he knew she'd be all right. Then I heard more hushed voices and more footsteps. There was a doctor's visit and then an ambulance arrived and Grandma was gone.

'She needs hospital care now,' said Grandad, patting my arm. 'Then she'll be home. Right as rain.'

Mum went to see her and asked if I could go a few days later.

'Shall I fetch Cathy for a visit?' she'd said to Grandma, holding her hand.

'Yes,' Grandma replied. And that was her last word. Before Mum had a chance to take me to see her, she died on 29 October 1957 of a brain haemorrhage.

Dad broke the news. For once he was sober. He came

into my bedroom while Grandad stayed at the hospital, gently took my hands in his and said: 'Your Grandma has passed on.'

Shaking like a leaf, the tears streamed endlessly off my face. I couldn't comprehend it. 'No,' I replied. 'No, no . . .'

Grandad came home later, quietly. He sat in his chair and stared at the wallpaper. His wireless, that usually filled the room with canned laughter or music, stood silent. I crept in. The ticking clock and our breath were the only sounds.

'She's gone,' he said, simply.

We sat for what felt like ages, saying nothing, just absorbing the emptiness of the house and our hearts. Breathing in the sweet smell of tobacco that clung to his clothes, I hoped as hard as I could everything would turn out all right.

Grandma was buried on Halloween night, 31 October 1957. Kids weren't encouraged to go to funerals back then, so I was sent to my pop's house, my mum's father, on the other side of Glasgow for the day.

Pop was a miner at Douglas Water mine, having joined up when he left school. He and his wife, also called Mary, had thirteen children, one of them being my mum. We weren't close though, as we lived too far away for us to visit him often. Pop didn't speak much to his own kids, let alone his grandchildren. His wife had died when my mum was fourteen, so Pop lived with his youngest sons. It was very much a boys' house and girls were rather sidelined.

That evening, watching his blackened face appear at the front door, I had my first insight into the world of coal mining. I knew he worked in a pit, but had never seen him come home for his post-work bath before. It was a revelation.

Covered from head to foot in black soot, all I could see were the whites of his eyes and his teeth. Leaving his shoes at the door to avoid footprints, he shouted to one of his youngest sons to run him a bath. I was shooed out of the room as his back was scrubbed pink again with a bristle brush.

'Harder please, lad,' I heard him order.

Then he sat down with a cup of tea, easing himself into his armchair and making an 'Eeee' of relief through his teeth.

Pop never spoke much. To me, the pit to which he disappeared was as mysterious as he was. He was a masculine character who did man's work in a man's world. Even though I saw very little of him, I sensed it was a hard life. He'd always look exhausted, his eyelids heavy and his eyelashes thick and black as if he wore mascara. I later learned this was known as the 'mark of a miner'. However hard miners scrub, they can never lift the soot caught in between their lashes.

Within days of the funeral, my family had had a meeting about what should happen to Grandad, who seemed like a broken man. It was decided I could go and live with him permanently, a decision that I was more than happy with.

Grandad never spoke of Grandma again. If anyone – usually my dad – mentioned her, he fell very quiet, staring at the floor with his mouth twisted in pain, so I learned never to speak of her either. I just concentrated on cheering him up, and looking after the big man, just like my grandma had done so well.

I took on all the cooking and cleaning around my school lessons while Grandad carried on working. He liked looking after me just as much, too. Every morning he'd knock on my bedroom door holding a tray bearing a bowl of steaming porridge, some toast and an egg, so that I could have breakfast in bed. There wasn't a choice about my plate being cleared or not!

I loved cooking for Grandad although there were some meals I couldn't eat myself. Even now my stomach grimaces a little at the thought of his favourite pigs' trotters or old-fashioned ribs. He loved his meat. He also picked up the mantle of Grandma's lessons and showed me how to skin a rabbit and clean and gut a chicken.

Meanwhile I'd treat him to his favourite dinners that Grandma used to make, like toasted cheese and potatoes, stew and mince – and of course my speciality, heart-warming soups so thick you could stand your spoon up in them. Whenever he was pleased with something I'd done, Grandad's face broke into the biggest of grins.

'I'll dance at your wedding,' he'd quip. Or: 'You'll no see what I'll give you.' And I never did, as he never did buy very much, but he was a character all the same with his funny wee sayings. We might have lost Grandma but we still had each other.

By the time I was fifteen, I wasn't interested in school one little bit and left without a backward glance or any exam passes. In fact I didn't even take any exams and refused to contemplate college. Some folk told me I'd regret it, and that I should at least try, but back then few people saw the point of learning after school. Girls knew their destinations would be factory work and then marriage; it was a given and the only choices available at that time.

I got a job working in a factory building electrical fans. It was piece-work so we were only paid for what we made. This sounded like a completely fair deal, except however hard we worked we often didn't make a bean. The fans were fiddly to make and when we checked the insides the wires broke all too easily when they were tested. After chatting to some of the other girls, we soon realised that many of us were working for nothing, as the wires broke on a regular basis no matter how careful we were with them.

Little did I know this would be my first taste of an industrial dispute! Always the first to speak my mind, I was angry we were working all day for absolutely nothing.

'This isn't fair,' I raged to one of the girls. 'I think we should organise a strike.'

They all laughed, thinking I was mad. But I was deadly serious. The company was obviously doing very well and we were making most of the machines. It was only the wire process that seemed to go wrong.

I stormed upstairs to see the manager. 'We're going on strike,' I announced proudly. 'This wire situation means we end up working for nowt, and that's not on.'

'Who's on strike?' asked the manager, peering through the door behind me.

'We are!' I cried, pointing at the room next door. 'All us girls.'

Luckily for me, he had a sense of humour, listened to my concerns and moved me to another production line. The strike never happened, but the seed had been planted. Even the lowliest paid worker had a voice if they wanted to use it. Little did I know it was a principle I'd stick to much later on in my life.

Meanwhile I was growing into a young woman, though I had few opportunities to exercise any real freedom. To look at the portrayal of the swinging sixties on TV programmes you'd think every teenager in the country was dancing around in mini skirts with flowers in their hair, listening to beat music all day long. This may have been true for a few lucky ones in London, but life in Hamilton, Scotland, couldn't have been further from that image. The vast majority of us were just scraping a living, and as far as our wardrobes were concerned we made do and mended. My favourite items were a lemon Charleston dress with a fitted waist and tiny pleats and a felt dress with underskirts I used to stiffen with sugar. Free love was also the last thing on our minds. Pregnancy out of wedlock was of course hugely frowned upon so us girls would hold back for as long as possible. When you started seriously dating a boy it was pretty much a given you'd get married, so I was always careful about who I chose to step out with.

Every week I went to the local Co-operative shop to stock up on fresh butter, milk and bacon for Grandad. The boys behind the counter would weigh out the butter and pat it together with wooden paddles or slice out the bacon depending on how thick you wanted it, all while they asked how your day was going. The shop had only just done away with the old-fashioned pneumatic tubes that propelled money along them, and it was the start of 'self service'. Two young men, Gordon and his younger brother Douglas Black, both of whom shared the same sandy-coloured hair, chocolate-brown eyes and cheeky smiles, would often vie to serve me first.

I had a craic with both of them, joking along or chatting about work as they weighed out my groceries. Then one day Gordon grew serious and quietly asked me for a date.

I didn't hesitate to shake my head. He was a nice enough lad, but it didn't feel 'right'. There was no chemistry. Plus he was a bit too young for me. He nodded quietly, and went off to serve someone else, his cheeks slightly flushed. But I couldn't be anything other than honest.

A few weeks later, I was back at the Co-op, about to pay for my goods at the till, when I reached into my back pocket to find the fiver I'd put there had disappeared.

'Where the blazes has that gone?' I said out loud. Grandad would kill me if I'd lost it.

Suddenly Gordon's brother Doug was by my side, beaming away, holding out a five-pound note. 'Looking for this, Cath?' he laughed.

I snatched it back. 'You cheeky bleeder!' I cried.

It was the start of a constant banter between us. One week, he began taking the mickey out of me for being small and for a joke he picked me up by my jacket and hung me on a peg for a moment or two.

'That'll keep you out of trouble,' he laughed as I kicked my legs like a toddler.

'I'll get you for this, Douglas Black!' I shrieked with laughter.

He did make me giggle, even if he went too far sometimes. We started flirting a bit and eventually he asked me out. This time I said, 'Yes please.'

Later Doug revealed that the girl in the sweet shop section had told him she'd overheard Gordon ask me out, spurring him into action.

'I had to have you for myself,' he laughed.

Off we went to the pictures to see *King of Kings*, starring Rip Torn, for our first date. In the dark, he reached for my hand. Giving it a little squeeze I felt a tingle up my spine. He was such a lovely-looking chap and he appeared to like me just as much as I liked him.

Soon we were meeting twice a week for a date. There wasn't a right lot to do in Hamilton so we mainly went for walks in the park or to the pictures. We also loved playing records. Unusually for a lad at this time, Douglas loved opera and introduced me to all the greats. In particular he liked Beniamino Gigli and even today listening to him reminds me of our young courtship. I preferred the Everly Brothers and the Beach Boys, and I loved Jim Reeves. Grandad had bought me a small record player in a vanity case, and let's just say it was put to some use.

Sometimes we went up to Denison Pally, a dance hall in Glasgow, to watch a live band play covers of the Beach Boys or Helen Shapiro and other popular songs. We may not have had much money, but any spare cash we did have we knew how to have fun with. Like two pieces of a jigsaw we matched each other, despite the fact we were complete opposites. I was more forthright and outspoken than my laid-back, easy-going, funny Douglas. But how we laughed together, over silly things.

'You're the top of the pops, you are,' he would say, picking me up to go to a dance or the pictures. Looking into his big chocolate-brown eyes made me feel as if I'd come home.

Chapter Two

Grandad met Doug a few weeks later. Before he asked him his name or even said 'Hello' he took one look at him and said: 'What colour are you?'

I expected this as we were Protestants (associated with the colour blue) and under no circumstance were we allowed to mix with Catholics (green). Straight away, his back as stiff as a rod, Douglas answered: 'Blue', and the pair of them smiled and shook hands.

It must have been hard for poor Grandad to see his granddaughter – his little girl – with a man, but he never said a word. He always let Douglas come in for a cup of tea after our date and he was very friendly towards him. He also kept a close eye on me too, mind. Once Douglas leaned in for a sly kiss on the front door to say goodbye when we both heard Grandad bellowing from the window upstairs.

'In. Now!'

He'd been watching our every move.

Not that we could get away with much in any case with neighbours like ours. The term 'curtain twitchers' didn't touch it, as they were constantly looking over fences and making comments about the comings and goings of other folk. Everything was everyone else's business.

One lady, Doris, was especially bad. She looked and sounded just like the Les Dawson character, Cissie Braithwaite, who was always sour-faced and passing sweeping judgements on other people's lives. I got sick of it. Then one day, I overheard she'd been gossiping that I was actually pregnant.

So me being me, I decided to play up to this. I borrowed a pregnancy smock off someone I knew, and went outside to hang the washing when I knew Doris would be out watering her garden. I leaned over, holding my back while picking up the pegs, as I'd seen pregnant ladies do. I had to concentrate hard not to laugh. From the corner of my eye I could see Doris doing a double take and then rushing inside, to spread malicious gossip about me, no doubt.

The next day, around the same time, I pulled on my tightest-fitting pair of jeans and a tiny top, again to put the washing out. Now, miraculously, I was no longer looking pregnant. This time Doris moved closer to the fence before shooting back indoors, obviously baffled.

Chuckling to myself, I vowed to carry the joke on for

as long as possible, so the next day I waited until I spotted Doris outside before popping the smock back on again as I took the washing in.

This time Mum spotted me from the window of her house. And she wasn't impressed. 'Cathy! What the heck do you think you're playing at?' she yelled. The show was over then, but I hoped it was a proper lesson for Doris.

The irony was, while Doris had her eye on me, she wasn't watching her own teenage daughter who fell pregnant that year to the shame of her family.

'Well, if folks just kept an eye on their own . . .' I said to everyone who'd listen.

Meanwhile, as our relationship grew more serious, I met Doug's family. His mum had already died so he lived with his dad and brothers. He was one of nine boys and two girls. James, the eldest, died after he was born, and was then followed by Harry, Archie, John, Tommy, Jimmy, Malcolm, Iain, Gordon, and then Irene and Anne. Doug was the youngest. All the boys except for the three youngest worked in pits across the area as underground men for most of their working lives.

His father, Thomas, started in a mine aged twelve. He worked right up until he was fifty-five, clocking up an impressive four decades underground. At the time I met Doug, Thomas was working as a deputy at the Cardowan pit in Lanarkshire, and he knew Hugh, Mum's neighbour.

Growing up in a busy household full of miners meant Doug saw first-hand every day what life in the pit was about. For every schoolboy, a miner was akin to a hero and it was seen as the place where big, strong men worked. But Doug was also all too aware of the hardships his brothers suffered.

Every morning he'd wake up to hear the sound of hobnail boots pounding the path in front of the house. At the end of the day shift and the start of the night shift he'd hear them dashing home. After school Doug and his brother Gordon would run outside and cry: 'Got anything for us?' to see what leftovers they had in their sandwich boxes, known as piece tins. As growing lads they were always hungry, looking for an extra mouthful.

Working conditions in the pits in the 1940s and 50s were primitive. Before the modern machines arrived, Doug's father and his brothers were at times quite literally going at parts of it with a pick-axe. Sometimes they sat in coal seams just two feet high, with running water at their feet. They were all injured at some point. It was par for the course. You worked in a mine; you risked life and limb.

Douglas grew up watching his brothers rise at an ungodly hour to return home much later completely exhausted and filthy. His brothers all had a constant, sickly pale pallor, due to the lack of sunlight and bad ventilation. They came home with hacking coughs but rarely took a day off sick.

His dad was the 'Oversman', their boss, but instead of showing his sons any signs of favouritism he came down on them like a ton of bricks, forcing them to cut more coal than the other lads or shouting at them to work harder. Sometimes the tensions were brought back home afterwards.

One day when Doug was just eleven, Malcolm, then twenty-one, came home, crying in agony. A blood-splattered bandage was wound around his hand and he'd been in hospital. He'd lost two fingers with the cutting machine. It wasn't a case of 'if' you have an accident, it was almost 'when'.

Poor Malcolm had not only lost his fingers, but he was terrified at what his dad would say when he found out he'd been so badly injured. Thomas wasn't one to suffer any fools gladly, even if it was a genuine accident, which in Malcolm's case it certainly was. Unable to go on in the pit, Malcolm quit on the day it happened and went off to find himself a job as a farmhand nearby. His fingers never healed properly and he was left with an ugly bunion lump.

It was also the days before electric lamps. They used paraffin to light their helmets. Once Jimmy thought he was being helpful when he filled his dad's water bottle with paraffin and had to run away for a few hours when he heard his dad gagging as he made the discovery!

Doug, Gordon and Iain were the only brothers who

didn't go down the mine at fourteen. Their dad and brothers told them they weren't to, either. His dad was especially aggressive in his stance. Desperate to protect his youngest sons from what life had in store as a miner, he'd stand over Doug if he ever overheard him mention the pit and wag his finger in his face, threatening him.

'I never want to hear you say you'll be joining them,' he'd growl. 'Ever! You find something better to do with your life. The pit is no place for no one with half a brain.'

Although he was as hard as nails on his older sons, his father had softened towards his younger boys. He wanted a different life for them.

Seeing and hearing stories of the injuries, and having his father so dead set against it, left Doug with absolutely no desire at all to follow in the family footsteps. Straight after school, he joined the Co-op, hoping he'd have a job for life. But a few months into our courtship he was let go. The self-service supermarket industry, in which customers picked up products themselves, had slowly taken over and large numbers of shop assistants serving customers were no longer needed.

That evening he went home to tell his dad, who told him what was to happen next.

'You'll be up at 4 a.m., you'll take a sandwich and a bottle of water, and you won't come home till you've got some work,' he ordered.

So that's what Doug did. He walked miles from farm to farm in the area, knocking on doors, offering to do any available job, until eventually someone gave him one.

Despite this setback, our courtship grew more intense and Doug and I became inseparable. We started to spend weekends together at his brother Archie's house in Cardowan. He'd invite along his friends and other brothers until the house was full. We'd be twenty people to a small room, all having a sing-song, or telling stories or even poems. Sometimes the boys would do their party pieces. Archie loved to show off with his mate called Dixie Dean. The pair of them, two hard men who'd built huge biceps from working at the coalface, would sit in the middle of the floor, holding a half-inch steel rod, then pull it so hard it bent in two. Other times people would bring a big salmon they'd fished from the River Earn and the winner who guessed the weight would get an extra drink. I'd often get it correct but was never allowed to drink any of the sherry, whisky and beer on offer, as I was still only fifteen.

Doug and I were happy enough, just being together. But the practicalities of life couldn't be ignored. Doug's job working for a pittance as a farmhand came to an end. He got seasonal work over Christmas at the Post Office but when that ran out he started to get desperate.

'I just don't want to sign on,' he complained. Signing

on the dole was for wasters and no-hopers and Doug didn't want to go there. There was shame for being on the social. I didn't blame him for not wanting to take that path. But this left almost no other options for working in the area. Except for the army.

Doug had already been in the RAF cadets, so I always knew it was on the cards for him to join up. I just didn't like to think about it. I'd miss him terribly if he went away. After a year of us dating, he suddenly turned up at my house, saying he needed a word.

'I have signed up, Cath,' he said, looking heartbroken.

'What?' I spluttered.

Turned out, that day, he'd gone to sign up for the dole, for the first time. He'd not worked for over a week and didn't have a penny to his name. But as he approached the dole office, the queue was four people wide. There and then, he decided he'd try the Territorial Army office and join up.

Seeing a fit, healthy, eager young man coming through the door, the army recruitment officer didn't waste a moment. As soon as he gave his name and address, they gave him a medical on the spot, a quick grammar and arithmetic test, and then he was whisked off to sign his life away to the forces. Straight away he was also paid: £3, 7d (32p) – not a fortune, but better than the dole and much better than nothing. They asked him if he could leave for training that very afternoon, but Doug had told the officer he'd wanted to see his girlfriend first.

As he kept talking, I felt myself getting choked with tears. It felt like my world had come crashing down. Doug was going! Tomorrow!

'But, but . . .' I kept stuttering. When would I see him again? When would he come home? What if he were sent to a war zone?

He did his best to comfort me, looking as sorry as I did.

'You know the situation, Cath,' he said sadly, holding my hand tightly. 'If we wanted to get married one day, you don't want me sat on the dole.'

'Aye.' I shook my head, wiping my face. 'Money comes before any love story in this case, for sure.' We sat and hugged each other. Tonight he'd pack his case and tomorrow he'd start twenty-two weeks' training down in Farnborough. It was unavoidable and we'd get through it.

I soldiered on myself in the factory, writing to Doug every single day, as he did me. We also called each other at allotted times. I'd run to the call box at the end of the road, timing it perfectly for when Doug had told me he'd ring, or I'd do the same for him. A couple of times the sergeant picked up the phone when I was expecting it to be Doug and he wasn't amused. Finally the long wait

27

came to an end, and I went to see Doug pass out as a sapper of the Royal Engineers.

For his big day, I splashed out on a green printed dress and new high heels to wear for Doug's parade and the army church service afterwards. Filled with excitement, I caught a coach from Hamilton to Victoria station in London, before getting a train on to Farnborough. But as I walked away from the station, I realised I'd left my high heels on the train. Sprinting back, the bag had already gone, along with my shoes in it.

'Damn!' I cried. Now I had nothing to match my new dress. Rather sheepishly, I arrived and watched the parade from the stands in my trousers and jumper but I felt I couldn't go to the church service with all the smart relatives.

Doug got two weeks' leave before he was sent to his first posting in Osnabrück, Germany, for two years, so we had a day together in London, visiting Buckingham Palace and the sights before returning up north.

The time we had together disappeared as fast as a snap of the fingers, though, and all too soon we had to say goodbye. This was to be the first real test of our relationship, now he was going to be away for so long.

We carried on writing to each other every day. Sometimes I'd run out of things to say and turned to humour instead. 'Here's just a few lines, Doug,' I'd write.

Then I'd draw three straight lines below. Or I'd write: 'Just a note to say hello,' and then I'd simply write the word 'hello' in the middle of a blank sheet of paper. Doug thought I was crackers, but it kept us both laughing.

Once Doug didn't seem to respond to any of my questions in my letters for about six weeks. Eventually I found out that he'd not even opened any of my letters during that time. Apparently, where I'd written his initials ('DAM' for Douglas Alistair McNae) after his surname Black, a new postman had mistook his name for 'Blackdam', and thinking no one of that name existed, they'd just piled up!

I was so proud when Dougie took up lightweight boxing and became the champ in his unit. In one letter he included a picture of himself alongside a twelve stone, six-foot-something brute, telling me that with a single punch he had taken him down in the first round. I showed the snap off to all the girls at work.

After six months, Doug got his first posting back, travelling home in time to see in the New Year of 1964. We drove back, holding hands all the way to my mum's house where she was holding a party. Doug handed me and my sister our presents. He'd got me an old-fashioned dressing table set, and Mary a music box. Then as the party got into full swing, he grabbed my hand and took me into a bedroom. Pulling out a box from his pocket, he got down on one knee.

'Will you be my wife?' he said.

He knew my answer as well as I did. Doug was a good man, I knew he'd be a provider, and I wanted to be with him for ever. There wasn't a second's hesitation. 'Yes, please!' I cried.

Only then did I peer into the box and notice the ring was made with a pearl. A pretty thing, except I hated pearls, always had done. As Mum used to say, 'Pearls are for tears.' Douglas didn't know this about his new fiancée, but what did it matter. I was to be his wife and that was all I wanted.

Mum, Grandad and some of Doug's family all chipped in for our big day. We both had enormous families so had to put 'no children' on the invite otherwise we couldn't have afforded to feed everyone.

The night before my wedding, Mum had a 'talk' with me. After being married to my dad for twenty-odd years, any rose-tinted glasses regarding marriage had been truly crushed. Shaking her head she looked at me. 'You've got to realise,' she said, 'it's no fun and games. Love soon goes out the window. Then you'll just have to chug along, like me and your dad.'

'I know, Mum,' I sighed, not really wanting to hear

this. I loved Doug, I was sure he loved me too. And he was very different to my dad.

'Well, you're too young to know what I mean,' Mum said. 'But with this wedding, you've made your bed now, too. So you'll have to lie in it.'

Putting Mum's comments aside, I went to bed and woke up the next morning feeling full of excitement. Really I wanted to be on Grandad's arm to be given away, but Mum wasn't having it. 'Your dad can't be alive and not give you away, it wouldn't be fair,' she said. 'He can't sit there and watch his dad do it. What would people think?' Although she knew what a rotten father he'd been, she didn't want to broadcast the fact. As for me, I was just thankful he managed to stay sober.

I wore a white silk dress with a full veil, and Dad walked me up the aisle with Mary following behind us as bridesmaid. Doug was so nervous he was standing to attention like he was on parade, not even looking round as I came in. He hated being in the spotlight and had never been so embarrassed. As I left the church on Doug's arm, a married woman, everyone gathered round the church doorway as the wind almost swept the veil off my head. Laughing, I grabbed it just in time. My wedding day almost literally blew me away.

We had a small reception. Doug stood up and said: 'Thanks for coming, the grub's all paid for so get stuck in.'

Our honeymoon – a week in a caravan in Anstruther, Fife – went all too quickly, as we'd decided to try for a baby straight away. But our happy bubble was popped when I returned to Mum's house to collect our wedding presents. A beautiful mirror and a portable wireless were among the generous presents we'd opened before our honeymoon, but they were missing from the bedroom where Mum had kept them.

We both looked at each other, not needing to say a word.

'It's Dad, isn't it?' I said quietly. He'd been known to pinch a suit out of Grandad's wardrobe for drink, and on one occasion he'd even given away the bike he'd bought for my tenth birthday.

Mum was furious. It was the straw that broke the back of their ailing marriage and she left him a few weeks later.

She didn't stay single for long, though. Just a month later she sat me down to tell me she'd got together with her bachelor neighbour – the miner, Hugh.

'You what?' I said, staggered.

Standing at just 5'4", Hugh was a stocky little fella, a hard worker down the pits but also someone who loved a drink or two. I never saw it coming that he'd get together with my mum.

Dougie raised an eyebrow when I told him Mum had fallen for him. All of his brothers had worked with Hugh down the pit at one time or another and they thought he was a bit of a nutter. A lairy character, he worked like a pack horse, and built up a thirst for beer to match.

'I never thought he was the type your mum'd go for,' chuckled Doug. 'But I guess at least he works hard.'

Hugh had always been nice enough, but I'd had no idea he'd had designs on Mum. Now it transpired he'd asked her out years earlier, before she'd met my dad. She'd said no and he had remained a bachelor until Mum divorced.

To avoid any gossip from the neighbours, Mum decided to move south with Hugh, so he got a mining job at Firbeck colliery in Nottinghamshire. They wanted to live together, but it'd take two years for her divorce to come through and to hook up with one man while still married to another was certainly not the done thing in those days. So they moved down to Langold, near Worksop, with Mary in tow, to start afresh. Hugh earned a good wage in the pit, and could provide well for my mum and sister, something Dad never did.

The decision to move turned out to be a good one, as the pits in Scotland were being closed at a rate of knots. The late 1960s were a time of turbulence, as the mining industry had been hit by the Labour government over the past couple of years. Doug read in the papers how the workforce had dropped from three quarters of a million miners ten years earlier to around 350,000. Scotland was hard hit, losing a lot of pits, and more closures were planned. But now that Hugh was working in a Nottinghamshire mine where the pits were rich with coal, he had no concerns about losing his job. Folk said there was enough coal to provide fuel for the next 1,000 years.

On one visit down south, Mum did mention the idea of Dougie coming down to work in a pit. She knew he wasn't keen after his father's experiences. But she also saw what a good life Hugh was now providing her with.

'Think of the pay, lass,' she said to me. 'The life isn't as bad nowadays for a miner. They use machines and the like. It's a job for life too. Doug'd never need worry again.'

I laughed.

'Bless you, Mum,' I said. 'But I think we're going all right. Dougie always gets by.'

Hugh stayed quiet with any career advice of his own. He told Doug later he didn't believe in telling younger lads to get down the pit. Just like Doug's protective father, he knew working underground could still be a dark world in every sense of the word and wasn't for everyone. Good pay and a roof over your head, yes; but he'd only recommend it as a last resort.

Doug quietly told me one day he thought Hugh was a hard man for the work he did. He pointed to the fireplace, just three feet high.

'Look at the height of that, Cath,' he said. 'Hugh told me he'd been two foot deep in water yesterday, hunched under a pit roof as high as that fireplace mantelpiece. Aye, Hughie must have nerves of steel to sit in that for seven hours a day.'

Yet of course we also knew that working for the Coal Board brought enormous benefits, not least of all a good wage, and a trade hopefully for life. What's more, many jobs came with houses. Mum and Hugh were doing well from the industry – that couldn't be argued with. In some respects I knew Doug must've been tempted and I didn't blame him. But it wasn't enough for him to sign away his life above ground – albeit tied to the army – for one thousands of feet below us.

Chapter Three

We returned home to live in Grandad's spare room and Doug was sent to Oman a week later. The British Army were helping to clear mines and guard the straits for the oil traffic. So I started married life as I'd ended it as a single woman – living alone in my grandad's spare room. Not that I minded. I still loved stopping with Grandad and we were so close I couldn't imagine life without him, married or otherwise.

Just after Doug left, I discovered I was pregnant, so I wrote to my new husband and told him in my next letter. He was thrilled, writing back to me enthusiastically the same day, full of excitement at the prospect of new father-hood. Neither of us could believe it had happened so quickly. Not only had I struggled with cysts on my ovaries, poor Dougie had discovered he'd only had one testicle when he joined up in the army. The chances of us conceiving, doctors had said, were pretty minimal. But it turned out that Doug just needed to breathe on me and I'd find myself expecting.

Doug's letters were censored now, so I didn't have much of a sense of what was going on. He'd write about going to the casbahs or say he wished I was there. Just small talk. Nothing about the dangers. However, the wireless and TV filled in some of the gaps. Two lads from Doug's regiment, the Royal Engineers, were killed in mine attacks. I was worried sick, but tried not to let it show in my own letters. I just had to focus on the new bairn.

At ten weeks though, I started bleeding and lost the baby. Devastated, Grandad took care of me after my D&C. Doug was granted a day's leave on compassionate grounds. Before I was discharged, I asked the doctor when we could try again for another baby. 'As long as you don't have any bleeding or discomfort, straight away,' he shrugged.

That night we did try again and a month later I realised I was pregnant once more.

'You must have your dates wrong,' my doctor insisted.

'I can't have,' I laughed. 'I only saw Doug for one day so that must be the day I fell pregnant!'

With Doug away, Grandad filled his place just fine, looking after me and seeing I had everything I needed. I had an intense craving for peaches so every few days he'd nip to the shops, sometimes walking miles as the bus drivers were on strike for better pay and conditions at the time.

'There you go,' he'd say, handing me a brown paper bag. 'Don't eat them all at once.'

I only seemed to be able to stomach sweet, juicy fruit and eggs this time around.

However, the excitement turned to fear again as at ten weeks I threatened to miscarry once more. Back in hospital, the doctors had bad news.

'You've lost the baby,' they said. 'You'll need another D&C.'

Lying on the hospital bed, in tears, I couldn't believe it was all happening again. I felt so alone, wishing Doug was there too, not hundreds of miles away, fighting a war I knew nothing about.

I was prepared for theatre and just had to wait my turn on the busy ward. Lying on the bed, I put my hand on my stomach with silent tears slipping from the corners of my eyes. Quietly, I said goodbye to the baby we were destined never to meet. But just before I was wheeled down, my operation was put back as a new emergency came in. More hours ticked by and another nurse took a fresh urine sample from me for testing.

'Just to make sure you're all ready, dear,' she said, marking me off her list. 'Won't be long now.'

However, as my turn finally arrived, the nurse came rushing into the ward waving a clipboard.

'Take this patient off the list!' she cried to the consultant. 'She is still pregnant!'

My tears turned from fear to joy in a flash as I rubbed my stomach in disbelief. Amazingly, I was still expecting. The nurse guessed I'd maybe lost a twin. But I'd come within minutes of losing them both.

I carried on as usual, working as much as possible, but as my bump grew I started to feel breathless, my heart racing. At seven months pregnant, I went to see my GP to ask him if something was wrong. He knew me well and had been my doctor all my life.

'Where's your husband, Doug?' he asked, looking concerned.

'In a warzone in Oman,' I said. 'Dealing with mines.'

I said it in a matter-of-fact manner, as that's how I felt. Doug had a job and he was off doing it.

'Are you upset?' he asked, peering at me over his glasses.

I swallowed a sob as it rose in my chest.

'I am just getting on with it,' I whispered.

Just a few days later, as I lay in bed, feeling weak as usual, a thunderous knock came at the door early in the morning. I hobbled downstairs to find two policemen on the doorstep. Instantly my heart started racing again, but this time for a different reason.

'What is it?' I said, leaning against the doorway to steady myself. 'Please don't tell me it's Doug . . .'

They looked at me and then looked at my bump. 'Were you in bed?' they asked.

'Yes,' I said.

Turned out they were police sent by the army. My doctor had contacted Doug's regiment to ask them to let him home for compassionate leave, and they'd sent the police down to check on my story. With confirmation I was indeed pregnant and bedbound, Doug got his leave early.

My heart didn't stop racing, though. I was to discover that I had a heart defect similar to Mum's, although luckily not as severe.

On our first wedding anniversary, I went into slow labour, which felt like it was going on forever. Susan was born on 24 May 1965 in Bells Hill maternity wing ward. She looked at me with her chocolate-brown eyes, the spit of Doug's, and we all fell in love with her.

Doug was thrilled to be posted back on British soil. Finally we were a family and were hoping to live as one at the Invicta Barracks in Maidstone, where Doug was stationed next. Now we'd get a married quarters and start life as an army family all together. But first they had to build our new home. Every month the army sent me a letter, informing me of its progress – when the windows had been fitted, how long the carpets would take to come, that sort of thing. Then, as the date drew near for us to move in, we were told it had been given away to a sergeant!

'What do we do now?' I asked Doug on the phone that evening.

'God knows, lassie,' he replied.

It was such a blow. We were due to move, but now we couldn't. Our dreams of a family life together had been shattered by a senior officer without a backward glance.

Meanwhile I fell ill again with terrible back pains. My ovarian problems had travelled to my kidneys. When Susan was nine months old I had no option but to have a major operation to remove most of my ovaries, leaving me with just one quarter of an ovary left. I was still only nineteen so they didn't want to remove all my ovaries, otherwise they'd have to give me a full hysterectomy.

'You'll find it very, very difficult to get pregnant,' warned the doctor afterwards.

I was gutted, but happy to have my health back and grateful to have one child already.

After a two-week spell in hospital, I was allowed home. But it was going to take a while to recover. Doug decided he couldn't stand being away any longer and chose to leave the army. He had to go and speak to the officer about being discharged. He didn't know what to expect, but fortunately the army were understanding. Anyone could see that the situation we were in just wasn't working. I couldn't cope being on my own with Susan, our house in Maidstone had never materialised, and there seemed to be no immediate prospect of us getting another one. If we'd all been together he could have stayed in, but this was no way to live as a family.

Doug was discharged just before Susan turned one, but any relief about being together again was quickly tempered by the big worry – unemployment. With no savings and a new baby, Doug needed something straight away. And for the first time in years, the subject of working in the pit reared its head again.

'What do you think?' asked Doug. 'Shall I just become a miner and be done with it?'

'I don't know,' I sighed. 'It's not my place to say, Dougie. I won't be the one who has to go down there every day.'

In fact we wondered whether we even had the option of getting a mining job at all. There were fewer pits than ever before in Scotland. It'd mean moving and starting again down south.

But before Doug had a chance to think too deeply about the mines, another job popped up. Doug's sister Irene worked with her husband up near Loch Katrine, for the Glasgow Co-operative, clearing the forest, looking after the water reservoirs and the freshwater trout. There was a vacancy up there to work near them. They provided homes for their workers too, so Doug accepted it.

To begin with it felt like we'd moved to paradise. In the heart of the Trossachs, we were surrounded by the most magnificent landscape you could imagine. You couldn't come in by car unless you lived there, so few vehicles were on the roads, adding to the overwhelming feeling of peace. Our little house looked straight out at the loch, which changed colour dramatically depending on the time of day and weather conditions. But although it might have been a paradise to look at, the wages were almost impossible to live on. Doug got just £10 a week and our rent alone was £2. It was barely enough for a single man to live on, let alone a family. The weather was also hard to bear. Being in a beautiful wilderness meant we were at the mercy of the elements. Some days it was so windy I had to loop a rope round my waist and tie it to the door handle just so I could collect wood outside and get back across the threshold in one piece. A few months in, I also fell ill with another miscarriage and, what with these problems along with our constant money struggles, this period of our lives became increasingly unhappy.

Not for the first time my grandma's lessons in making good, hearty soup helped Doug and I to survive on such low wages, but long term it was no way to live. We couldn't afford very much at all. Then we had another miracle. Two years after Susan was born I fell pregnant again – a complete shock to us both knowing I only had a quarter of an ovary left.

The doctors gave me painful hormone injections into my muscle to make sure I kept the baby for the first few months. Luckily this time there were no complications.

In May 1967, I was rushed to Airthrey hospital after a six-hour labour and gave birth to our second daughter, Lorraine. A pretty wee thing, with long eyelashes framing dark eyes the same as Doug's, we all fell in love again instantly. She boosted our morale, but obviously gave us another mouth to feed, so when she was two weeks old we decided to move back to Hamilton to find more suitable and better paid work.

One of my uncles had a job as a tarmac supervisor so he gave Doug a job tarring roads, which paid a better wage of £30 a week, enough for us to afford a tiny mortgage and buy our first home. All we could afford was a two-bedroomed flat in a tenement block in Motherwell, near Glasgow, bought for £2,000.

Motherwell might have been in Scotland still, but it was a world away from Hamilton.

The charmless grey sink estates and the undercurrent of despair felt around the city at the time was palpable. A grey tarpaulin appeared to always cover the sky, to match the mood beneath. Every day I'd wake to hear screaming matches from our neighbours and a trip to the shops meant navigating drunkards staggering across the roads. As soon as I stepped foot outside I wanted to go back in. The whole time I was there, I never made a single friend.

Then, in February of 1968, the unthinkable happened and I fell pregnant again. As likely as infertility had been for us, given our medical conditions, we realised the doctors must have got it wrong in our case.

Just as we were wondering whether to move and what to do, fate intervened. While visiting Doug's brother Gordon, who was now also working in Loch Katrine, a huge storm began brewing outside as we ate dinner. As the dark clouds gathered I had an ominous feeling. I just wanted to get off home, although it was three bus rides away and of course we had the two wee girls with us.

'C'mon,' I said to Doug. 'Sup up and let's get going. Those clouds are giving me the shivers.'

Just as we gathered the girls' coats and shoes, the skies burst open, sending lashings of heavy rain against the windows. The rat-a-tat sound made us all jump, as the gale force wind blew bits of stones straight on to Gordon's front panes. In a hurry, Gordon and Doug grabbed an old mattress from upstairs and held it against the window, fearing it would crash in, shattering glass over us all. As they did so we watched with open mouths as pieces of a nearby gamekeeper's roof and shed flew by like something out of the tornado scene in *The Wizard of Oz*. Even a kennel with a dog howling inside flew past.

We had no choice but to stay put and that night we all lay huddled together on the sofa, getting little sleep, listening to the screaming wind outside.

The following morning, we woke to a scene of devastation. Trees, roof slates, bits of wood, fencing and glass littered the roads. On the wireless we heard how two people had been killed by falling trees. The winds reached 120 mph.

'C'mon,' I said to Doug. 'Let's just get home safe now.'

The ride seemed to take forever as the bus was battered and pummelled with the dying breath of the storm. Finally, as our grey tenement pulled into view, I was the most grateful I'd ever been to see it. I couldn't wait to get the kettle on.

We pulled the pram up three flights of stairs and I allowed myself a sigh of relief as I twisted the key in the lock.

'Right, tea or coffee?' I said to Doug. But as I pushed the door open, a rush of icy draught hit me straight in the face, almost taking my breath away.

'Doug?' I began, as he followed me. I carried on in, following the draught, which turned into a breeze, whipping my hair into the air. Stepping into the lounge, I could see that the carpet and sofa were a funny colour . . . and wet.

I didn't have to go any further to realise what had happened. The grey angry clouds and spitting rain we thought we'd left outside were clearly visible in our living room, which now stood without a ceiling. The wind had blown our tenement roof clean off!

'Oh my God, Doug!' I screamed, my hand flying to my mouth. Doug was standing behind me, his head skyward, mouth agape.

After a few seconds of taking in the sight, we both flew into emergency mode, gathering as much as we could carry and putting the girls in the bedroom. Doug ran downstairs to see if the water on the floor had seeped into the flat belonging to the old lady who lived below. Luckily it hadn't. A council official turned up and told everyone on the top floor to sleep in the hallway as it was the only safe place left on that floor of the building. They feared the other part of the roof would cave in at any minute.

That night we bedded down on blankets and pillows by candlelight. As we lay there, trying to drop off, I just felt sick to my stomach. We'd been unable to afford insurance as well as the cost of the house and there was no way we could afford to replace the roof.

After a sleepless night we woke to find the Territorial Army pulling tarpaulin over the exposed part of the building.

'We can't stay here,' I said to Doug, unable to contain my tears. 'We just can't.'

In desperation to get away, I asked to go down and stay with Mum and Hugh. Living in a tenement in Motherwell was bad enough ordinarily, but with the roof blown off, it was unbearable. The following day our living room looked like a bomb had hit it, with the odd bird diving down to peck at the remains of our carpet.

As we pulled up outside Mum's little house in Langold, everything seemed a bit brighter. A busy pit village, it had friendly local shops and a sense of community I'd never experienced in Motherwell. Neighbours said 'hello' even though I was just a visitor. Hugh was working on the coalface and had just been promoted to deputy, one of the highest-paid workers, bringing home a decent wage. As much as he liked a drink with the lads afterwards, he could provide for his wife too.

Mary, meanwhile, had left home. Aged nineteen, she had married a miner called Robert, known as Chippy, as his father worked in a chip shop. I didn't click with him, as I thought he was a bit lazy and not a worker like my Doug. He also mimicked my Scottish accent and borrowed money to gamble. But who was I to criticise? They seemed happy enough.

My sister and her husband were what Doug and I called 'club people', meaning they liked a booze-up and a laugh. They were always found down the Miners' Welfare whenever we dropped by.

Now, don't get me wrong, I liked to laugh where I could do, but the kids and my home came first. I didn't like drinking much and the thought of getting dolled up to sit in a pub and get drunk just wasn't me. Mary used to twist my arm a few times though and she'd get me into the Miners' Welfare for an orange or lemonade if she tried really hard when I was on a visit. To listen to us nattering you'd never believe we were sisters. After living in England for so many years my sister had lost all her Scottish tones.

That wasn't the only difference between us. Mary's existence seemed positively carefree compared to what we were going through.

'Oh Mum,' I complained, as we took off our coats. 'I am not happy.'

She listened quietly, pouring me cups of tea and jiggling Lorraine on her knee. She could see I was at the end of my tether.

After a few more cups of tea down me, I began to feel a bit better and decided that whatever was going to happen there was little use now in worrying about it.

Doug arrived later on. I could tell by the way he held

his head high something good had happened. Strange, I thought, considering the 'home' we had to go back to.

'Are you OK, Douglas?' I asked, stirring sugar into his tea.

'Yes,' he grinned. 'So what do you think of your mum's place?'

'Lovely,' I sighed, looking round at the cosy little sitting room.

'And the area?' Doug pressed.

'Just as nice,' I said, staring out the net curtains at the row of neat houses across the road.

'Well, how would you like to come and live here?' he said, taking a slurp of tea.

I stared at him. 'Live here? How?'

'There's a guy retiring on the surface of the pit,' he explained. 'I've been offered a job. I know it's at the pit, but it's above ground and isn't all that bad. It's not an underground job, it's digging the slack heap with a bulldozer.'

I opened and closed my mouth like a goldfish, unable to find the words as Doug explained that the job came with a pit house in this area. We'd have a job, a home and a stable wage. It was like winning the pools.

'Oh, you're brilliant,' I laughed.

Back in our tenement block, I cheerfully packed up all our furniture, clothes and ornaments. I was heavily pregnant with my son and we were about to start again but life couldn't have felt better.

In the autumn of 1968, the job finally came up at Steetley pit and we got a lift from Motherwell to move down there. As I watched the fields speeding past our car, I rolled down the window to catch a sniff of the fresh air, which smelled like sweet grass. I already felt like I'd come home.

We arrived outside a three-bedroom home in Beech Grove, Carlton-in-Lindrick, Rainworth. A smart new Coal Board house, with clean red bricks, it really did feel like a little piece of heaven after where we'd been living. The village, pronounced 'Renoth' by locals, had been built especially for the pit and had some lovely rolling green fields, farmland and lake areas nearby.

'This place is perfect for the kids,' I smiled as we crossed the threshold. I just wanted to cry with relief. We were finally leaving the dark days of Motherwell behind us.

But just as we arrived, we got a letter from our neighbour in the tenement block. Doug's face changed when he ripped it open. Scanning the words, he went a funny colour.

'Oh, spit it out,' I cried. 'What's happened?'

His voice shaking a little, Doug explained how our neighbour, who'd had a key, had gone to check on our flat and found the lock bust. Every stick of furniture we owned had been stolen. I grabbed the letter to see for myself in black and white. It meant we'd have to start again. I couldn't believe it. But even then I was relieved we never had to go back to that place.

At first we could only afford a settee, which doubled as a bed, and a second-hand pram on Hire Purchase – but it was a start. We might have lost everything but we still had each other and a wee one on the way. The following day, Doug went off to start his new job in nearby Worksop. He was set to earn £14 a week. Not much more than the Loch Katrine job, but a slight improvement. His job was to use a bulldozer to move and flatten the piles of slack brought up with the coke. It was a busy, noisy job, with the pile continually growing higher all day and needing constant levelling off. I could see the machines whirring and grinding into action day and night from my kitchen window. I felt so proud. This was a job for life; we didn't have to worry any longer.

I don't think either of us could believe that after all these years Doug had joined a pit, but he wasn't going underground, so it was a good alternative and not as hard. This showed in his wage. The surface workers earned about a third of what a miner below the surface did, but to Doug it was a sacrifice worth making – after all, he knew all too well what underground life meant. Especially the coalface workers. They earned treble what he did, and deservedly so, as they had the toughest job of all.

He got some stick once he'd started his new job, though. His colleagues who did work under the ground gave the lads on the surface constant ribbing, especially when it was a hot and sunny day at the start of a shift.

'You'll be basking in that sunshine then, eh, Douglas?' they'd tease. 'Be lovely and warm behind your wheel under the blue sky in the fresh air . . . You'll be bathing in the bloody top while we're grinding down below, eh? Think on that!'

Doug knew they were envious. He also knew, from memories of his brothers' working lives, they were suffering far more than him thousands of feet under the earth, so he laughed it off. All he cared about was having a regular income and after such a hectic few years both of us were so relieved he had a job at all.

'Aye,' he said. 'I know what you're talking of, lads. My father and brothers were down the pit. It's a tough one.'

He may have brushed the comments aside, but there was a proper 'class divide' between those on the surface and the underground men. Doug and his digger were on the bottom rung.

While Doug got used to his new job, I threw myself into making our house a home. With little furniture the least I could do was try and make it warm and cosy. Our central heating was fuelled by coke, and I soon realised the eight bags the Coal Board dropped off every week weren't enough to keep it warm. With coke proving too expensive, we also got a paraffin fire to keep the bedroom warm.

To be living back nearer my mum and sister Mary was an enormous treat for the whole family. They lived around fifteen miles away, and we started to reconnect. Mum would get two buses over as often as possible, taking the kids out to the park, or going for long walks with them in the fields and woods. They loved collecting blueberries and blackberries, and anything else they could pick and eat in an instant. Coming home with full bellies, and black smudges round their chops, they'd grown into contented-looking country kids within weeks.

To have my sister back in my life was also wonderful. We'd grown apart since I'd got married but now we were able to go food shopping together sometimes or just meet up for a coffee.

As much as it was good to be living closer to my mum and sister again, we did have several close fall-outs with Hugh. The more we got to know him the more we realised what a strange character he was. Compared to my dad he treated Mum like a queen, and although he liked a drink, he always put her first. They were happy. But he had an eccentric side too. My pop once said after meeting him: 'He's either really, really clever or really, really stupid.'

Whatever job my mum gave him to do in the house, he'd mess it up, so he ended up getting away with murder, lazing around doing nothing. He couldn't have been stupid though as he'd been promoted as a deputy in the pit, which is a job where you have to keep on your toes as it involved being responsible for some of the explosions at the coalface. For centuries, miners had used dynamite, but now the mines were more controlled, with health and safety being paramount. It was up to the deputy to implement the rules and regulations. The deputy had to plant the explosive, made from a substance used in washing powder, and he was the one to press the detonator after the men were made to move 250 yards away for their safety. The men trusted their deputy with their lives. The buck stopped with that position so it was only entrusted to the most serious and capable men.

Hugh loved talking about his job if he were asked. Despite my reservations, he was an eager worker even if we thought he could act the fool. Sometimes, though, his foolishness appeared borderline madness. Once Doug offered to teach Hugh to drive. He'd failed his test eight times, though we wondered if that was deliberate too, so he wouldn't have to drive around on errands. Anyway, during one particular lesson, he was approaching a roundabout and Doug told him to stop.

'Yes,' he said, hitting the accelerator.

Seeing they were heading straight towards a wagon on the far side of the road, Doug screamed and grabbed the wheel, sending them skidding across the roundabout, a hair's breadth away from the truck.

'Jesus Christ!' yelled Doug as they screeched to a halt. 'You nearly got us both killed. What you playing at?'

Instead of looking even the least bit sorry, Hugh gave a little giggle, which cranked up to a full belly laugh. Furious, Doug drove him home and threw the keys at him. 'That's me finished. You can teach yourself,' he said.

Mum tried to calm them both down, and told them to go and get a wee drink. Reluctantly Doug joined him, but even in the bar, Hugh started telling the story to the barman, laughing and joking again.

Doug slammed down his drink and left. 'If I don't leave I'll bloody kill you,' he said.

Doug called him a madman after that. I think he put his eccentricities down to the fact he tolerated such poor conditions in his job, too. Mining life didn't bother someone like Hugh, Doug said.

I'm glad Mum found him as he obviously made her happy, and he always got on well with my sister. But I don't think Doug and I ever understood his character.

Chapter Four

By coincidence, my sister Mary fell pregnant with her second child at the same time as my third, and our due dates were on the same day, 27 September 1968. The previous year poor Mary had lost a stillborn child after it was born so badly deformed you couldn't even tell the sex. So Mum and I hoped a fast second pregnancy would heal the pain of loss. By now any sibling rivalry between us had long gone and I loved and wanted to help my baby sister.

And bless her, my sister needed help. A hopeless house-keeper, Mary's head was always in the clouds and she couldn't keep a room tidy even if her life depended on it. Clothes were strewn across the floors instead of in the drawers, dishes were piled up in the sink and the ashes were always left in the fire. When it came to keeping our houses clean, my sister and I were like chalk and cheese.

Mum was always ribbing Mary for it, telling her off or

running her finger along her mantelpiece to show her the thick grey fluff she'd allowed to build up.

'Mum, let me be!' Mary cried.

I agreed with Mum though, so poor Mary often had it in stereo. In my eyes she was still my lazy little sister, getting out of doing chores, even when they were in her own home.

However, with our new bairns on the way, we sat nattering for hours about babies and I'd knit bonnets and booties for her wee one, again something Mary had never learned to do.

As fate would have it, we both ended up in Kilton maternity hospital with labour pains at the same time, both ten days late. Mary had a boy, Ian, in the morning and my son, Douglas, arrived at night time on 4 October 1968 after barely any pushing, and before a midwife even reached me. It was like he couldn't wait to get out.

'He's brought himself into this world all by himself,' I murmured, as I held the wee thing for the first time. Both of our babies weighed 8 lb.

The nurses put our beds together. As it was my third baby, I was able to help Mary get used to being a mum. It was a special time for both of us and drew our bond even closer.

After we'd had the bairns we were both dying for a fag, so we slipped on our dressing gowns and started walking

out. Although I winced a bit in pain, I walked as confi-
dently as possible, knowing the ward sister wouldn't let
me out otherwise. Mary, always one to feel sorry for
herself, was almost doubled over and so the sister noticed.

'You need to get back to bed at once,' ordered the sister.

'Mary,' I chuckled, when I got back, 'you should've
pretended you were OK if you'd wanted a wee smoke.'

She gave me a wry smile.

'You've done this three times, Cathy,' she said. 'You're
a pro!'

A few months after the bairns were born, Mum was
fretting more than ever about the state of Mary's house.

'Right,' I said. 'I'm going to get a few bits together and
I'm coming over.'

An hour later, Mum and I descended on Mary's doorstep
armed with mops, sponges, buckets, bleach and a scrubbing brush. Like a pair of locusts we systematically went
from room to room, pulling out all the rubbish, folding
clothes and cleaning walls and floors, all while Mary
looked on in bewildered amusement.

'Do you have to?' she kept asking, while pacing the
floor, burping Ian.

'Yes!' both Mum and I replied in unison.

Sometimes a new baby brings family bonds closer and
with two bouncing baby boys to coo over, Mary, Mum
and I became a tight unit. But just when things started

to tick along, after a few short months at Steetley Doug was made redundant. Private contractors were taking over the jobs at the pits more frequently as the government sold off the mines. Rumours were constantly swirling around about whether more planned closures would take place. But then the mines in Nottingham were so productive it didn't seem likely. Luckily there was still plenty of work about in the area, as straight away Doug got a post at the nearby Rufford mine. Now we understood why miners were known as 'Gypsies', as they frequently moved around for work, sometimes leaving for new communities and sometimes travelling further afield. Later on, Hugh would travel as far as Yorkshire main as his pits closed or downsized. It became part of the job.

As always, Doug was just grateful to have a regular livelihood, meagre as it was. He was doing the same work as before, digging on the surface for a pittance, and we'd grown used to struggling on the wage, but the squeeze was getting tighter and tighter. We relied on our few pounds family allowance to keep food on the table. I'd always been good at eking out food but we needed so much more for our growing toddlers. My knitting could barely keep up with them.

After settling in and having my wee boy, I started to get to know some of the neighbours a little better too. Up until then I'd not seen many folk. Many of the other miners' wives were working and after Motherwell I'd grown used to keeping myself to myself. But Barbara next door, whose husband Paul was a deputy, was lovely. A very pretty young woman from Manchester, we'd chat for ages over cups of tea. Barbara had four kids and was a natural mum. Far more patient than me, I'd marvel how she'd sink to her knees and play with the kids, drawing or baking for hours without getting bored. She loved kids and kids loved her.

Doug often bumped into Paul at the start and end of shifts and to Paul it was madness working on the surface for such a small wage when jobs were available underneath. One day he spotted Doug coming home, looking exhausted after a long, fourteen-hour shift. Some weeks Doug was working eighty hours, although barely bringing home enough money to keep us.

'Why are you killing yourself for such little take-home pay?' he asked. 'You can earn yourself three times the amount underground! Why don't you come underground with us?'

Doug shook his head. 'I know what life's like underground,' he said. 'It's not one for me.'

Although I supported whatever decision Doug made about the mine, I started to wonder how long we could go on for. We still had so much furniture to replace aside from buying food and clothes.

Our three kids' needs were endless and daily life felt like a non-stop whirlwind of nappies, feeding and changing. Of course in those days before disposables we used terry towelling squares. I had around twenty-four of them, and would constantly have some on soak in a bucket in ONO, the cheapest powder on the market. Then I'd get them rinsed, dried and hung up, before the next lot went in. My hands were wrinkled and left raw with all the detergent.

I didn't have a washing machine either. I had two sinks, one for the heavily soiled stuff to soak in and a glass board to scrub on. They were more pricey than the tin boards, but I found tin caught strands of cotton and snagged the sheets and clothes. Every evening as soon as the kids were in bed, out came the washing. I'd scrub all evening and then get things hung up to dry. It was never ending.

Doug pitched in to help when he could. He'd boil up water for the bottles, and was a dab hand at shaking up the baby powder to make sure the baby didn't suck up lumps. There were sleepless nights for both of us, although I always leapt up first to try and get the baby back off so that Doug wouldn't be too exhausted for work. I'd walk the floor with Douglas for hours to get him to nod off. Right from the start he was full of beans.

But something had to give. Two weeks before Christmas, I arrived home from the post office having picked up the family allowance, when suddenly I felt overwhelmed with exhaustion. Pushing the pram and shepherding the toddlers certainly kept me busy but my mind was also whirring away non-stop, trying to work out how to make our few pounds eke out even further for presents and the like. Back indoors, I threw my purse on to the kitchen table and went to put Douglas down for his afternoon nap, leaving Lorraine and Susan running around.

'Just give me a minute, you two,' I said, clutching Douglas to me.

A few minutes later, I came back downstairs to smell a funny burning aroma coming from the kitchen fire.

'What the hell's that?' I thought, leaning into the fireplace. I lifted the lid on the boiler and peered in.

There, among the embers, and already frazzled to a cinder, were the remains of my leather purse, along with the few pounds from the family allowance of course. Either Lorraine or Susan, still only toddlers, must have chucked it in while I was upstairs.

My heart palpitating with despair, I slumped down on the kitchen chair, put my head on the table and wept. Susan and Lorraine rattled around looking at me like they didn't know what to say. They knew Mummy was crying and upset, but had no idea why. I didn't even have the strength to tell them off. It'd be no use anyhow. Susan patted my arm and Lorraine brought me her dolly. I picked it up and held it tight. I felt the weight of the world on my shoulders in that moment. How on earth would we manage now?

That evening I rang my mum, who was living with Hugh in Doncaster after recently moving. I never liked to ask her for anything, but I couldn't see how we'd cope unless I did so this time.

'Please can you lend me some money?' I sobbed.

'Of course,' she said, without hesitation. She told me she was on her way over.

I put down the phone gratefully. We'd had our ups and downs when I was a child but I always knew Mum would be there for me.

I watched the clock as the hours ticked past and there was still no sign of Mum. When it got to midnight I called her again.

'You never came!' I cried. 'What happened?'

'We did!' she said. 'We went all the way to Rufford and asked around but we couldna find your road.'

'No, I don't live in Rufford!' I cried. 'I live in Rainworth. The colliery is called Rufford main.'

People always made that mistake. The whole saga made me cry even more.

Doug came home to find me in floods, not something he was used to seeing.

'Cath, whatever happened?' he said.

'We can't go on like this,' I sobbed. 'I know you're doing your best but your wage isn't enough, Doug! I'm scrimping and eking out what we do have. The bairns barely have enough clothes . . . the house is cold. This is not the way I want to live my life. It is not!'

I saw his mouth set into a grim line. I knew my words cut him to the quick.

'It's just too hard,' I whispered, wiping tears with my sleeve.

Doug prided himself on being a breadwinner, but facts were facts and surface work wasn't paying the way. We couldn't afford to go on like this; we had to face it.

'I'm going to get a job myself,' I said, swiping at my face with the back of my hand. 'That's the only thing fer it.'

The jobs available to women in the area consisted of factory work either on the farms or in the hosiery mills. So I opted to work in the turkey section of Eastwood's factory. As a lifelong hater of all things needlework the thought of darning tights was my idea of hell, so blood and feathers it was.

I was offered a daily shift from 8 a.m. to 5 p.m. and two nights a week until 8 p.m. Doug did a twelve-hour shift, 6 p.m. to 6 a.m., and when he got home, I gave him the children and went out to work myself. We'd only see each other for five minutes a day, but at least we'd have money in our pockets.

My boss liked me from day one, as I stood up to him and was always outspoken but also worked terribly hard. At first I did packing but one day he came in, looking glum.

'What's wrong?' I asked.

'I need a killer as one hasn't turned up.'

A killer was the person who slaughtered the turkeys.

'I'll do it,' I said, without a second's thought.

Petrified, minutes later, I found myself standing with a stun knife in my hand. I wondered why on earth I'd been so quick to offer. The birds were so big with huge wingspans. They would be shepherded into shackles, and you had to grab their beaks and stun them. Then, with a quick slit of the throat, they would be dead.

As I tried to pluck up the courage to do this myself, a massive bird started flapping and making a fuss. He was so fat his legs wouldn't even fit into the shackles. Panicking at the size of him, I turned and ran as he swooped up towards me. Yelping, I legged it around the factory floor, while some of the others laughed. I swear he chased me around, but in hindsight he was as panicked as I was and ran in any direction to get away. After all, he had more reason to fear being in there than I did!

Someone managed to grab him and, stunning him in one movement, he was held up.

'Stab him,' someone else said. So I closed my eyes and

plunged my knife into his chest. I didn't know who to feel sorrier for, myself or the bird. Horrible work, but someone had to do it. After Grandad had taught me how to skin a rabbit I was less squeamish than most. These birds were just food for the table at the end of the day.

After a few months of this intense work schedule, I started to worry about the safety of the kids. Doug was so physically exhausted after his shifts he'd drop off even if he sat down for just five minutes. I feared the kids would be put in danger without an adult constantly supervising. Once I got home to find him half asleep, while Douglas was pulling himself up on the furniture trying to walk. I knew anything could happen, however good a father Doug was.

'No,' I said. 'I won't be able to work after all.' But how we'd live off Doug's wage, we didn't know. I handed in my notice. We might be completely skint again but at least the kids weren't in danger.

For the first time we felt truly trapped. We'd no money left at the end of the week for anything, aside from the absolute basics.

One afternoon, I was walking out of a grocery shop – having counted out pennies to just about pay for that night's dinner – when I bumped into Barbara.

'What's up, Cath?' she said. 'You look like you've lost ten shillings and found a penny.'

'You've knocked the nail on the head there, Barbara,' I agreed, sadly.

'Come on over and have a cuppa,' she said.

Tea and a natter heals everything, but in this case it wasn't going to buy the new clothes for Douglas or school uniforms for Susan and Lorraine.

'I just don't know how we're going to manage,' I sighed. 'I need to work as well to make ends meet, but we could never afford the childcare if both of us are working. Doug's exhausted and we just can't go on . . .'

Barbara smiled. 'Yes, you can,' she said. 'I could do with a job too now we have four kids, so let me take your children and you can pay me.'

For the first time in what felt like ages, I smiled. 'You're on,' I said.

Barbara would look after Susan, Lorraine and Douglas and I'd give her £5 a week – half my wages. It suited both of us.

I worked every day up till 6 p.m., then went home, cooked the kids their dinners and got their jammies on. It was all go, and I didn't have a minute to myself or for my husband. I saw Doug for about half an hour before he left for the night shift. We'd manage a quick 'hello', 'what's fer tea?' and maybe a quick moan or groan about the day. Then he disappeared into the night.

Being ships passing in the night is never good for any

marriage and ours was no exception. Although funnily enough I could actually see Doug at work, as our kitchen window looked out on to the slack heap and I could see the machinery he was probably driving in the distance. I could see that, like me, he was flat out. But it felt like a terrible irony, that although we were both working all these hours, due to the very low wages money worries continued to loom like a never-ending black cloud.

An honest day's work was the only solution to dragging ourselves out of this poverty, but sadly not everyone had the same attitude. Although on the whole, we took the mining community to be a very honest one, this wasn't always the case. In the January after we moved, Barbara told me about a burglar who'd broken into a few of the houses, pinching stuff while the men were at work.

'It must be a miner,' she said. 'After all, he seems to always pick the times when the women are on their own in the house.'

I shivered. 'Well, we haven't got a right lot to pinch,' I half-laughed. 'If he rifled through my drawers he'd find no pieces of jewellery or extra cash lying around, that's for sure.'

We had always left our back doors open previously, as we felt no sense of fear. Things like this hadn't happened before. But news travelled fast and the wives started pulling latches across and double-checking bolts. I tried to remember to do ours when I could. But I hadn't been joking about having nothing of value. And there was no reason why we'd be unlucky enough for the burglar to pick our house.

But of course, there was also no reason why our house would be exempt either. A few days after she'd warned me, I was lying in bed after Doug had left for the night shift when I heard something strange. The stairs were creaking as if someone was walking up them. But the footsteps sounded out of place. And Doug wasn't due back from his shift yet.

My heart started banging so loudly I thought whoever it was would hear. As quietly as possible, I slipped out of bed, crept across the room and grabbed a wooden chair. Holding it in front of me, legs first, I made my way towards the door.

Whoever was out there faced getting a chair rammed into his chest – the only way I could think of to defend myself and my family. I held it aloft, breathing deeply to steady my nerves.

'Come on then,' I thought, defiantly.

Listening intently, I counted the number of creaks on the stair. One, two, three, four . . . he was edging ever closer. I felt sick, hoping against hope the children wouldn't wake up and open their bedroom door. I feared I couldn't protect us all.

Creak number five, then six. I felt sweat pool on my top lip, as my arms quivered under the weight of my chair.

Then, suddenly, I heard the sound of a car pulling up outside our house. My neighbour must have come back from a late night out. The creaking stopped, as it appeared the burglar was also listening intently. I held my breath, barely daring to move. Then rapid creaks and footsteps in quick succession followed as the intruder rushed back down the stairs and out the door.

I raced to look over the banisters to see who it was, but he was long gone, the door left banging open in the wind. Checking the latch, I saw no sign of a broken entry. Although he'd not needed to as I'd stupidly left the door open.

Later on, when Doug got home, I told him what had happened and he was furious. 'Who the hell could it be?' he raged. 'Miners stealing from miners? I can't believe it. Just make sure that door is bolted now.'

A week later, when he was back on day shift, Doug went to lock the back door before we went to bed, and as he put his hand on the handle to try it he could feel someone on the other side also giving it a wiggle! In a flash Doug unlocked the door and flew outside to see a jacket turn in the darkness and the burglar disappear into the night.

It took a few months, but eventually the police arrested a miner called Mark and found piles of TVs, radios and tape recorders in his home. Everyone knew him. He was married with three kids and seemed a good type, Barbara told me. The day after he was arrested his wife and kids moved away. The Coal Board knew they'd be picked on, so moved them quick. Later on we all heard he was sent to prison.

Chapter Five

Drama seemed to follow us during our time in Rainworth. Even keeping our house warm soon proved unexpectedly life threatening. The bags of coke provided by the Coal Board were simply not enough to heat our home, and winter was especially harsh that year, with ice crystals forming on the inside of the bedroom windows by the morning. We went to bed watching our breath rise. Even extra blankets weren't enough to keep out the chill. So I bought a cheap paraffin heater for the bedrooms, just to get a bit of extra warmth going.

One night, in February, I said goodbye to Doug on his night shift and got the kids and myself off to bed. I flicked on the paraffin heater, thinking I'd turn it off before I dropped off to sleep. But, exhausted after a day at work and dealing with the kids, I couldn't keep my eyes open by the time I hit the pillow.

It felt like I'd been asleep only for a few minutes when

I found myself being shaken violently awake by Doug, screaming like a banshee.

'Cathy!' he yelled 'Wake up! Oh my God, are you all right?'

Gasping with fright, I came to with a jolt. The room flooded with sunshine as he pulled open the curtains.

Then the smell hit me. Thick black smoke stung my eyes as I opened them, and I started coughing. I knew instantly what it was. The paraffin heater. It'd been left on all night belching out acrid fumes that could've killed us all.

'The kids!' I screamed, waving my hand through the smoke.

Doug was already down the hallway to find the children, and I ran after him. We flung open the doors to see Susan and Lorraine opening bleary eyes, with rings of black soot around their noses.

I gathered them up in my arms, and just held them for a moment as they coughed. 'Thank God,' I whispered, kissing their warm heads while Doug ran around, flinging open the bedroom windows.

He turned off the heater and pushed it outside. Then he came in, tears pricking his eyes. 'Seeing your bedroom window from the street, all black and streaky, I thought I'd find you all dead,' he said, his voice breaking. 'My whole family.'

We'd been lucky. If Doug hadn't come home when he had maybe we'd all have died of smoke inhalation. I vowed never to use a paraffin heater again, however cold the bedrooms got. I chucked it out and got a Calor gas one instead.

In between the drama of burglars and ridiculously dangerous heating devices, we still had the daily rush round to get the kids up and away to Barbara's.

The children only had two or three outfits each as we'd lost most of our stuff in Scotland. That was another reason why funds were so low – we were still trying to replace all the furniture and clothes we'd lost. The rest would have to wait. I knitted constantly to try and clothe the children too. I had a knitting machine, which I found very boring to use, but in one evening I could knock up a cardie for Lorraine, who was eighteen months old, and then sew it together during my break at work. I certainly used every hour of the day; there was no time to waste. It took its toll, though. I was constantly so tired I was either losing my temper or bursting into tears at the slightest thing. I felt quite alone during this time. I never got to know any of the other neighbours, as we were constantly at work or at home getting ready for the next day. It was a whirlwind.

During the short times we were together, Doug and I

started snapping at each other with increasing frequency. We'd end up fighting over the kids. One day he'd accuse me of being too hard on them, the next day I'd do the same to him. If I said 'black', he said 'white'. We couldn't agree to disagree either. With exhaustion setting in, our tempers were frayed to the max and something had to give. Our house became a battleground of petty rows and we were filled with a bone tiredness neither of us could shake. At one point I thought we might even split up. I just couldn't see a future married to the bad-tempered man he'd become. He also found my constant working hard to live with. As a man he felt belittled: he wanted to be the provider. And I wanted him to be the main breadwinner too – I missed the children terribly, and felt like I never saw them. Working all these hours suited neither of us. Doug felt caught between the devil and the deep blue sea. He'd enquired about going underground, but would have to leave his job at the pit and the house first for six weeks before re-applying and retraining. He couldn't just swap jobs.

After one row I asked Doug what was wrong.

'What's really the matter?' I said. He looked so distraught I couldn't believe the petty row about house-work and the children we'd just had was at the heart of it. 'Talk to me,' I insisted. 'Sit down and talk.'

Doug stopped mid-sentence and sat down.

'I miss Scotland, Hamilton, my brothers . . .' he said, sadly. 'I want to go home, Cath.'

I took my husband's hands and nodded. We'd only just got settled here, but I knew what he meant. We were working all hours and still barely scraping a living. We knew hardly anyone and I missed Scotland too. The dream of working in the pit wasn't living up to what we hoped. We might have a roof over our heads but we could barely afford to feed our kids under it. And I knew that the last thing Doug wanted to do was go underground.

'I'd do it, you know I would,' Doug said, sadly. 'But I'm scared, Cath. I won't manage. I promised Dad too . . .'

'Shhhhh,' I said. 'You don't need to explain. We've come this far, we'll just keep going.'

And so it was decided; Doug would go back to Hamilton, try his hardest again to find a job and then come back for us. Meanwhile we managed to buy a small four-berth caravan, and moved on to a caravan site in Bellshill, Lanarkshire. Fortune was on our side and Doug soon found a job driving buses in Hamilton.

It was 1972 by now and decimalisation had just been brought in a year earlier. Neither of us were especially happy about it, after all it made day-to-day living even more expensive. And it hit the poorest hardest.

Doug came home from work incensed one evening.

'The poor old dears on the buses are still trying to pay

with old money,' he said. 'And the conductor didn't want to let them on. Well, I told them to hop on anyway. A bus ticket is twice the price now!'

Luckily the conductor saw sense not to make a fuss. Eventually Doug left the buses and found a job driving a bulldozer for a building site, and between Doug's two jobs, and with low living costs, we soldiered on. Then we managed to buy an old bigger caravan, which Doug slowly started to do up, painting the insides and getting new curtains. After a few months it was finished, so we were back in Scotland and finally had a decent-sized home, albeit a temporary one. Some peace at last! But of course, life never stays peaceful for long . . .

One afternoon, I was walking back from the Turkish baths, when I spotted black plumes of smoke rising from the area where our caravan was parked up.

Running towards it I vowed to speak my mind to one of the residents. One man in particular was always burning rubbish and it was too close for comfort to our caravan this time. It might just be an old one, but it was our home and I wished he had more respect. I was about to give him what for. But as I picked up the pace, I started to feel sick . . . the smoke wasn't coming from a nearby rubbish fire, it was coming from our caravan. As I turned the corner to see it in full view, I realised angry flames were licking at the windows and burning the curtains.

I just stood there, wanting to scream, but no sound was coming out. Neighbours were running from their caravans as the acrid smell started to permeate the site.

'Cathy! Where are the kids?' One of them yelled.

'Away,' I cried. 'Thank God.'

I was so grateful the children hadn't been in the place at the time. They were still safe, being babysat by neighbours in another caravan nearby. At that moment, I saw Doug running towards me, having just come home from work.

'Oh my . . .' he gasped. 'Cathy!'

Everything, every single thing we'd owned was in that caravan, and no, we had no insurance. We couldn't afford it. It was sheer stupidity with hindsight, but food and clothes took precedence then. Unbelievably, for the second time, we'd lost everything we possessed.

A feeling of strange numbness overcame me. Feeling light-headed and detached, I just turned my heel and started to walk off. I couldn't bear facing such a catastrophe for the second time. It just wasn't fair. I started to run. No idea where to, but anywhere seemed like a good idea.

Doug ran after me and caught my sleeve.

'Cathy,' he said, gently. 'Come here.'

With no energy left to resist, I fell into his arms.

'Not again, Doug,' I sobbed. 'Not again.'

A fire brigade investigation found the TV caused the blaze by blowing up. Apparently I'd inadvertently made the situation worse by polishing the TV set every day with spray; the chemical build-up had helped ignite the explosion. If the children had been in at the time, we'd have lost them too. It didn't bear thinking about.

After days to-ing and fro-ing to the council, we were eventually rehoused in Motherwell again. It was in a flat other people had turned down, so it was the roughest of rough council estates. We started where we'd left off before, with absolutely nothing.

The day we moved in couldn't have been more depressing. Every room was bare, and the walls were covered in damp, mould and brown streaks of filth.

We didn't have a cooker so had to make do with a gas stove and Calor canisters. All I could manage was to heat up a tin of vegetables or beans and dish them out on the few pieces of crockery we had left. We'd managed to get a three-piece suite on Hire Purchase, and they had to double up as beds.

That first night was dreadful. We pulled out the sofa to make it into a bed, with nine-year-old Susan and seven-year-old Lorraine sleeping alongside us on it. How four of us didn't break it I don't know. And of course there was almost no space. For Douglas, I shoved two armchairs together for him to sleep on. As we lay in the dark, listening to the sounds of our children's breath, I fought back tears. How we'd ended up in this situation I didn't understand.

The following day, I went to see the council to see if we could get any help with the flat, hoping they could provide proper beds or bedding at least. The lady at the counter shook her head. Because Doug had a job, even a low-paid one, we were not entitled to a penny of help. What made me sick was I knew that few of the others in our block worked. Out of twenty of us, I knew of only us and two other families who worked. The others sat on handouts.

To add to the burden, we all began to notice we were being bitten half to death by fleas. The wee buggers were everywhere, leaping over the carpets, sofas and curtains. We were infested but we couldn't understand where they were coming from.

Doug was complaining about it to his line manager at work one day.

'Ah,' he said. 'That estate is infamous for fleas. It's built on an old pit and they love the coal dust as it traps heat and keeps them snug!'

We had to get the council in, who sealed all the windows and let off chemical bombs to get rid of them. It was humiliating.

Doug was desperate to earn more money so that we could rebuild our lives faster. He went to his boss. 'I need overtime,' he explained.

'I know,' said his boss. 'And I could give you work twenty-four hours a day, but after seven days you'll be no good to anyone. So how's about I give you £100 and you can pay it off through your wage?'

Doug and myself had never borrowed any money – it was our way not to. But these were truly desperate times, so indeed we took this desperate measure. Straight away we used £50 to redecorate, getting rid of the damp and the bugs. It made our rooms slightly more inhabitable.

That Christmas, things were simply worse than ever. We had nothing, so it took careful planning. We'd managed to buy a hamper to pay off during the year with a shilling a week from a catalogue Doug's brother Gordon had given us. It contained tinned fruit, vegetables and a tinned chicken, something we could have instead of turkey.

I prepared the children's presents weeks in advance, too. I got a tomato box, a wire coat hanger and some lace and materials to make Susan and Lorraine a doll's rocking basket. This would be the only present they'd get this year.

Using the wire for the rocking part, I sewed the sides with fabric and padded it with cotton wool. I could only do it at night-time after they'd gone to bed. We bought Douglas a very cheap plastic dumper truck.

We couldn't afford a tree, so Doug took a hacksaw down to the woods near the River Calder and came back with a three-foot tree. We had no decorations so I made a fairy using a toilet roll and some lace. Someone gave us some broken fairy lights, which we fixed.

On the big day, we gave the girls their presents and happily they were pleased. Of course we played along with the idea that they were from Father Christmas to try and inject at least a little magic into the day!

Doug and I didn't buy each other anything. We had no TV either so could only listen to the radio for a little bit, again a second-hand one someone had donated to us, that cracked and popped, making it barely audible.

To prepare the dinner, we screwed open the tins, then heated up the contents on the Calor gas stove. Doug and I looked at each other as we tried to swallow the chicken. It was tasteless and so full of bones we could barely eat it, but we pretended it was good anyway and implored the kids to eat up. Thankfully the fruit and vegetables went down all right. We couldn't even afford any crackers so that we could wear coloured paper hats. As I cleared away, to rinse the plates, with what little washing-up liquid we had left, I felt my heart breaking. I could hear the kids playing with their toys, making the best of what they had, but I so wished I could give them more. All we had to do now was play a game of cards or a board game. There would be no delicious cakes or extra presents this year.

We had to make do, but it just wasn't good enough. Considering what hard workers we were, this position seemed doubly unfair.

Mum did what she could, sending clothes or food up when she was able. But I didn't like to keep asking her. She'd started to speak to Doug on the phone sometimes about the pit again.

'There are jobs underground going, you know,' she said, quietly. 'Hugh told me.'

I could tell when Doug had been having chats about the pit again, as he started bringing it up in conversation. 'Cathy, it might be the answer,' he'd say.

After all we'd been through, returning to Scotland, I felt less prepared to throw in the towel. Plus it all had to come from my husband. It was his decision.

Doug's brothers helped out too, but we both felt a keen sense of embarrassment taking handouts. And if the poverty wasn't enough to grind us down, the neighbours definitely were. There was so much thieving going on we could barely keep up. If it wasn't nailed down it went missing.

Wee boys, aged around nine, would come along and

pinch the wooden pegs from our washing lines. They'd bleach them and later that evening come along the doors and try to sell them back.

Once I took off my shoes after putting out the rubbish. I left them to dry on the doorstep before wiping them off. An hour later I opened the door to find they'd disappeared. That evening, a young lad knocked on the door, with my shoes all polished up in his hands.

'Would you be interested in buying this lovely pair of second-hand shoes?' he asked in the voice of a salesman.

'You cheeky beggar!' I cried, swiping them off him. 'Trying to sell me my own shoes back!'

Amongst all the thieves and bad apples, our kids stuck out like sore thumbs. Our Douglas was bullied especially badly as he was the same age as a lot of the troublemakers. He'd come home, full of fury. 'I wish I could clout them back, Mum,' he cried.

I felt sorry for him, as he knew if he fought back they'd come running in their gangs and they'd beat him soundly.

Eventually after he was pushed and shoved one day coming home from school, I'd had enough. I knew I needed to stand up for my son myself. I went and found Christine, a woman whose nephew was one of the worst perpetrators.

'If your nephew hits my Douglas again, I will hit you

next time to make up for it,' I said. I was that cross.

She looked shocked and knew I meant it. The next day the lads left Douglas alone.

Susan and Lorraine were almost confined to their bedrooms. They couldn't stand all the mouthing off going on outside, so hid away from it. Although I kept myself to myself, one day Christine asked if I wanted to share a lift with some other neighbours to the local supermarket. None of us could afford one minicab ride each and I needed to do a cheap shop so I said yes. We waited outside for the car to arrive. After a few minutes, I leaned down to take my purse out of my bag ready for the taxi. But once I'd done so, I looked up and saw that the four neighbours I'd been standing with had disappeared.

'Eh? Have I imagined this?' I thought, completely bewildered. I looked around me and couldn't work out where they'd gone or how they'd managed to melt away at such speed. When I peered back at our block, I could see them all frantically opening their doors and legging it back inside their houses.

Then I looked down the road and saw the electricity meter reading man coming up the road. Suddenly it all became clear. They'd all fiddled their meters so they were desperate not to be seen.

It was only myself and one other neighbour who ever

opened our doors to him. Later I spoke to Christine. 'Why don't you fiddle yours?' she asked.

'For a start I don't believe in it,' I said. 'And secondly we don't use enough electricity in the first place!'

I got given the nickname 'the Queen Mother' because they said I had airs and graces. Every morning I'd be knitting on my doorstep at 8 a.m., with the kids out for school and all of my jobs done, while most of my neighbours were still in bed. Doug called our road 'DHSS Row' and he couldn't have been more right.

I often found myself on the phone, sobbing to Mum and sometimes Grandad. She was staggered at how things had turned out and wanted to help. But being so far away there was little she could do. Besides, things had been hard at her end, with Hugh off on strike. The National Union of Mineworkers (NUM) had called a strike after becoming incensed about the way the government was using their pay packets and a ban on wage rises to help control inflation.

'The government has to listen to us,' sighed Mum. 'It's not fair the way mining is going.'

The terrible weather was helping win public support for the miners' campaign but the country was facing electricity shortages as they cut off the movement of coal to the power stations.

'What a state of affairs,' Mum said. 'But at least we've got work.'

I fell silent. Neither of us had to say anything, but we both knew Doug's situation had to change. Without a doubt, returning to Scotland had been a huge mistake.

Something had to give and once again Doug and I sat down to talk about our options. Once again the idea of mining came up. We just kept coming back to it.

It was also apparent that we needed to think seriously about where we wanted to live. We may have been back in Scotland but I soon realised I felt more at home during my time in England.

'I think we had a much better life in England,' I said, quietly. It was the first time I'd said it out loud.

Doug looked at me in surprise. Then he frowned.

'Yes,' he said, slowly. 'I think you're right.'

Chapter Six

Part of us wondered if we hadn't left it too late to join the mining industry. It wasn't just our futures that felt uncertain. By mid 1973, the NUM had encouraged miners to work to rule. As a result, coal stocks slowly dwindled and we saw on the *News at Ten* how an oil crisis had ensued and the price of coal was rising. The government moved to reduce electricity consumption, and by the end of that year Edward Heath announced the start of the three-day week. Shops and businesses could only use electricity for three days in seven, to try and stop a total shutdown.

We'd never been ones to notice much about politics, bar Mum letting us know what Hugh and his pit were up to, but suddenly politicians' decisions were affecting everyone's day-to-day lives. There was no escape. The kids were not allowed in school on the days of the electricity shortages due to health and safety concerns, so I'd be picking them up early.

'Make sure you've got hold of Doug,' I said to Susan, as I pushed the pram along a gloomy pavement in the pitch black. Woolworth's was one of the few shops able to keep its lights on, by using a spare generator. The rest relied on candles. I often found myself picking out apples and oranges in the grocer's by a flickering flame. Some days it felt like a literal return to the dark ages.

Then, five years after Douglas came along, I'd found myself expecting again. It was a huge shock. We'd never used contraception, but after five years we'd all but thought our chances of having more kids were over. However, it would have been unthinkable for us not to go through with the pregnancy. All babies are a blessing.

Around this time, I bumped into an old friend, Liz, who lived nearby. She'd recently had a miscarriage and faced having a D&C.

'I'm not going to Motherwell hospital,' she said. 'I've heard they carry them out without any pain relief.'

I laughed. 'Don't be silly, Liz, this isn't the Victorian era. Of course in a modern hospital they will give you pain relief. Go and have it done, it's important.'

The following day, I went to visit Liz in Motherwell. I soon realised it was a basic maternity hospital, but seemed clean enough. As I approached her bed, I saw she looked deathly pale, her starched sheet pulled to her chin.

'They didn't use any pain relief . . .' she whispered. 'Three of them had to hold me down on the bed.'

I was stunned. I couldn't believe what I was hearing. The place was barbaric.

'Gosh, I had no idea,' I said. 'I am so sorry.'

Back home, I described the place to Doug.

'Dear God!' he cried. 'You want to stay well clear of that place, Cath!'

I agreed. But when my labour pains began, it was all too late to make other arrangements and the ambulance took me there automatically.

Carrie was born on 7 October 1973. As with all my labours, it was long, hard work. Afterwards at home, I lost lots of blood and was in huge amounts of pain.

Doug called the doctor who came to see me and ordered me to go back to Motherwell hospital. 'No way!' I said. 'I know what doctors do there!'

'My wife goes there, nothing is wrong with it,' insisted the doctor.

'Well, that's your wife, not you, isn't it!' I retorted.

In the end, I stayed in my bed and eventually passed a ball of blood and veins.

'Urgh, what's that?' I said to Doug, who looked equally shocked.

He picked it up with a piece of tissue.

'Something for the doctor to see,' he said.

The doctor came back and gave me an injection for the pain. He looked at the ball and told me it was likely an undeveloped twin.

'I'd no idea,' I said, softly. But I didn't have time to dwell on what could have been or what I'd lost. With three busy kids and another newborn, there wasn't much time to sit and feel sorry for yourself. We just had to get on with it.

Meanwhile our money worries continued while we decided what to do. Of course we now had another mouth to feed. The truth be told, we just couldn't afford another one.

During this time of despair, Doug just soldiered on, working on the building sites for a pittance, but all the while the idea of him going down the pit was rumbling away in the background. One Saturday afternoon Doug was having a rare sit down, flicking through the local paper with a cup of tea, when he ripped out a job advertisement to train up miners down in Bevercotes colliery in Nottinghamshire.

'Take a look at this, Cath,' he said.

It read: 'We'll move your family and your belongings, pay you £50 on arrival and £50 after you stay for a year. You'll be trained within a few weeks and get a job and house for life . . .'

My eyes widened. In every which way it was tempting. We knew through Hugh that Nottingham collieries were lucrative places to work, boasting busy production lines with hundreds of years' worth of coal left in them. Mum had recently told me how new machines to help the men cut the coal, all introduced under new health and safety acts, had made the profession safer than ever. It sounded nothing like what Doug's dad and brothers had endured. Miners were more like engineers these days, put in charge of big machines, protected by strict rules and regulations. You could earn a decent wage for life in this industry. The pits down south were attracting workers from all over the country, that's how popular they were.

Perhaps Mum had been right all along. Maybe it wouldn't be as bad as Doug had feared.

Doug sighed as he looked me in the eye. 'This time I could train to go underground. Become a proper miner. I could just go for it. What do you think?'

'Ah, Dougie, you know it has to be your decision,' I said for the umpteenth time. Despite all our financial troubles, I couldn't bring myself to tell my husband what to do. He had to come to his own conclusions. My own thoughts on the mine, I kept to myself. In all honesty, I hated the idea of kissing Dougie goodbye every morning to send him into what sounded like a life of hell. I'd never forgotten the story of his brother Malcolm or how my pop came home black and exhausted. No, entering a mine was a life of mystery as far as I was concerned, and from all accounts not a particularly happy one.

I'd felt like Doug had had a lucky escape serving in the armed forces, and being a miner seemed to me like he would just be facing a new danger on a daily basis. In an ideal world I'd want to keep the man I loved a million miles away from a coalface, with its dirt and stench. Why anyone would choose to work underground was beyond me. But for the first time, when he pulled that advert out, I saw a sparkle reignite in those chocolate-brown eyes. I could see his pride returning. Maybe, just maybe, he was right?

For all my own private thoughts on the subject, things were looking pretty desperate by now. I'd just found out I was pregnant again, this time with our fifth child. That was something we had never expected, for sure. But as hard as life was, we didn't want it any other way. To be living in the fleapit of Motherwell though was such a far cry from what I wanted for my kids, I couldn't be happy about it.

Later on, after the children had gone to bed, Doug brought up the subject again.

'There's no escape; mining is in my blood,' Doug said. 'I know what's involved. I know how tough it is, but I need to do this for you and our family now. We'll get a good house and a decent wage. They are the only things that matter now. I want to do it, Cath.'

The mining industry was never far from the headlines at the time. The Tories had used a slogan a few months earlier, in February 1974, which read: 'Who Governs Britain?' alongside a picture of some miners. Heath had called a snap election that had led to a hung parliament. There was real anger from the government about how powerful the miners' unions had become. But in our eyes they were merely ordinary hard-working folk voicing an opinion. A proud, dignified, hard-working class who kept the country running and the lights on. To be part of it would in many ways feel like an honour.

Doug spoke with determination, but as he squeezed my hand, I knew just how hard this decision had been. After all, Doug had done as his father had wanted and avoided the pit for years. He'd watched his brothers, six of them at one point, all working in the pit, and he'd witnessed the accidents and heard the horror stories. But he was right. We were on a crossroads now and needed a home and good wage more than ever. We simply had to escape from this hell-hole. He'd tried to live a life outside the pit and failed. If we had a second chance to properly make a go of life in a pit, and living in a pit village with all the community it has to offer, something my mum and sister had enjoyed for years now, we'd feel so lucky.

'If you're sure,' I said.

Doug nodded. We both knew it was the best way out of this situation and it couldn't come quickly enough for me.

Without another moment's agonising or hesitation, he grabbed a pen and filled in the form.

'Done!' he said, triumphantly.

Just a few days later, he was booked into Boston training centre for miners where the new recruits were given a thorough health check. Just like in the army they were examined head to toe. They checked their chest expansion and made them take fitness tests. That many lads of all ages, from all over the country, wanted to join, they could pick and choose the fittest men. Thankfully Doug was one of them and a few weeks later Doug had been accepted for training at Bold colliery in December 1974.

My husband was finally going to become a miner underground.

Now the decision had been made, we moved to Parbold, near Skelmersdale in Lancashire, to live with some friends, Jessie and Sam. They'd kindly agreed to put us and our children up for a few months while we got sorted. Luckily the children were all still young, so we managed to squeeze into their one spare room. It was a tight fit but we were grateful for the roof over our heads while Doug found jobs driving buses and taxis as he waited for his training dates to come up.

When they finally did, Doug set off to Bold colliery every morning for twenty days. He had to get into a cage lift and then plunge 600 yards down into a relatively shallow mine shaft, for a day of instruction from the oversmen (bosses). He also needed to acclimatise to pit conditions. For anyone new to it, the darkness and the intense heat combined to form a completely alien environment. For many of the trainees – known as 'green labour' – who had worked in the outdoors and open fields for years, it couldn't have been more different. Cramped, dark, and reaching temperatures of up to 120 degrees, the conditions were like nothing anyone would have experienced before.

The days of pick-axing at a coalface with a paraffin lamp torch on your head were long gone, though it was still a very dangerous place, with many injuries occurring. The instructors hammered home the facts about the extreme dangers during the lads' training, telling them one in three miners can expect to have a bad accident at some point. And one in twenty could expect to lose their lives.

When Doug's father and grandfather were miners, thousands were injured or killed every year, but even with safety having improved hugely the risks remained. Aside from the walls coming down on top of them, miners were mainly fearful of fires or gas. Coal dust is highly flammable and one single spark can cause an explosion. All men were issued with 'self rescuers', gas masks that would give vital minutes to escape. And one lad would always be down there carrying a Davy lamp to check for gas – though Doug couldn't believe it when he found out that the lad only got an extra five pence a day, for all the responsibility of the lives of the ten men he was with.

Haulage was another dangerous job as each coal tub weighed a tonne; imagine one of those rolling towards you! A nurse was on constant standby to provide immediate medical attention and the local hospitals dealt with miners' injuries very swiftly as they were used to seeing so many. Relatives were always called by the 'sister' on duty at the mine the day anything happened. It was the phone call everyone dreaded.

Despite his new appreciation of the risks, Doug came home in high spirits on the first day of his training. To him, the biggest surprise was the sense of camaraderie below the ground. The lads were all being trained together, and they joked, laughed and bonded as they realised that the success of the mine and its safe running depended on a team effort.

'It's a bit like the army down there,' Doug laughed. 'An army underground.'

I smiled too. At long last we had something to smile about. I was proud of Doug for taking this on. It had been something he'd dreaded for years, always putting it off and trying other jobs, but now he'd done it, he looked happier than I'd seen him for a long time.

The first day he got home, I noticed something strange about his eyes. He looked like he was wearing mascara, just like my pop had done. It was all too familiar to Doug, as he'd grown up seeing his brothers' black-rimmed eyes. Another sign of a miner was their livid scars from any cuts, which turned blue after soot got caught under the skin. This usually happened only with deep cuts, if the deputies didn't wash it out with sodium hydroxide fast enough. The men were scarred for life and the cuts were also known as 'Mark of the Miner'.

But Doug seemed not to mind these things. In fact, in a quiet moment, he expressed regrets about not making his decision sooner. 'If only I'd known it wasn't so bad,' he said. 'I should have gone underground a long time ago. It would have been easier to do that than face all the desperate times we've done.'

He was right. The Motherwell tenement, the factory work, the low wage on the surface, living in a caravan for a year . . . he'd tried everything to avoid the pit. Now he was there, it wasn't so bad.

'But you weren't to know how it'd changed, Dougie,' I

soothed. There was little point in having regrets. We'd made the decisions we'd made and that was the end of it.

After he'd completed his training, Doug had to wait to start his job properly, as men were trained in 'batches' and started in teams. So he took a job driving buses in the meantime and we were allocated a house by the Coal Board while we waited. At the start we were given the offer of an old or a new house. I picked an old one. Not just for the charm, but also because it had a coal fire whereas the new ones ran on coke. I'd already learned my lesson from Rainworth about how coke doesn't go very far.

On the way to our new house, in Ollerton near Newark-on-Trent, we packed up the car and my grandad came down to help. I was expecting my baby to arrive any day now, so the race was on to get us indoors and settled. With the car packed with boxes and kids, we set off on the 130-mile journey to Nottinghamshire.

'Aye up,' said Doug as the car slowed down. 'Think we've got problems here.'

The car ground to a halt as he pulled over on to a grass verge. After leaping out, he scratched his head and announced it was a flat tyre.

Everyone piled out as he jacked up the car, doing a quick change before we all piled back in.

After a few more miles a familiar clunking feeling rocked us in the back.

'Oh no!' cried Doug, as he pulled over again. Now another tyre had gone like a burst balloon.

I just started laughing. I could feel my baby moving around impatiently and the kids were bouncing around with excitement. In many ways it couldn't have been more stressful, but nothing could faze me. To be leaving our old lives behind and getting this second chance in a pit village where Doug would be earning a good wage made me want to punch the air with joy. I just sensed all our lives would be changed for the better now and it would take more than one or even two flat tyres to bring me down.

As our car, driving slowly on two spare wheels, turned into Ollerton, the mining village, I just couldn't stop smiling, soaking up the views of the smart houses. Square-fronted, they had two windows at the top, one large one at the bottom and neat white front doors. All their lawns were well kept with wooden picket fences, some with gates, along the front lawn. All of them exuded an air of respectability, and just looking at them made me feel welcome.

'I feel like I've come home again,' I said to Doug.

He laughed. 'I think we all have.'

Our new house, on Whitewater Road, was a typical

Coal Board place, with the bottom half brick cast with three steps at the front. One path led to both our door and the other house next door. It was a lovely place, so big compared to what we were used to. We unpacked the car, and the kids all ran around like banshees picking their rooms. We didn't have a huge amount of possessions and very little furniture, so it only took a couple of hours to get ourselves in and the door closed.

We spent that evening unpacking kitchen items and getting the house straight. Outside the window we could see other families arriving at the same time as us, unpacking their cars. We still had very little compared to everyone else, but this time it didn't seem to matter. With Doug's good mining wage coming in, we'd soon be able to afford more bits and pieces ourselves as time went on.

After I'd got the kids to sleep, Doug and I stuck the kettle on.

'Let's have something stronger to celebrate,' Doug said.

He'd bought a six-pack of Carlsberg to share with the workmen, who had been helping us unload. Never one to drink, I poured a glass of lemonade. Sitting down together on our old sofa, we looked at each other and clinked glasses.

'Cheers,' I grinned.

'Cheers,' Doug replied, his voice breaking a little.

'We've done it, lassie,' he whispered. 'I'm going to be a proper miner. We don't have to worry any more.'

'And I'll be a miner's wife,' I teased. 'Fancy that.'

We both admitted the same thing. We felt hugely grateful to get this second stab in the pit. With this lovely house, on its friendly looking street, in the middle of the green swell of the East Midlands countryside, we both felt at home already. And come Saturday, Doug would be guaranteed his first decent wage in years. It all seemed too good to be true. I almost wanted to pinch myself. I just couldn't stop smiling. Doug squeezed my hand and as I glanced at him, I realised his eyes were glassy, full of tears.

'Thank God, Cath,' he said, quickly wiping his cheek.

We both fell silent, sinking into our settee, sipping our drinks. We barely had a stick of furniture; the place needed a good clean; I was about to give birth – but at that moment I could not have felt happier. A safe port, at last.

Chapter Seven

That night I barely slept, but not through worry of bills or being woken by babies, but I kept waking with a sense of excitement. I just couldn't wait to start getting our new place ship-shape.

After getting the kids up for their breakfast, I set about cleaning and sorting things out, ignoring my big bump as I had plenty to be doing. The house was lovely but needed a good clean, especially the soot-covered windows and step outside.

As I was buffing a window at the top, half-standing on a window ledge, one of the neighbours came rushing out.

'Oooh! You OK, my love?' she shouted up.

'Yes, fine thanks,' I said. 'Just cleaning my windows.'

'Oh gosh, do be careful,' she fussed. 'You're about to pop!'

I smiled. 'It's number five,' I laughed. 'I'll manage.'

Another knock came at the door soon afterwards. It was another miner's wife from down the road who'd come to ask me if I'd like to swap her new house for my old one. She'd already realised she needed more than the weekly eight bags of coke she was given to keep the house toasty and it was costing a fortune. I just laughed. 'No thanks,' I said. 'We're settled in here already.'

After she left, I thought to myself I'd rather have an efficient fire than a fancy new house that costs an arm and leg to heat.

Later on I was on my hands and knees scrubbing the front step and a woman who introduced herself as Miss Wilkinson came over.

'I'm from the Coal Board,' she said, her kind face beaming. 'And it's my job to make sure you're all settling in. Please let me organise for someone to come over tomorrow and help you clean. You must be about to give birth any day now.'

'No, I'll be fine, honestly,' I laughed. 'What's the worst that can happen? I'll just go into labour!'

I'm a tough cookie, but she didn't seem to realise this. After four babies, I wasn't worried. I thanked her for her kind offer.

'To be honest,' I said, 'if I ever had a cleaner I'd want to get up even earlier to get things spick and span before they arrived. I'd end up even more stressed than before!'

She laughed, but said if I needed anything just to ask. As she waved and walked off, I found myself smiling again. What a wonderful change this was to the Motherwell estate. This place was full of proud, kind, hard-working people. People who cared.

Later on, she popped over again and this time I asked if she could lend me some bleach. I wanted to get the doorstep shining.

Happy to help, she came over with a cup of Domestos. She put it on the windowsill and as my back was turned just for a few seconds Douglas had run over, grabbed it and downed it in one!

Grabbing him, I rushed him to the kitchen tap and frantically poured water into his mouth as he screamed. Miss Wilkinson dashed back over as I yelled, 'Please! Call an ambulance!'

We managed to get him to hospital, where luckily he was given the all clear. Not that we knew it then, but my cheeky little boy was hyperactive and we had to be on our guard with him. What a dramatic way to mark our first day in our new home!

My new baby, who we named Allan, eventually arrived ten days late, and suddenly we were a family of seven. It was just in the nick of time that Doug started his new job. He was assigned to work at Bevercotes pit, working day or night shifts for £28 per week, an absolute fortune compared to the paltry £3 daily rate on the surface.

Bevercotes was known as a demonstration mine, meaning it had remotely operated machinery, which was seen as a very modern invention at the time. Men in this pit could cut vast pieces of the coalface all at once. The days of chipping away with a pick-axe were long gone. Lads from Scotland, England, and Wales came to work here, as they were recruiting a lot of 'green labour' – people who had worked on the land, as farmers or farmhands, who'd run out of work and wanted to earn a good crust. Doug was to work as an 'underground general', which meant he'd do a variety of jobs. He planned, though, to work his way up, learning all the jobs and then one day becoming a deputy.

On the morning of his first day, Doug got up and dressed in old jeans, a T-shirt and pit boots then set off at 5 a.m. to start the day shift at 6 a.m. He was feeling a tad nervous, but I made him up a packed lunch of a doorstop cheese sandwich, and sent him on his way. The pit was a couple of miles away and the Coal Board sent out a bus to pick up the men at the end of the road.

'You'll be back before no time,' I said.

Waving him off, I felt a knot in my own stomach. I tried not to think of the reality of his situation. Getting into a lift and dropping deep underground, swallowed up into the 'unknown' black hole. I closed my eyes for a few seconds as the old worries flitted through my mind: the danger of gas, fire, ceilings caving in . . . It just didn't bear thinking about. Without Doug I didn't know what'd become of us. Not only would I lose my soulmate, but our home and our community. Usually the Coal Board would give the family a one-off payment of £100 or so in the event of a fatality, and a basic death grant from the government. Then you'd have a few weeks to find somewhere else to live and off you'd go. But it didn't bear thinking about now Doug was going out the door.

Just as their father left, Susan and Douglas came running downstairs, rubbing their eyes with sleep. The pair of them were always together, thick as thieves.

'Dad!' Susan cried.

Doug turned and knelt down to give them a quick kiss and cuddle.

'Hope it's not too dark,' whispered Douglas. He'd already been given a helmet with a lamp on it to play with by a passing neighbour. Like all the kids he was fascinated by it and he and Susan had set up a mini camp under their duvets, playing 'miners' until they dropped off to sleep.

I shooed the kids away to let Doug off, and closed the door.

'It won't be too dark, silly,' I laughed to the children as I took them back up to bed. 'He'll have a light on his head all the time to show him the way. That'll keep him safe until home time.'

I was smiling brightly, but found myself swallowing hard. Please let him come back in one piece, I thought.

Turning back to hear Allan waking for his next feed, I went into the kitchen to get a sterilised bottle filled. Whatever Doug had to endure during the day, the fact was I had four kids and a baby to care for. Whatever my worry was for Doug, it had to stay locked inside me. It was no good making a song and dance about it. I'd have to learn to swallow the anxiety down and focus on the here and now.

After getting the kids up for breakfast, a knock came at the door.

'Yoo hoooo!' A smiling face emerged as I opened it. Thrusting her hand into mine, the lady introduced herself as 'Sheena'.

'I'm your new neighbour,' she said, pointing a few doors down. 'I hope you're settling in OK.'

I nodded and invited this small, birdlike lady with blondish hair in for a cuppa. She talked nineteen to the dozen, telling me all about what was around the pit area, how good the local shops were, how the Miners' Welfare did right good turns every week and I wasn't to miss the Bingo. And all in a single breath!

I could barely keep up. Soon I'd become used to Sheena's 'drop-in' visits, always with little notice and always breathless with news. She'd plant herself at my kitchen table and whether I was busy or not would make me listen. I could be up to my elbows in scrubbing dirty nappies or washing four bottles at once, and she'd still chat away nonstop. Then she'd up as quickly as she arrived and take off to the house next door. I soon realised she worked her way all along our road by lunchtime. By the end of the road she must've been high on caffeine with all the teas and coffees.

The afternoon of Doug's first day whizzed past and I soon heard the key in the door again. He finished his shift at 2 p.m., getting home for around 3 p.m. When he came through the door he looked exhausted, and still a bit hot and bothered. He'd had his shower before he'd hopped in the minibus home, and was clearly still digesting his first full day below.

'How was it, love?' I asked him.

He sat slowly in the chair, half smiled and blew out his cheeks. 'It were quite an adventure, Cath,' he said. 'But it's another world down there. Coming up out of it feels a bit like a holiday already.'

On the way down all the men had been given a brass tally, with their own number on it. Doug's was 642, one that'd last him throughout his career. All the men also got a silver container with a small gas mask to put on their belts, a four-pint flask filled with water and orange powder with salts to rehydrate them, and a hard hat with a light on top attached to a battery. Then he was led into a lift cage with sixty men and for seventy seconds they plunged down below the surface of the earth. The mine stood at 3,000 yards deep, much deeper than the training mine at Bold colliery.

'It was a bit of a shock, that lift,' Doug laughed. 'We were all packed in, thirty on top and bottom, like a double-decker bus . . . except it was like no bus I'd ever been on! The lift plunged down a shaft with a sopping wet wall and it stank to high heaven. Best get used to it, though!'

I wrinkled my nose. I knew the lack of fresh air would get to me.

At the bottom of the shaft they were then sent to their place of work. Some had a two-mile walk before they reached their patch. Doug was put on a 'paddy' – a wee train – and taken six miles further into the pit. I shuddered a little as he told me about it.

'I can't imagine being that far under,' I said.

'Aye,' he nodded. 'It's a different world, Cathy. But there are beautiful parts to it too with the stalactites and all.'

He pulled a piece of rock from his pocket with an imprint of a fossilised leaf on it. The kids all gathered round, oohing and aahing.

'This'll be millions of years old,' he chuckled, letting them all run their sticky hands over it. 'Imagine that!'

Before the men had arrived for their shift that day one of the deputies would have used a Davy lamp to check for methane gas to make sure it was safe. Thankfully I knew Doug wasn't a risk taker. He'd be methodical and careful, I was certain. But it wasn't the avoidable things that worried me, it was the unavoidables – like a ceiling collapse or an explosion going wrong. On the coalface especially there were so many unknowns, so many possible mishaps, sometimes even human error was not to blame.

For now, though, he just needed to learn the ropes and all the safety tips he could.

'I'll likely be doing one of three jobs,' Doug went on. 'Either track laying, dust spreading, or making manholes.'

Track laying was for the tubs of coal to be wheeled on and involved using steel girders and bolts to make new tracks for the tubs as the coal was cut away.

Dust spreading was getting rid of the tonnes of dust created every year down there, including chalk from the ground. 'It's like bags and bags of flour,' Doug chuckled. 'You don't turn black in that section – you turn white from the chalk dust!'

Making manholes involved constructing the arches of steel and drilling them into the ground to support the new ceilings of parts of the pit. He'd find out soon enough which task he'd be put on.

Doug had been teamed up with three other green labour men: Garland, Roberts and Williams. All were from the north and all 'soft lads' in Doug's eyes.

'Nice enough but won't last in the pit, I reckon,' Doug tutted.

Although Doug was viewed as green labour too, he was quickly spotted as a hard worker, someone who listened to what he was told to do and didn't mind pitching in. But that was Doug's nature and, as he'd often tell them, mining was in his blood. Besides, he'd never been one to mind getting his hands dirty.

The men were still being trained up to work in different pit areas. The coalface was one of them and one of the biggest jobs. This was the place where the new coal was cut from, and was the deepest area of the pit. Doug would now be working 3,000 ft deep, and up to six miles along from the entrance.

As he spoke, I swayed with Allan on my hip while trying to feed Carrie some carrot puree. Although motherhood could be a hard job I wouldn't swap our roles for anything in the world.

'Is it hot down there?' I asked.

Doug pulled a face. 'Hot,' he said, 'is not even the word!'

The mine was cooled with ventilation shafts and pipes bringing water in, but parts of it still reached 120 degrees.

'The men work in their underpants,' he chuckled. 'Not a pleasant sight in some cases, but needs must.'

'How did your sandwich go down?' I asked.

'It was like toasted cheese,' he laughed. 'I won't be taking one again. The heat turned the bread stale and the cheese turned to liquid. I'd prefer some grapefruit or something thirst-quenching.'

After working his seven-and-a-quarter-hour shift with a twenty-minute break, Doug came back up. Of course they had to allow their eyes to readjust on the way up and the way down. The lamps on their heads were so bright and strong they dazzled the men's eyes if someone swung round, beaming it into your face. So on the way down, they half closed their eyes and did the same on the way up. All the men had a shower straight away on their return, entering the room on the 'dirty side' and leaving it on the 'clean side'. The room was heated to dry out their clothes as well, and then they were free to go and take a bus home.

'Fresh air never tasted so good,' said Doug.

While Doug was getting used to his new life, so was I. My day revolved around getting the kids to their new school, settling them in, then getting back and sorting out the house. It didn't leave much time for nattering. I got on well with Miss Wilkinson, who still always stopped by to chat, to see if I needed anything. I always politely turned her down – used to being independent, I never liked to rely on any folk for help – but just the fact she cared was lovely. And of course Sheena had started to drop in almost on a daily basis, but I didn't mind. She was kind enough. She filled me in on all the gossip in the street. There was more going on than any episode of *Coronation Street* it seemed!

Doug had also started to find his feet within the community. Although he didn't click with the green labour lads he had trained with, Doug hit it off with Les, the miner next door, and three other lads in the pit: Jonny Green, Geordie Maddox and Brian White. They were all Geordies and the three of them shared the same silly sense of humour and dry wit.

Les had gone into the pit aged fourteen but left when he was eighteen to join the army. At the time, the safety wasn't as good and he'd wanted to get away. But lured by bigger pay packets and the mechanisation of Bevercotes he came back. Jonny was a real character. He was always trying to worm his way out of working if he could but he made the boys laugh so much they let him off.

Some of the other wives I didn't click with so much as they were very different characters to me. Geordie Maddox's wife Agnes was a rather toffee-nosed lady, with airs and graces I didn't get on with. She swanned around in heels and a fur trimmed coat, even to take the kids to school, and I could see she spent a lot of her money on her clothes. It came as no surprise to me that Agnes had a best friend like Ruby. Every time I walked past the hairdresser, Ruby seemed to be installed underneath one of the hair drying machines, reading a magazine or filing her nails. The two of them looked more suited to a life working in a cabaret than being miners' wives. I sensed they thought the rest of the wives weren't good enough company for them.

'On their way to the hairdressers, no doubt,' said Sheena one day, as the pair clip-clopped past my window.

I couldn't help but laugh. Even dyeing your hair was a waste of time and money in my book. After all, we all get old and go grey eventually.

Despite my private thoughts about them, I often met the pair of them in passing as Doug got on so well with Geordie. Agnes spoke as if her mouth was full of marbles, with a cut-glass accent. I'm sure she put it on, as she was so unlike her down-to-earth husband. He used to be a deputy at another pit until it had closed. He'd had to join Bevercotes as a general worker with the idea he'd work his way up to be a deputy again, but Agnes lost none of the airs and graces of a deputy's wife. I rather suspected she was shocked at life in Ollerton and thought we were all beneath her. Most of us were just working-class folk, happy – grateful even – to be part of the mining world. There wasn't much glamour in the village.

Even between them the glamour pusses fell out sometimes. Once Agnes made a dig at Ruby's cooking. Despite her high and mighty airs, Ruby was still a Geordie at heart and loved baking pease pudding, a basic but popular northern dish. One day Agnes popped her head around her kitchen and told her 'that', pointing at the dish, was 'letting the side down'.

It wasn't only that pair who thought they were above the rest of us. The deputies' wives were terrible, some of them. Now, deputies earned more money and had more responsibility. For example, they had to rigorously enforce the safety measures and do the 'shotfiring' – setting up and triggering an explosion at the coalface, something Hugh had explained was his job. The miners tended not to mix with the deputies, and vice versa, and a couple of their wives were very la-de-dah, despite the fact that Doug had told me there were times he'd ended up doing the job of a deputy at the coalface.

Once I overheard a deputy's wife as she pushed past a young lass buying apples in the grocer's. 'Don't you know who I am?' she actually said. I did a double-take. Did I really hear those words come from her mouth?

'No,' said the grocer, confused.

'My husband is a deputy,' she smiled, offering some money for a bunch of grapes.

'I don't care,' I interrupted. 'And neither does he, so wait your turn, madam!'

She stuck her nose in the air and walked out. I don't think she paid for the grapes in the end either.

Chapter Eight

Although the village gossip was all quite fascinating, my hands were so full during the day that I didn't have too much time to join in. I spent most of my time on my own with the kids, just seeing everyone was fed, watered, and got off to school, and that all the housework was done. Susan and Lorraine became involved in the local mining marching bands and needed to-ing and fro-ing to different competitions, too.

There were three bands, called the Blue Jays, the Nomads and the Tartaneers. Susan and Lorraine learned to play the kazoo, and practised twice a week in the local school grounds. Susan joined the Blue Jays and Lorraine went into the Nomads. Don't ask me why, they just chose them themselves! The bands catered for a range of kids from age five up to eighteen, and they put on displays all year round, at village fetes and fairs. They'd also enter competitions and were graded on how well they did. If they were even a fraction out of time, they'd lose points.

We soon realised the depth of pride and competitiveness of each pit village. The leader of the Blue Jays was a former army officer, who screamed and yelled at the kids as if they were about to go off to war. Well, it was a war in a sense. All they were fighting for was the prize of a plastic trophy, which us parents had to pay for to boot, but it was all taken deadly seriously. If so much as a speck of dirt was found on their white plimsolls the kids would be sent home with a flea in their ear. But they loved it. The film *Brassed Off*, with Pete Postlethwaite, portrayed the camaraderie and sense of competition of pit bands very well. Our kids' bands were like the junior versions, although in our area the adult band wasn't quite as big a deal.

If I wasn't ferrying the kids around, I was baking, always ensuring that Doug had a hot and tasty meal to come home to. After years of eking out the food budget, I was still in the habit. The kids' favourites included corned beef and tatty pie, which was a mix of tins of corned beef, onion and carrot with mash squashed on top. They also loved Freshman's pie – minced beef wrapped in a pastry case – or a cobbler, which is minced beef topped with little dumplings. They also loved my Quiche Lorraine, and the doughnuts I made were so fluffy and fresh straight from the oven, I often didn't get chance to fill them with jam before eager fingers had whipped them off the tray. It was a good job I had a big family, as Doug would joke how I didn't know how to cook for less than ten anyway. My portion sizes have always been as generous as possible.

Getting new furniture and paying for clothes is a challenge for any housewife and after all our bad luck with our things being stolen or burned it was tough, despite Doug's new job. His starting salary was £28 a week to begin with and it went straight into the bank and then straight out again into my purse to pay for our household expenses. Bigger items like furniture either had to wait or be bought on HP.

Debt was inevitable and although it wasn't something the neighbours broadcast, we all used the loan company called Paggetts down the road. It was just like the Provident in terms of how it worked, but it was a local company run by a local lady, Nancy Stewart, and luckily for all of us she possessed a heart of pure gold. Every week people would be queueing to ask her for help. She'd sit down and sympathetically nod as she heard how a family needed a new bed, motor, school uniforms or even just cash to buy food with. Then her pen would come out, she'd ask us to sign a few pieces of paper and you could opt for cash or a voucher.

Often I went to her asking for cash. We still needed it quite desperately to get the kids their uniforms. Shoes and kids' clothes cost a fortune then. They lasted longer than they do now, mind, but £4.99 was average for a pair of shoes, and later on that'd be half my week's wages. With two or three pairs a year for five kids it all added up. Most of the clothes were bought in Nora's, a lovely village shop catering for all at the pit. They were reasonably priced compared to many and knew what people could afford. But also they had the monopoly. The nearest other shops were a good twenty miles away in the market town of Retford.

Every week, Nancy would knock on the door and ask for the debt to be paid back, usually £1 a week. I was always honest with her.

'Hello, Nancy,' I said one day. 'You're wasting your bloody time this week, I'm afraid. I'll have it for you next week.'

Quickly she trusted me as I always did give it when we had the money. Best of all, when we got the next loan, if we had a little left to pay she'd carry it over to the following time. She never had to do it but she chose to help the hard-working families.

Folk did get ripped off sometimes with HP stuff though, as with some companies the quality wasn't always brilliant. The worst episode we had was back in Motherwell, when Doug bought a fake leather button-backed sofa for £140, paying it off at £2 a week. Within three months the thing looked ten years old, with the edges all frayed and the sponge filling bursting at the seams. We could barely sit on it.

He rang the HP company and told them. He got a soothing response from the boss but no offer of a new sofa.

'Well, I am not paying for it,' said Doug, 'unless you replace it.'

Things turned nasty when the boss point-blank refused. Soon afterwards, I was getting the tea on when I found myself opening the door to a debt collector.

'If you don't repay your money we won't be knocking next time, as we'll be bringing the bailiffs,' he snarled.

Quite shocked, I found myself lost for words. Doug wasn't, though, when he got home and I recounted the doorstep visit to him. With a fury in his voice I'd not heard before, he borrowed a neighbour's phone to have it out with the boss again. Then he arranged to have the sofa dumped outside our block, and told the council to bill the HP company, which thankfully they did. Doug got his money back and we got rid of the sofa – though of course that meant sitting on cushions on the floor for a while again.

But Ollerton was a world away from Motherwell. Although we struggled a bit with the clothes and furniture, luckily food seemed to be cheap and in plentiful supply, with so many farms in the area. Once my sister Mary rang me up from her place in Langold, sounding beside herself with excitement.

'You'll never guess what, Cath,' she said. 'I've just bought a whole pig. A man in the market wanted it gone. Do you want to go halves? We'll never get through it!'

I love my meat and half a pig would feed an army.

A few hours later I found myself pushing Allan in the pram, while balancing half a cut pig on top. Wrapped in a bin bag, it weighed a ton and smelled of fresh flesh and blood. I could hardly wait to get started on it. Once I got it indoors, I set about chopping and cooking, until the entire street filled with the smell of roast pork. After filling up the fridge, I banged on Sheena and Miss Wilkinson's doors to offer them some chops. I didn't have enough space for it.

When Allan was a few months old, my thoughts turned to work again as we needed both wages. Although we expected Doug's wage to increase, he'd need to be fully trained first, and this would take some time.

While I was out shopping I bumped into another neighbour, Jackie. She was a kindly sort, a proud-looking tall woman, with a flicked fringe in the seventies style and big hoop earrings. More of a glamour puss than me, but nice enough.

'Ooh Cath,' she said, sighing a little. 'You know me and Ruby are desperate for a job at the moment. But you know, around here, there isn't a right lot.'

'I'm needing work too,' I said. 'Are there any factories around here?'

Jackie frowned, fiddling with her necklace. 'I don't know about that,' she said. 'I've never asked.'

I grinned. I love a challenge and decided to see if I could find some work that very day.

So after Allan's nap, I set off to a nearby industrial estate, to see what I could find myself. They had factories for all sorts and knowing I didn't ever want to work in hosiery, as I still hated sewing as much as I did years ago, I only went to the other outlets.

A man told me there were shift-work jobs from 5 p.m. to 10 p.m. going at the metal works, on the production line, putting flues together. I went straight there and found an advertisement on the wall. I took a copy of one and went back home feeling triumphant. I've always believed anyone can find work if they look for it.

I bumped into Jackie on the way back. Her eyes opened wide as she saw the ad. 'I'll let Ruby know,' she said.

I wasn't too keen on working alongside Ruby, as I couldn't imagine she was a grafter. But I was glad at the chance of applying for something myself anyway.

On the day of my interview I overheard a familiar Scottish accent. It was Sidney, my boss from the turkey factory. Before I even opened my mouth to say anything in the interview he gave me a hug. 'When you starting then, Cath?'

he asked. I got the job and it was just what we needed. That extra fiver a week made the world of difference.

With Doug laid up on the sofa, I'd get the children ready with their tea and then Susan and Lorraine would help put the little ones to bed while I shot off to start my shift. Those two were a godsend.

The work itself was hard and boring. We had to join the pieces of metal together to build the flues, and did as many as we could. The edges of the sheets of metal were as sharp as razor blades, and everyone was always getting nicks and cuts on their fingers.

One evening, I was so tired a sheet slipped off my table and it fell sideways straight down on top of my feet at the ankle like a guillotine. For a split second everything seemed to stop and I daren't look down. The pain of the cut was so bad it brought tears to my eyes and I feared I'd cut my feet clean off.

Someone rushed over to pick it up, and then we both pulled up my trousers to see the damage. My feet were bleeding badly but it was just two small deep cuts. The last thing I needed was to end up footless! I stuck to the job for three or four months until the plant closed down.

The pit village gave our kids a newfound freedom they'd never enjoyed anywhere else. Susan was now ten, Lorraine was eight, Douglas was six and Carrie was four.

They'd already found firm friends in the Houston family down the road, who had kids the same ages as our eldest three. They loved running out into the streets with their balls and prams. The noise of the kids playing in the streets wasn't always welcomed by the miners, though. The work was in shift patterns and whoever was doing the night shift often felt short-changed. Kids screaming with laughter on bikes is not a pleasant sound when you're trying to squeeze a night's sleep in during the day time.

We all did our bit telling them to pipe down. And on the whole, they were good kids and they listened.

One Saturday evening I got home from work to find Doug asleep on the sofa and the house eerily silent.

'Wake up,' I hissed. 'Where are the kids?'

Half groggy still, Doug looked shocked as I shook him off the sofa.

'Dear God, Cathy, you could wake the dead,' he cursed.

'But where are they?' I cried.

It was gone nine o'clock and dusk was upon us. And our house was empty except for Allan who was asleep upstairs. It wasn't like the kids to be this long. My head felt giddy with worry.

I grabbed my coat and started running up the road. As I turned to the end I spotted Susan, Lorraine and

Douglas all pushing Carrie in a buggy, looking like a scene from an Enid Blyton story. Carrie was wearing a cardigan and a felt hat, and pieces of straw were poking out from the top of her shirt and trouser legs.

'Penny for the guy,' Lorraine giggled. The cheeky devils had dressed their baby sister up and touted their walking and talking 'guy' around the streets. Pleased as punch, Susan held up a bagful of jingling coins. 'We made a fortune, Mam,' she laughed.

That Guy Fawkes night, we had a little bonfire out the back for the kids, and as soon as the smoke started to rise we found ourselves surrounded by dozens of neighbours we'd never met before. Our bonfire turned out to be the best icebreaker you could have. I'd already made some toffee apples, but after they were all taken, I went back into the kitchen and started making toffee pears when the apples ran out. I couldn't make them fast enough. The kids sat around, their teeth stuck together, telling me how delicious they were.

We were settling into pit village life happily and every-thing seemed to be falling into place. Grandad remained a big fixture in all our lives despite the distance between us. He was as pleased as I was about Doug's new job. He knew how we'd struggled.

'He's made up for life now, so he is,' Grandad said.

'I know,' I sighed. 'We're lucky. But I do worry about

him sometimes. It's a long way down there. There are always stories of someone being injured in the village. It's not a case of if, it's more like when!'

Grandad laughed my concerns off. He was never one to worry without good cause.

'You just be grateful you're a spoiled southerner now,' he said. 'Nothing bad will happen, Cath.'

My lovely grandad had the ability to reassure me and make me think everything would be OK, even now I was an adult. I only wished I could believe him.

My children had always adored him and called him 'Grandad' even though he was actually their great-grandfather. Whenever his car pulled up, the five of them would pile out the door and race to hug him first. He'd arrive up the path, his pockets brimming with sweets for them. Then he'd struggle in the door with the kids dangling off his arms and legs, barely able to move. 'All right, you lot,' he'd laugh as they all grabbed the sweets, thanking him for their favourites.

As he got over the threshold he'd always laugh and say cheekily, 'STBD!' We adults knew it stood for: 'Shut that bloody door.'

Grandad was diabetic and would give the kids pocket money to go to the shops. Of course they always chose what we called 'rubbish' sweets, the ones with all the additives and nothing but sugar. But Grandad would ask for his favourites – Maltesers or Mars Bars – ignoring his doctor's orders regarding his diabetes.

Grandad was incredible with those kids and would sit and listen to them intently for hours rabbiting on about whatever it was. I was sure his ability to zone out was even better than mine. I just didn't have the patience and would often switch off and nod automatically as I was cooking or cleaning. Grandad would sit and listen with a look of fascination on his face.

Sometimes, though, he would wind me up as much as the children. Lorraine was great on the piano so we bought her a little keyboard and, boy, did Grandad love sitting down and bashing out old Scottish tunes. On and on he'd go, filling the house up with what I called 'dirge', although he was on the whole a fine player. In the end I removed the fuse from the keyboard plug when no one was looking.

Later in the afternoon, Grandad sat down again to play and started pressing the keys over and again, eventually realising it wasn't working.

'Oh, do we need another 50p in the meter?' Grandad asked, dipping in his pockets. 'Has the electricity gone off again?'

'Nope, it's OK,' I grinned. 'Just the keyboard playing up.'

I did feel guilty but I just couldn't stand the racket. To have a moment's peace in that house was rare enough without any extra din.

Chapter Nine

Because we were working so hard, we had to rely on the kids to do their own jobs. As soon as they were old enough I gave them tasks to do and expected them to stick at it. With a brood of five and a small budget, I couldn't do it any other way.

Susan was a godsend. She was growing up into a bonny girl, with sandy hair and dark eyes like her dad's. Full of life, she was very sure of herself and what she wanted. Although she didn't have much of a brain for school she was very home-minded and helped get everybody up, made the beds, got breakfasts and took the older ones to school. I was able to take the others to nursery and pick them up later on.

Lorraine was much quieter and kept herself to herself. Although when she was with her younger brothers and sister she drove me crazy, always winding them up and telling stories. Once I asked them all to clean their room and they all sat on the sofa looking at me, deadly serious, shaking their heads.

'Go on,' I repeated. 'Go and do as you're telt!'

Again they all shook their heads. A bit flummoxed now, I realised something was going on and I asked them what they were playing at.

Douglas and Carrie looked at me with their big brown eyes, just like Doug's, and pointed at the pattern on the carpet.

'Lorraine said the next time you ask us to do something we have to say no or a giant hand will pop out of the carpet and grab us,' they said, shuddering.

I didn't know whether to laugh or shout louder. But at least now I knew which little madam was to blame.

'Lorraine!' I yelled up the stairs. 'Get down here now!'

She also had her share of jobs, but was so lazy. When all the others had done their chores by the time I'd got home, Lorraine never had done. One time the kids started leaving their shoes on the stairs. When one did something, usually they all did, and when you have five kids that's a lot of shoes!

One morning I tripped on them on the way down. Luckily I grabbed the handrail before I fell but I vowed there and then that the shoe habit had to stop.

'Right,' I said over breakfast. 'I nearly broke my neck this morning, so can you all just stop leaving your shoes lying around from now on? The next time I see a pair I will chuck them in the dustbin.'

The following afternoon I picked up Allan and Carrie from nursery, turned my key in the door and sure as eggs a pair of shoes was laying on the stairs . . . and of course they belonged to Lorraine. Always true to my word, I picked them up and dumped them in the outside bin.

A few hours later Lorraine wanted to go out. 'Where's my shoes, Mam?' she asked.

'Where did you leave them?' I replied.

'Um, maybe on the stairs?' she said.

'Well, in that case they'll be in the bin now,' I said.

'Maaaaam!' Lorraine wailed, dashing outside. But she was too late. The rubbish men had been and they were her only pair.

Half an hour later I heard more screaming. This time it was Susan. Cheeky Lorraine had managed to go out, but was wearing her sister's shoes. I had to laugh.

I did rule the house with an iron rod, though. I had to, there were so many of them. So if one of them did something wrong, I'd punish them all. Usually, though, it was Lorraine's fault. Once I came home to find the rest of them had stripped Lorraine to her bra and pants, tied her hands behind her back and had her on a kitchen chair outside as they threw buckets of cold water at her. They were fed up of losing their privileges like time on the record player or being allowed out because Lorraine wouldn't do her jobs. I had to put a stop to it, and told them off for attacking her, but I did feel for them. Of course, as soon as Lorraine was untied she poked her tongue at them all and told them to get lost. The next day she 'forgot' to do her errands, to boot.

As much as I loved the hustle and bustle of our family life, sometimes I felt like I never got a minute's peace. Even when the kids were off to sleep, my own bed was no longer a place of rest. A few months after we'd arrived, Doug developed a loud crackling sound in his chest as he lay next to me at night. It was like having a crisp bag rustled in my ear. It was so loud, I gave him a prod with my elbow.

'Doug,' I hissed. 'What's up with you?'

He let out a cough and rolled over. 'I don't know, Cath,' he said, hawking up a cough again.

He didn't have a cold, and wasn't smoking any more than usual.

'I think it's just the pit,' he mumbled, before dropping off again. A bit later he went for a medical at work and was given the all-clear. The miners usually were, even if it was obvious that something was wrong on their chests. We all suspected regular cover-ups, as the Coal Board didn't want to be saddled with having to dole out compensations.

'You're right as rain,' the doctors would nod, signing off whatever was needed.

Sometimes they were given time off sick or diagnosed with URI, which stood for 'Undiagnosed Respiratory Infection'. The lads used to called it a 'U R Idle' certificate, as a joke. That was the way it was, you laughed it off and you still had to work.

Doug always had a cough, but we just passed that off as a smoker's hack. We both liked a cigarette. We couldn't afford ready-made so I rolled my own, and we'd have around twenty a day. Everyone smoked, it was just what you did, and it settled your nerves!

In fact I was having a cigarette outside when a friend from round the corner, Shelly, passed by one day. She looked morose, so I offered her a fag and we got chatting. Seeing what the other miners sometimes got up to made me feel all the more fortunate to have Doug as my husband. Shelley's husband was a rogue, always out on the piss, never taking her with him and generally treating her like a skivvy. I don't know how she put up with it.

Many of the lads Doug worked with went straight to the pub for a few pints before they went back to their wives. I was lucky with Doug that he took his family responsibilities seriously and we never had the spare money for beer anyway, plus there was the small matter that I'd never let him get away with it!

In comparison to some couples, Doug and I only had a few major fall-outs. One week Doug agreed to do a string of double shifts for extra money. He was exhausted, and after bolting down his tea, he immediately fell into bed and was out for the count. In the morning he got up and went straight out again.

That morning as I pulled back the sheets to air the bed and make it up, I spotted a great swathe of soot all over Doug's side of the bed.

When he got home I gave him the rollicking of his life. 'You make sure you wash properly!' I cried. 'Don't be climbing into my bed in that state!' Oh, I was fuming. Eventually, after I calmed down, Doug explained he just hadn't scrubbed his back properly as he was so exhausted and wanted to rush home. I ended up feeling quite guilty that I'd been so hard on him.

We might have had separate lives all day, but as soon as Doug stepped over the threshold he was back part of the family hub. Always a talkative one, he would tell me about his last shift, giving me a right rundown of how good or bad it was. As his wife, I saw it as my job to listen, even if I had half an eye on the kids, or a pot boiling away or my knitting on.

A few times after he joined the mine, Doug would be working away when he'd hear a familiar accent. 'C'mon Black, get stuck in, no hanging about . . .'

Then an older miner would slap him on the back and he'd turn to find one of his dad's or brothers' friends. A blast from his past in Scotland.

'I thought your dad said he'd break your back rather than let you down the mine,' said one. The mining community was a small one and despite there being hundreds of thousands of miners still, everyone seemed to know everyone.

Doug laughed. That was a saying of his dad's and he hoped it'd never come true. But times had changed; mines were not such terrible places to be in comparison to how they had been before. After the journey we'd had, there was no doubt in our minds that the mine was the best place for him to be now.

Rightly or wrongly, Doug had gone against his father's advice in the end, but the dangers of the pit were never far away and a constant reminder that this was a job that commanded respect, especially with regards to safety.

I refused to let myself ever listen out for the phone ringing, though. It would just paralyse you if you started doing that. Besides, with all the kids my mind was kept occupied. It was the same for all the wives. We just couldn't think about what our husbands were doing thousands of yards below our feet. It was just a job, albeit one with terrible risks.

All we could do was hope nothing would happen to

Doug. Luckily I knew he was a careful sort and would always stick to the rules and stay out of trouble. I knew that much.

The stories he'd come home with sometimes, though, made my stomach spin. Once one of the green labour lads Doug had trained with nearly had them all killed. The men were always frisked for contraband when they went into the mine – things like fags, lighters and matches. Yes, unbelievable, but some of the men were stupid enough to try and sneak them through.

One day, Doug was sent on a job with this particular lad. They were supposed to be laying some sleepers for the train track. After a few minutes of trying with the spanner, the lad dropped it, hurting his own foot.

'Get him out the way,' yelled a deputy. 'Go on, go and get some fresh air.'

The man moved off and Doug took over. After a few moments of clanging about, they turned to see a big flash followed by an overpowering smell of sulphur.

Due to the pitch-black darkness, it was as clear as day: a match had been lit.

Now it was Doug's turn to drop the spanner. 'My God, did you see that?' he said.

Running down the shaft, the deputy went to look. The green labour lad was found, a terrible look of guilt on his face.

'What are you doing?' cried the deputy. 'Where is the fag?'

He shrugged and shook his head, but Doug caught up and, kicking a pile of coal next to him, uncovered a pack of Park Drive cigarettes and a packet of Swan Vesta.

Not only was this a sackable offence, but worst of all, he was down the 'fresh air' ventilation side of the piping, meaning that if the coal dust had caught alight a fire would have devastated the area within seconds.

The deputy was furious. 'I'm a husband with kids and so's he,' he yelled, pointing to Doug. 'Are you trying to kill the lot of us, eh?'

Doug was spitting feathers when he told that story after the kids had gone to bed. He didn't want them to overhear and worry. It angered me too. What the hell did some of these men think they were playing at? It beggared belief.

Generally, though, the miners were a close bunch. I suppose the ongoing fear of an impending disaster played a big part in bringing the men together. Doug was so close to Les, Geordie and Pete (another neighbour) especially.

One of the things they most dreaded down the pit was hearing a sudden 'tinkle' followed by some dust falling from the ceiling. Sometimes it was the sign of the start of a wall or ceiling collapse, something that was completely unavoidable, however careful any of them could be.

'Oooh, it sends a shiver down your spine, lass!' Doug said, turning slightly pale. 'Everyone just stops. Their eyes widen and we all just look at each other, barely daring to breathe.'

The intense danger they faced together helped create an incredible sense of camaraderie. Down that mine every man wasn't for himself. He was for others, too. If one man got himself into trouble, the chances are they were all in danger.

Doug was continuing with his training, first moving on to being a 'pipe fitter', making sure all the piping was working to bring fresh air and remove the gases from the mine, and then finally making it to the coalface.

Now this was a prize role, as the pay was triple what you got as an underground general. Once again the high salary reflected how dangerous it was. In effect it was danger money. The men had to wait their turn for training, which took the form of a 100-day intensive course.

One of the younger lads was the first of Doug's team to be trained on the coalface, but the following day Doug was called over by the training officer, Ron Fox.

'You need to come down,' he said.

'Already?' said Doug. 'I thought you were training up the other fella first.'

'Ah, he couldn't handle it,' Ron replied.

Doug didn't ask questions and just went down the next

day to take his place. Part of the training was to sit on the machine as the coal cutter moved across. In an instant the coalface would shudder a bit and 'drop' down a few inches, sending a plume of coal dust everywhere, and turning everything pitch black as it was literally cut before your eyes.

This poor lad wasn't expecting the 'drop' to happen so fast. As his vision suddenly became obscured by thick black powder, the fright sent him spinning backwards, and he actually soiled his trousers.

Doug shook his head as he told me that evening. 'I dunno ken why some of those boys are trying to be miners,' he said. 'They want the money but are not up to the job.'

I had to admit, it did sound frightening enough to me.

The tunnel of coal was cut with two roadways in it, and then one face of the tunnel was cut through the coal by a loading machine. This acted like a giant bacon slicer, but instead of a blade it had steel picks on a fearsome-looking spinning drum.

This monster machine ploughed up the coal and then it all fell on to a conveyor belt running at the bottom. While this happened the roof had to be supported by new girders bolted into place.

It could take a whole shift to advance just two feet, but advance they did, at all costs. The managers had their targets of a certain number of tonnes a month. Come what may they wanted to hit them, too.

'Are you going to get a mask to wear?' I said. 'All that dust can't be good for your chest, Doug.'

He laughed. 'That's why we all try and chew a bit of tobacco,' he said. 'Sees you through. Makes the stress less bad. A few of them wear masks, but they're made of cardboard and only last five minutes.'

Not all the miners took the work as seriously as Doug. One day, Doug, Jimmy Garland and another lad, Brian Green, were shadowing the trainer Ron Fox at the coalface. They had to stay by his side as he showed them the ropes.

But when they turned around Jimmy wasn't anywhere to be seen.

'Where's he gone?' asked Ron, rolling his eyes.

Doug and Brian shrugged. As far as they were concerned Jimmy had been following them. They all looked around the darkness then Ron turned his head to look down the miles-long tunnel they'd just walked, where the coal tubs sat on the rails.

He strained his eyes and Doug followed his gaze. They could all see a single faint beam of light shining upwards from the coal tubs to the ceiling.

Ron tightened his mouth and Doug followed as they tramped back up the tunnel.

They peeked over the side of a coal tub and there lay

Jimmy, sound asleep. He'd turned off his strong beam light but unfortunately for him he still had a small beam on. After a night of drinking he'd slipped off for forty winks!

Doug couldn't help but laugh but really he didn't approve. As far as he was concerned, Jimmy was a scallywag.

The lads were shown how to use explosives safely too. Dynamite had stopped being used long ago in the pit, and instead they used Panodel, an ingredient like the caustic soda that is used for cleaning. After boring holes and packing it with the stuff, it was a deputy's duty to press the button, with the men standing at 250 yards.

Without a doubt it was one of the most dangerous parts of the job. The lads never knew if the ceiling was going to cave in, and often it caused water to build up. The men often found themselves working up to their knees in water. But still they only had their pit boots on for protection, and they got sopping wet. One thousand feet down and nine miles in, Doug found the conditions hard. The water pouring down the walls on to their skin was very salty and burned into the men's clothing.

One day he came back late. 'After seven hours down there they obviously thought we didnae had enough,' he said. 'They asked us to do an extra four hours overtime. We must be mentalists.'

Doug was incensed too by some of the treatment dished out by some of the more ignorant managers. Once when the men asked for more protection from the burning water, a manager bellowed over the tannoy: 'All we've got is bin bags,' he said. 'Punch three holes in them and away you go.' Sometimes for the workers on the front line, it felt as if they were being shown minimal respect.

With incidents like this happening almost daily, Doug didn't always tell me the details of the more dangerous parts. Only after he retired did dribs and drabs of stories emerge. He didn't want to worry me. And our family was what dominated our lives and that's what we chose to focus on. Not the danger. Doug spent seven hours a day in a mine, with danger everywhere, but as long as he was careful we just had to hope luck was on his side.

He'd always give me a quick peck goodbye when he left the house, and I'd always give a silent prayer in my heart I'd see him again. If the worst was to happen, we'd cross that bridge when we came to it.

Chapter Ten

Doug had been underground for just six months, and although the stories he came up with were enough to make anyone's hair stand on end, I trusted his methodical, hard-working character not to make any silly mistakes. Many accidents were caused by stupidity, Doug said, and I knew he'd avoid danger. Every time he brushed my lips goodbye, I wondered if I'd see him again, but only for a few seconds. I pushed any negative thoughts away, and what with the kids and my jobs there was no time to dwell.

But as is often the way, just when you think something might not happen life throws you a curve ball.

Just a few months after Doug started work I had a phone call during the day.

'Hello, Mrs Black,' said a female voice. 'This is the sister.'

I felt my stomach lurch, as I clutched the phone. A 'sister' ringing could only mean one thing.

'Yes?' I asked breathlessly.

Doug. Not Doug. Please.

'It's OK,' she said quickly. 'Doug is going to be OK.'

I gasped. My knees had already turned to jelly.

'But he's had an accident and is in Worksop hospital having emergency treatment . . .'

I barely heard the next few words about his knee and his accident. My mind was already racing to where he was, and how I was going to get there.

I dropped the kids off with a neighbour and dashed to be by my husband's side. Running down the ward, scanning bed after bed, I just didn't know what to expect.

Then I found him, writhing around on the bed, his leg held up, his knee the size of a small balloon.

'Oh, what a mess,' he said when he saw me. I squeezed his hand.

'What happened?' I asked.

Grimacing as he spoke, with beads of sweat on his forehead from the pain, Doug explained. A pipe one of the lads had been carrying had been carelessly dropped. It fell on to the hard coal floor, bounced and flew upwards, hitting Doug hard on the back of the knee. He buckled immediately, landing awkwardly. The result was a very badly torn knee, quickly swollen with fluid.

'It's killing,' Doug panted, trying to sit up.

'Who dropped the pipe?' I asked, thinking of how careful the men usually are.

'That bloody Paul,' groaned Doug.

I'd already heard Doug talk of this fella, Paul. He was a young lad with a big attitude problem. He didn't follow instructions and didn't enjoy his work. But his carelessness put the lives of the men at risk and he'd injured people inadvertently a few times. He gave a few of the lads a 'black nail' – when something is dropped on a finger or toenail and it becomes blackened with bruising. Apparently butterfingers Paul was always dropping girders or not lifting things properly. Every single lift or movement in the mine needed to be carefully coordinated to avoid mishaps.

'He's green labour,' sighed Doug. 'He boasts about earning the good wage, but that's all he's keen on. Safety is of no interest to that silly boy.'

Some of the lads even refused to work with him and others threatened to punch his lights out. There was no room in such conditions for anyone to be anything other than a team player.

'Someone's going to kill him one day,' said Doug. 'Before he kills them first!'

I touched Doug's head. I could see a letter 'M' had been marked in pen on his forehead.

'What the hell's that?' I said, just noticing it.

'The nurse wipes your forehead and writes the letter "M" after she's given you a shot of morphine,' he explained. 'So's the ambulance medics know you've had some.'

146

I held Doug's hand as the nurse drew off the fluid in his poor knee. Wincing again, Doug went pale and bit his lip. I bit mine too. To have such an injury so early on in his mining career seemed so unfair. I wondered how long this knee would trouble him now. Sick pay wasn't much, even if we were eligible for it.

But neither of us said anything; we accepted it as part and parcel of his job. I knew we'd soldier on somehow.

In fact, we were still able to enjoy a laugh together, even while Doug was still in hospital. We had a giggle after a joke I'd played on Doug a few days earlier – which I'd long forgotten about, what with all the drama – came to light.

When Doug was injured, one of the men went to his locker to collect all his clothes to send to the hospital. The nurses had gone through his bag and pulled out a pair of underpants I'd stitched for Doug for a laugh.

They read: 'Constructed in 1960. First erected 1965.' The nurses thought it hilarious and were waving them around the ward like a banner. I couldn't help but crack up too.

Doug's face went redder than I've ever seen. 'When did you put them in my locker?' he cried.

'I cannae remember, Doug,' I giggled. 'A few weeks ago, I think. But at least it gives us something to smile about now.'

The nurses and doctors were fantastic. As it was a hospital in a mining village, they were used to seeing miners coming through the doors. They didn't mind a craic with the lads. They saw the same injuries every time, and so were able to quickly work out effective treatment.

When I got home from hospital, I felt drained after all the adrenaline rush. As I put the kids to bed, they looked at me, worried. Mummy didn't cry often, but the red rims of my eyes and Daddy in hospital told them something terrible had happened.

'He's going to be OK,' I soothed to Susan, Lorraine and Douglas as I tucked them in.

'He won't die, will he?' said Susan, her lip wobbling.

'Nah!' I laughed, trying to make a joke. 'He just won't be playing football for a while.'

As I went downstairs to start the washing, the door went. It was Geordie Maddox, his face etched with pain and worry for his friend.

'He's a tough nut,' I said, quietly. 'It'll take more than a rogue pipe to stop Doug.'

Later on Miss Wilkinson popped in. One touch of her hand sent the tears I'd tried to hold back all day on to my cheeks, and the words I'd been swallowing down as I'd sat with Dougie suddenly poured from me.

'It's happened so soon after joining the pit,' I sobbed. 'We've only been here a few months. Why Doug?'

'I know, pet,' she said, giving me a cuddle. 'You just never know when it'll happen. Could be two months or twenty years. No one can tell.'

I wiped my eyes with the tea towel I was holding.

'Aye,' I said, taking a deep breath. I felt embarrassed I'd broken down a little. But needs must. 'I'll stick the kettle on and that'll put me right.'

The pain kept Doug off work for two months and he was on the sick for a while. The sick pay didn't stretch far enough. To get full pay you had to be in hospital for a whole week and he fell just shy of that. So we had just £34 a week to live off. We didn't have any insurance for Doug; we just couldn't afford it. Sounds crazy now, what with the adverts you see today, but no one could afford the extra few pounds insurance cost in those days. You just knew if the worst came to the worst you'd have to deal with it. The only option was for me to go back to work.

Luckily there were still plenty of jobs going in the farm factory, Eastwood's, where I had worked when I lived in Rainworth. Doing everything from potato picking to chicken killing, I soon joined the ranks of the other women needing a bit extra. It wasn't much so I had to do double shifts to make it worthwhile.

Poor Doug stayed at home and minded the kids while I went. We had to rely on Susan and Lorraine to help keep things afloat, with them taking the wee ones to school and nursery.

It was a terrible time for me, as I would literally get home just as they were off to bed some nights. Then I'd do the washing and cleaning and cook the meals for the following day – all the jobs Doug couldn't manage as he lay on the sofa, his knee upright as much as possible. Neither of us could wait until he got better.

By 1977, Doug was back at work, albeit getting regular gip from his knee, and things continued to look up when the Coal Board gave us another house. This time a four-bedroom place around the corner from where we lived came up, at 11 Petersmith Crescent. This house was very much like the last, with a half-brick front and a shared gate with the neighbours. But I was immediately blown away by how friendly the sixteen or so families were who lived nearby, even more so than our neighbours in Whitewater Road. Now Doug was bringing a wage in again, I stopped doing double shifts and had more time at home, getting to know the other miners' wives. Some of these women were to become lifelong friends who saw me through thick and thin.

Our immediate next-door neighours were Ann and Pete Jackson, at number 9, both in their late thirties. They had three children: a grown-up son, Kevin, who was a miner in the pit, a teenager, Alan, and Julie, who was the same age as Susan.

Ann was a quiet, smartly dressed woman who had a wicked sense of humour. The first chat we had over the short brown picket fence was about our husbands. It was a subject we'd come back to a fair few times!

'If you need anything at all, just ask,' she grinned. 'Especially a husband who moans all the time, as I've definitely got one of those I'd be happy to loan out.'

I nodded; I couldn't have agreed more. Doug was a rotter to live with when he was tired in the mornings on shift. Everything I did or the kids did he snapped at, even down to criticising the colour of the cup of tea I made him. I was glad to hear I wasn't the only one to suffer a tongue-lashing.

'Oh, I've got one of them, thank you,' I laughed. Straight away I trusted Ann, and soon we were always popping into each other's houses, sitting at the kitchen table to talk about the latest gossip. I knew whatever I said around that table stayed there and vice versa.

Ann and Pete were a sociable couple, always off to the Miners' Welfare, the clubhouse especially for miners and their families. They were always inviting us to go with them, though we never went as we couldn't afford the extra costs of a night out. But we appreciated being asked!

Next door on the other side were a young Scottish

couple called Sean and Esther Young. Esther was a big lass with strawberry-blonde hair and a job in an office. She really was Sean's long-suffering wife, bless her. They were both as big as their characters and treated me and Doug like a second mum and dad.

Soon after we moved in, we got the measure of Sean. I opened the front door one evening to find a young man looking frantically worried.

'Is Doug in?' he asked breathlessly. He'd already met Doug working in the mine.

'Yes,' I said, calling him.

'Please come quick,' said Sean, grabbing Doug's arm. The pair rushed into his house where Doug found water gushing everywhere.

Sean was a character who needed keeping in hand and sometimes it was too much for Esther and she would disappear to her mum's house for weeks. During these times, Sean took advantage and would invite the other miners round for a night of drinking. This particular raucous night got out of hand during a game of darts. One of them had struck the central heating pipe and burst it, spilling water all over the carpets. So Doug found himself on his hands and knees trying to stem the flow to save Sean from Esther's wrath when she got home!

Another new friend, Margaret, lived a few doors down at number 7, with her miner husband Billy and their four children. A very smart woman, she was every inch a stay-at-home mum, doting on her kids and keeping her house and garden spotless. She was very jovial and always up for a giggle, and I hit it off with her immediately, just like I did with Ann.

The Queen's Silver Jubilee in June 1977 was a great occasion to get chatting with the neighbours. The whole crescent came out in force and the Miners' Welfare put on a gala. All the villages nearby joined in, tying colourful bunting to the lampposts and decorating tractors and trucks as floats while the jingle-jangle of Morris dancers filled the air.

The Coal Board didn't give Doug the day off, and we couldn't afford to take it as a rest day, so he had to go to work. But he packed up at 1.30 p.m. and joined me and the kids at the party. He gathered the kids around and with a flourish pulled out a silver Queen's Jubilee coin he'd bought in the Post Office as a memento. It was a lovely day and brought the whole street together.

As much as I loved our new neighbours, though, I've never been one to try and 'keep up with the Joneses'. For a start we never had enough money to attempt it, but also Doug and I were so used to pinching every penny we had, it never occurred to me to splash out on unnecessary bits and pieces.

Doug and I joked that Margaret kept her Billy working

hard as she loved having top-notch things in the house. She always had the latest cooker or gadget. One day we watched in awe as builders started taking out her windows.

'What's going on there?' I asked Doug.

We both craned through the curtains to see. A couple of workmen were carrying white frames and thick glass. Unable to contain my interest, I walked outside to see.

Margaret 'yoo-hooed' me over to her.

'What are you having done now?' I asked.

'Double glazing,' she said, proudly. 'I'll be the first one in the street. Isn't it exciting?'

I had to laugh. I'd seen it advertised on TV and it was all the rage. The trouble was poor Margaret got cowboys to put it in. The window frames started to crumble after a couple of weeks and she had to have them replaced again.

Another couple we got on well with were called Linda and Martin Boswell. They had two little girls and a boy. Susan babysat for their son sometimes for pocket money. They were a lovely couple, always so cheerful, and I didn't mind helping them out when they needed it – which was quite often, as it turned out.

Linda was a young lass and seemed to struggle with keeping up with life sometimes. She was always popping across asking for a cup of flour or sugar as she'd run out. Once she turned up in a tizz asking for 50p for the gas meter. But as ever, I was happy to help – and equally I knew she'd do the same for me.

Chris and Jackie Knighton lived the other side of them. Jackie worked for some time with me at the flue factory and at Eastwood's. Her marriage wasn't a happy one so she tended to steer clear of conversations about relationships.

Doug soon got the reputation of being the handyman of the crescent. He loved working on his garden and doing DIY – like me, he's never one to sit still for long. Billy popped over one day for some advice after he'd spotted Doug building a lovely patio path on the front lawn.

'How much sand did you need for the concrete, eh Doug?' Billy asked over the fence. Doug rubbed his chin, worked out the dimensions of Billy's small path and gave him some weights and figures.

Two days later we were sat outside when we saw a big lorry pull into the crescent. It reversed on to Billy's front garden. Then the back of the lorry flipped open, tipping an enormous mound of sand – enough to fill a small beach – on to Billy's driveway. Then it promptly drove off.

Billy came running out as we walked over. 'Oh my . . .' he said.

Unable to help himself, Doug had to put his hand over his mouth to stop laughing.

'Is this your sand order, Billy?' he laughed. 'Do you think you've got enough, eh?'

We stood, barely able to see the houses across the road over the pile.

Sean and Doug came out with shovels and wheelbarrows and started putting it into bags. Doug moved some to our back garden and then called the local DIY shop to pick up the rest. Billy didn't live it down for weeks.

Doug's DIY accidentally got him into trouble with Pete too one day. He decided to build a wall down our side of the garden so Ann and Pete could have the front gate to themselves, an idea they were pleased with.

But he had to pull a tree down to do so. Ann and I pitched in to help, so we sawed up the trunk and branches and then wrapped ropes around its stubborn roots and stump, pulling with all our might. After a few 'one, two three, and heaaaaaaves', the tree gave a satisfying crack and pulled clean away, taking up the roots with it.

'Hooray!' Ann cried, as we collapsed with exhaustion.

Just as we were sitting there assessing our victory, we heard a yell.

Then Pete, his face purple with rage, came flying round the corner.

'You cheeky lot!' he yelled. 'You've pulled my prize roses up.'

'You what?' asked Doug, surprised at this showing of

anger from our usually placid neighbour. 'But your roses are round the corner, aren't they?'

Almost stamping his feet with rage, Pete was shaking. 'The roots of your tree are attached to my prize roses,' he said through gritted teeth. 'And you've pulled every single one of them up with it.'

We all said how sorry we were, but couldn't resist a giggle. Luckily once he'd calmed down Pete saw the funny side and realised we didn't mean to do it.

In fact generally Doug and Pete got on well. Pete often wandered over to see what was going on in our garden. Doug liked him; the camaraderie they shared underground was the same as that standing in their gardens. He'd come and watch Doug, always chewing on a match in the side of his mouth, rocking on his heels and quizzing him on what was happening. 'What's going on here then?' he asked. Pete wasn't as talented at DIY and liked to get tips.

'Just building an aeroplane,' Doug teased, when he was obviously fixing a fence.

Once, after another neighbour had told Doug there was plenty of sand under the topsoil in this area, he set to digging a huge hole in the back garden to collect it for cement. Every weekend, he'd get down to it, until it was big enough to put a ladder down there. As usual, Pete wandered over to have a look.

'What you building, Doug?' he said.

Doug grinned, a cheeky glint in his eye. 'A swimming pool,' he said.

Pete's eyes nearly fell out of his head. 'Wow!' he said. 'Really!'

'Yep,' said Doug proudly, leaning on his spade 'We're going to build a slide coming down to it from the kids' bedroom, too.'

Pete looked up at the kids' back bedroom window and blew out his cheeks in wonder.

'That's some ambitious project,' he said. 'You'll have all the kids in the crescent descending on you!'

It took several days of people asking me before the truth emerged. But now we had the sand, we weren't sure what to do with the hole.

So we invited our neighbours to dump any unwanted items in it to burn. Ann and Pete came over with an old table and chairs, Billy dragged across a sitting room chair and we shoved in other bits and pieces. Chucking on some lighter fuel and a match, I bought out teas and coffees and the men had pints as we watched it go up. It created a right stink, so it was a good job the neighbours were involved! The embers burned for days afterwards.

Chapter Eleven

Doug and I settled very quickly into life on Petersmith Crescent. We were as busy as ever but we did have a laugh when we could. Once all the wives were round ours when Esther started complaining bitterly again about Sean not doing anything with the front garden.

'He never mows the lawn and I have to nag him to just look at it,' she moaned. 'He keeps promising me he'll plant some new flowers but he never does.'

The gardens in the crescent were very much the men's domain. The miners all got a few extra days off a year and every one of them was usually spent in the garden. Maybe after being cooped up underground for so many hours of their lives they felt a desperation to be outside in the fresh air as much as possible. Miners being fanatical gardeners made sense!

But poor Esther's husband hadn't caught the gardening

bug and she was left staring at a wasteland every time she looked out the living room window.

Ann and Margaret both smirked at me, and afterwards I asked them what they were laughing at.

'We've got a plan,' they winked.

A few days later, Margaret came over with a bag full of fake plastic flowers. Ann was giggling her head off. 'Tonight it's Operation Garden,' she laughed.

That evening, after the sun went down, we snuck over to Esther and Sean's front lawn and quickly poked the plastic flower stems into the soil and the grass. Under the moonlight it looked like a colourful wonderland, and it certainly jazzed up the bare stone-ridden soil and long unkempt grass.

The next morning, we all poked our heads around the curtains to spy on the result. Sure enough, Sean opened his front door to collect his milk bottle, yawning . . . then he looked up then swiftly did a classic double-take.

We could hear him calling Esther.

'What's all this?' he was crying. 'Look! This lot have come up quick!'

Esther came running out on to the step. Straight away she spotted they were fake and guessed we were behind it.

'They are fake flowers, you fool!' she laughed, glancing round at our houses. I waved to her through my window.

'And I think I know who did it,' she grinned. I started

laughing so much that the tears were falling down my cheeks.

Living in a pit village is a bit like living in a big family, so people look out for each other and support each other in ways they might not a few miles away in a normal town. The Coal Board did their bit to help the community too. Further on, down into New Ollerton village, the old houses were snaking with massive cables.

'What are they?' I asked Doug one day.

'Methane gas,' he said. 'To heat the homes.' Somehow the mine was bringing up the gas and putting it to good use at the top, providing free heating. Even some of the electricity was made from there.

We got plenty of freebies from the mine too, including a big load of coal every week. Our houses were always warm as toast. We also got coal scuttles, pokers and even a washing line. Rightly or wrongly, the men often helped themselves to left-over paint and other DIY bits and bobs. There was simply so much stuff down there and deputies often turned a blind eye, unless of course something expensive was stolen.

One afternoon Doug started to notice Pete's attempts at concreting his patio looked a little suspect. Whereas Doug would do one long smooth section, Pete was doing a tiny part every week. 'What's going on?' Doug asked, pulling back the curtain.

I had a look. Pete's path was looking distinctly stripy as he laid a thin strip every weekend.

I started giggling. 'Aw, he's not got your knack for DIY, Dougie,' I laughed.

Doug went out to see and caught Pete at work.

'I just get the cement when I can,' winked Pete. Turned out Pete was swiping a bit in his pit bag every shift. Even for a big man like Pete it was a struggle to stand solidly upright as he walked past the deputies into the lift. The silly bugger was weighed down on one side!

While sometimes the managers turned a blind eye to small things going missing, on the odd occasion the miners stole so much it became a criminal investigation.

One miner set up a side job as a mechanic, working from his garage. He was so proficient he quickly gained popularity, fixing cars quickly and at little cost. But the oversmen heard about him and after a few months they asked the police to investigate. Plain-clothed CID officers turned up at the man's house, pretending to be customers, where a neighbour pointed them to a tannoy system – the same one used in the pit! They found the miner working in his garage, filled with top-notch tools pinched from the machine-fixing areas down below. He'd set up quite a professional operation by all accounts, even digging a hole to work under the cars in his garage.

Another time a miner was spotted leaving the mine with the same barrow and shovel every Friday evening. The security officer suspected he was up to something but had little proof. After many weeks the fiddle was uncovered. The miner who cheerfully walked past the security man had been pinching a different barrow and shovel to sell on every Friday, but as they looked identical the guard had thought it was the same one he was bringing out each time. He'd sell them for a tenner and use the money for weekend drinking.

After getting to know Ann and Margaret, they invited me to join them at the local Bingo nights at the Miners' Welfare. In Scotland, it was only the 'loose' women who went out on their own without their husbands to pubs and clubs, so, bar the odd drink with Mary, it wasn't a way of life I felt comfortable with.

However, I liked the pair, we'd hit it off, so I decided to join them on occasion.

'The Welfare' was a big building, with an area for acts to come on, a bar and seating for around 400. It was more like a theatre than a pub and was always packed out. It had function rooms and all kinds of things going on. It even had its own football team.

There was also a pub down the road, a proper sawdust and spittoons place called the Silver Bullet, but us wives never really set foot in there. It was more a rough and ready place for the miners to let off some steam.

The Bingo nights were big business, with some of the men getting even more excited than the women. You could win up to £100, a decent amount of money, and everyone wanted to have a go.

To be truthful I found Bingo a little boring, and wasn't overly keen on nights out. I'd so much to see to what with the job, and my evenings were about catching up with the cooking, cleaning and ironing, not nattering. I didn't like to drink, so I'd sit there with my soda and orange, wondering what Saturday night TV I was missing on the box. Doug and I loved to sit together and get absorbed in *Perry Mason* or *Hawaii Five-0*. A world away from our little pit village!

So I decided to only go and join the girls when I was 'feeling lucky'. My instincts seemed to do me right. One evening I had a strong feeling I'd win, but my neighbours wanted to go in together on joint lines.

'No thanks,' I said. 'I want to keep the winnings!'

They all laughed at me. After all, what were the chances I'd win? But sure enough I won on each occasion I felt like this. I never spent the money on myself though – it always went straight into the house or the kids' school clothes.

One evening, on a rare night out for both of us, Doug

and I went to see Neil Diamond at the Welfare. Big acts sometimes came down to the club, like Showaddywaddy and Lulu. Again though, I wasn't overly keen. But I did go with Doug to see Mr Diamond put through his paces, singing all the old favourites like 'Sweet Caroline'. It was a hot summer's evening and the doors of the social club had been thrown wide open, allowing pigeons to flap inside. Some of the people without tickets were rather rudely talking loudly as he started to sing.

So in between songs, he put down his guitar, and with his deep sultry voice said into the microphone: 'I'm going to sing a song about a pigeon.' He picked up a Spanish guitar and started off a riff singing: 'If I were a pigeon I'd fly around and shite on yoooou!' Everyone laughed and thankfully those at the back started to quieten down.

A year after Doug's accident, now Allan was in nursery, I decided to get a job at Herman's chicken factory in Tuxford, alongside Jackie and Ruby, doing evening shifts.

Doug's always called me a workaholic and he's right. I love making my own money and treating the kids. I wanted to buy Carrie a toy Silver Cross pram she wanted for her birthday. Remembering how Susan and Lorraine had to have toy cots made from tomato boxes made me feel more determined to give the younger ones a better life. The community we were now among was obviously already a step up.

Any road, the new chicken factory was a family business. They were tight buggers. They didn't give away anything for free and we had to pay for our own chickens we bought from there, for just a few shillings less than what they cost in the shops.

I did all manner of jobs, but was asked at one point to be a supervisor. This would have meant an extra few pounds in the wage packet, but in the end I turned it down. I knew the other girls would turn against me and I knew what the supervisors were like – they were very unpopular. Many were a bunch of skivers, smoking in the toilets, whereas I preferred to turn up and work hard instead. I knew I wouldn't fit in.

In the end I was put on to quality control, but did oversee some of the younger members of the team. One girl, Lucy, was always nattering and not looking at what she was doing. I liked to natter as much as the rest, but in a busy chicken factory you had to pick your moments and on the killing line it wasn't one of them. We were given a pair of electrical secateurs, an evil implement that you had to be careful with. It was for cutting the bird's neck clean off.

One afternoon Lucy was joking away to her

neighbour, and caught two of her fingers. They were snipped clean off.

For a split second, she stared agog as blood squirted from her hand, then she opened her mouth and let out an almighty scream.

The first aiders leapt into action, grabbing her hand, and mistakenly covering it in cotton wool – the worst thing to do as it kills the nerves at the end of your fingers. She was carried out, waving her hand like it was on fire.

'Help me!' she screamed, as the production line came to a halt. I dropped my clipboard, and ran over, picking up her fingers as carefully as I could and dropping them in a bucket of ice. I pushed the bucket into the hands of the first aider who'd called an ambulance.

A day later we heard how Lucy had been taken to Retford hospital but they didn't have an A&E so they had to rush to Worksop, but by the time they made it she'd lost any chance of saving her fingers.

A few weeks later she turned up looking very glum. 'Cath, I am making a claim,' she said. 'They were negligent. I need you to be a witness, they made a mistake with the cotton wool and hospital. It's a health and safety issue.'

As much as my heart went out to her for losing her fingers, I shook my head.

'You weren't looking what you were doing, Lucy,' I said gently. 'I told you that before. I am not lying to get you money . . .'

She stuck her chin out at me and stormed off. The first aiders were at fault but she also had to take responsibility. I'd have backed her up to the hilt if it'd been any different.

Jackie worked like a Trojan alongside me, but I didn't get along with Ruby any better than when she was with the other miners' wives. Even while killing chickens she brought in unnecessary airs and graces.

'Hello, Mr Herman,' she'd smile, giving a little wave as he came past. She was always sucking up to the management. I found her hard to stomach.

However, it was worth putting up with her to earn my 'pin money'; the job brought in the extra wage for us all to live a slightly better lifestyle. Already we were taking on the traditions and joining in with the spirit of the pit. For our first Halloween, all the kids dressed up in their dad's overalls and spare miners' helmets then covered their faces in soot to go trick or treating. Even the lassies put their hair up and joined in. The girls were as fascinated by the pit as the boys.

A new TV series called *The Stars Look Down*, about mining under the sea, was being shown every Saturday night and they'd sit in silence with a bottle of pop watching it attentively. It was based on a real-life mine in Ashington where Geordie had worked and it showed some terrible conditions.

On the last episode, we all sat agog as the miners played out their last scene. Seven or eight of them were trapped in a small area as the water started gushing in, reminiscing about the good times but stoically facing death in the face.

Doug watched intently too, but was also acutely conscious that our kids were next to him, mesmerised by it.

After the credits went up, Lorraine turned her big eyes on Doug.

'Is it like that for you, Daddy?' she asked.

Doug reached out and hugged her. 'No, sweetheart,' he said. 'Those lads are working under the sea – it would never happen like that for me.'

I didn't like the programme much. I thought they glamorised the mines and it was enough for us to live with the worry of the danger day-in day-out, without having to watch it for entertainment too. But the kids and Doug loved it so I joined in watching it.

Another series, *When the Boat Comes In*, starring James Bolam, was also a 'must-watch' TV show for miners in the seventies. It showed a man returning to his poverty-stricken town in the North in the 1920s and was another sobering view of the mining industry with all the ever-present dangers providing high drama and cliff-hanging episodes. Doug always reassured the kids there were good health and safety rules down there to protect him now, but I didn't like seeing them worried needlessly.

In any case, there was enough drama in real life without needing to watch more on the telly. Around this time there was a bread strike on, and the East Midlands was badly hit. It was all part of a series of strikes in 1978 that became known as the Winter of Discontent, after trade unions rallied against the pay freeze imposed by the Labour government. Bakers went on strike and people started panic buying bread, causing a national shortage. I'd always made my own bread anyway, but suddenly I couldn't even get my hands on a packet of yeast. My aunt Mary, my grandad's daughter, lived in Manchester and she started sending me packets down in the post. I wanted to share them with Ann and Margaret, as they had plenty of mouths to feed too, but there wasn't enough to go round. So I carried on with my own baking, and still managed to do Doug's favourite, cob rolls.

He came home laughing once, as the other miners had turned green with envy when he'd got his lunch box out down the pit. They watched in awe as he opened his mouth to take a large bite of a cob. 'My wife's a Scot,' he joked, 'and the best baker in Ollerton. If anyone can still get their hands on bread it will be her!'

They all asked for a bit and Doug jokingly said no, before handing them a small mouthful each.

Around this time, Doug experienced one of the single most frightening moments in his career down the mine. The coalface had two 'loader' and 'feeder' bays running off it in a U shape. The feeder area brings in the cool air, and the loader area takes away all the gas and the hot air. With the coal dust from the face hanging in the air too, this was the most deadly place for any ignitions or sparks to catch fire and all the men were aware of this.

One day Doug was on a break, sitting with Geordie, when the pair of them heard an unmistakable sound.

The hiss of a match being lit. Both of them stopped dead still, their hearts beating so hard as they waited. The even more unmistakable smell of sulphur from a freshly lit match filled the air. This was different to the match-lighting incident, as this was happening in the most flammable area of the pit.

Doug's faced turned puce. Both men were stock still, mute with terror as they hardly dared breathe in fear of what could happen next . . . namely a huge explosion. It could take a few seconds to catch, usually from some dust in the air. Powerless, all they could do was wait.

A deputy was nearby and had heard and smelled the same thing. 'Who the fucking hell is lighting up?' he screamed down the tunnel. He started running towards the light, but after a quick search found nobody. Whoever had been stupid enough had vanished like a ghost – after nearly making ghosts of them all.

For about three months after that incident, Doug's nerves were shattered. He woke up a few times at night, the sheets damp with cold sweat. He'd set off to work with a heavier heart than usual, sometimes looking pale and withdrawn. Those few seconds had filled him with such terror it was hard to shake off.

No one ever found out who the culprit was. It was just accepted that it was someone either suicidal or mentally subnormal. Doug always said you got the whole spectrum down there.

Chapter Twelve

While I worked at Eastwood's, a few of the other wives joined me, wanting extra money themselves now their kids were at school. Soon I found myself on a minibus which picked up me and the other wives every day – such as Pat Lockery, Jackie Knighton, who lived at number 17 in the crescent, and a woman called Alison who lived in the next road along from us. I often saw her out and about. She had three kids and her daughter was mentally disabled. This girl was fourteen at the time, but would often come and play with Carrie's toys outside our front, in her own little world. They got along very well.

Our job this time was to 'riddle' the tatties for eight hours a day, which involves the workers standing in a mobile tent behind a tractor, pulling out the bad potatoes and muck as they are churned up by the plough. We earned £25 a week.

On the first day, we all stood in the tent, almost

stifling giggles, not knowing what to expect. Already it was heating up with the four of us in it. Then, suddenly, as the tractor roared into life, the 'riddler' machine started up and suddenly we were in action. Soon we were in business, chucking out green potatoes as they surfaced and whatever else got thrown up, including an occasional unlucky hedgehog or rabbit. After filling up a bag, we had to tie it up and chuck it in a big box. Little wonder we all ended up with biceps like steel!

We had some interesting discussions in that tent. Something about the enclosed space meant we felt able to reveal our innermost thoughts. There were some outspoken characters so at times the conversations became quite heated as we put the world to rights.

One time we were having one of our usual debates, when suddenly Jackie stopped talking and started listening intently.

'Have you noticed something different?' she said, as the ground beneath us seemed to turn bumpy.

We all looked at each other, then suddenly we felt something like an earthquake beneath our feet. The floor of our tent seemed to give way.

'Arghhhhhhhh!' I screamed, as we fell into each other.

The tractor engine fell silent, and we stared at each

other in shock on the floor for a few seconds. Then Jackie let out a big yell.

'Owww,' she cried. 'That bloody hurt.'

Climbing out of the tent, we quickly realised the tractor, along with our tent, had fallen into a ditch, taking us with it. And the tractor driver was having a snooze at the wheel.

Alison climbed up and thumped his window.

'Hey!' she yelled. 'You could've got us killed!'

He woke with a start, full of apologies.

'You idiot!' Alison yelled.

From then on we were always on the ball, listening out for the sound of any changes in pace to the tractor. It was a boring job for the driver just going up and down a field all day, but he should've been thinking of us ladies in the back of his wheels! Whenever we realised he hadn't changed gears at the edge of the field, we'd start shouting, throwing potatoes at the Perspex of the tractor until he roused himself.

When the potato picking work had run out, and the season was over, the farmer found other jobs for us ladies to do.

Handing us all a paint pot and giant extendable ladder, he pointed to all the buildings on the farm. 'You can get started on that lot,' he said. We painted everything from hen sheds to fences – if it was wooden it got painted.

Then we reached the barn. Standing at around forty feet high, it made our necks ache just to gaze at the top of it.

'I don't fancy climbing up that far . . .' gulped Alison.

'Me neither,' said Jackie.

'OK,' I sighed. 'I'll get myself up there.'

Careful to stare straight up, I climbed the rungs, not daring to look down. At the top, with my paint pot swinging, I started whistling to myself, just concentrating on getting the job done. It wasn't so bad after all.

I soon needed to move across, so instead of climbing all the way down again, I just did a mini jump to 'shunt' the ladder across.

After twenty minutes I heard a man's voice yelp. It was Doug. He'd come to pick me up at the end of my shift. Looking down I could see him jumping about like he had hot coals under his feet.

'Cath!' he yelled. 'Don't jump the ladder. Bloody hell, lass, you've nearly given me a heart attack.'

I climbed back down as he told me off for taking such a risk. Looking back up at the half-painted apex, I realised he was right. I'd been so intent on getting the job done though I didn't really think.

Our safety wasn't the only thing low down on the farmer's priority. Our wages were only around £5 a day, but out of that the farmer took off tax and National

Insurance. We all knew he wasn't paying it out to the taxman, though. It went straight in his pocket.

Although I got on with my 'working wives', it was still my neighbours Ann and Margaret I turned to for true friendship. We'd grown into the habit of popping across to each other's houses for chats and catch-ups whenever we could.

All three of us knew implicitly that whatever was said around our kitchen tables stayed there. We'd spend the odd half hour in between getting the tea on swapping stories about the kids or our husbands. We all suffered with their grumpy moods when they were doing night shifts.

'You know,' I moaned, 'Doug even complained I'd not made the tea the way he liked it this morning when he came off shift yesterday. The bloody cheek, as if I've not got enough to do.'

'You want to hear Billy,' sighed Margaret. 'I told him to do every double shift he could lay his hands on so I can get new curtains for the sitting room. You'd think I'd asked for the crown jewels.'

Ann and I caught each other's eyes. We all felt a little more sorry for Billy than for Margaret, if truth be told.

It meant the world to me, having those two to mouth off to. I could clear my head, get it off my chest, and the pressures of family life were eased for a while.

Having the odd break away from home also served the same purpose. We could never afford a proper holiday abroad, so Doug and I decided to get an old caravan and a small beaten-up, second-hand minibus to pull it so we could get away to Sutton-on-Sea from time to time. It meant we only need pay for petrol money as I took all the food with us.

Once the caravan was packed up with the kids, enough food to feed a family of seven for three days, all the bedding and the tents, we could barely close the doors.

To get to the sea, we travelled through Lincoln and up St George's Hill, and our groaning minibus would have to climb a steep one-in-four gradient hill. Every time Doug would put his foot down, the van would shudder and strain and we'd all keep our fingers crossed it'd reach the top at all.

'Yous lot will have to get out and bloody push,' Doug would joke.

When we reached Cleethorpes, we'd catch a glimpse of the sea through the houses and the first one to spot it would scream with delight.

'We're all going to Blackpool,' the kids would sing.

Once we arrived, things quickly became regimental while we got set up. Everyone had their own jobs. First we had to empty the caravan, then set up the tent store, sort out the electricity and collect some water. We had a separate tent for the kids as the caravan wasn't big enough.

The kids were always dying to make a mad dash to the sea.

'Mam, can we go? Can we?' they cried.

'Get your jobs done first!' I smiled.

Then as soon as they were finished, we all changed into our swimming cossies, and off we ran down to the sand and the sea.

Doug and I loved the sea. It was so therapeutic, a world away from the pit and the factories. Feeling the waves lapping on my head as I lay back was the only time I felt truly free and relaxed. Of course the water was cold, seeing as it was the North Sea, and we rarely saw a blue sky, but even in the spitting rain we'd still dive in.

'Once you're wet, you're wet,' Doug laughed.

Sometimes Doug's face twisted as he got into the cold water. It had set his knee off again. Looking at my husband wincing as he waded into the sea, a couple of 'Miner's Mark' scars on his arms (where he'd been cut and the black soot had got in and however hard you scrubbed it didn't come off), I thought of how he'd actually given his body to mining. He was like a battle-scarred soldier. Scrapes and pains were an inevitable part of the job that he'd had to accept. He hadn't just given his time to his shifts, he'd given himself physically just to get that coal cut.

Before our excursions, Doug had visited a scrap merchant to pick up an inner tubing of a tractor tyre.

'The scrap dealer wanted to know what on earth I wanted it fer!' Doug laughed after bringing it home. Pumping it up with a foot pump and attaching a rope to it, he'd chuck it into the sea to let the kids play on it. We couldn't afford any proper inflatable toys from the beach shops but this was a brilliant alternative.

We were always mindful of the strong cross tides coming down from Hull to Skegness, so Doug took a firm grip of the rope and called the kids in when the tides came.

Sometimes, for a treat, we'd give the kids a few bob to go and play in the fair in Mablethorpe. We banned them from the penny slot machines, though.

'Nobody wins except the person who owns the machines,' their dad would tell them.

Afterwards the kids would get back on the bus and we'd maybe pick up some fish and chips on the way home.

If it was raining there was always plenty to do as well. Sometimes Doug would go to the pawn shop and pick up a couple of batteries so the kids could watch a black-and-white mini-portable TV to watch the quiz shows or *Saturday Night at the Palladium*. We loved our games too, like Snakes and Ladders and Ludo. When the packet of cards came out for a game of Happy Families or Snap, the roof of the caravan would almost blow off with the arguments and heated debates about who was cheating who.

Lorraine, as usual, was normally at the centre of any scrapes or games. Once the kids had a full-on water fight, which got very heated. Grabbing buckets and sponges, they started an all-out war, with even little Allan toddling around and joining in. Later, again wanting to punish Lorraine for something or other, I caught the others all holding her head under the water in the big sink we used to collect water for the caravan.

'Stop!' I yelled, trying to rescue her. 'You'll drown her!' Douglas and Susan, who had her head, dropped her like a hot potato as I batted them away. But as she caught her breath Lorraine was laughing as hard as the rest of them.

'Thanks, Mam,' she said, that cheeky look still in her eye.

The water fight went on all day. As I sat outside scraping potatoes for dinner, I looked up and copped a flying wet sponge square in the face. I didn't know whether to laugh or scream at them. So I did both.

One evening Doug was walking past the children's tent, when he stopped and then called me quietly.

'Come and listen to this,' he grinned.

We crouched nearby the tent, as we saw the five heads all lit up by a torch and heard the sound of Lorraine's voice.

'And then,' she whispered, 'the headless beach lady walked straight through the wall of the castle . . .'

I could hear Carrie and Doug cry: 'Oooh!'

'Trust our Lorraine to be scaring the living daylights out of them,' I whispered to Doug. He laughed.

We listened for a few minutes, as Lorraine reached the climax of her 'story', and as she neared the ending, Doug reached out and rattled the top of the tent. All five kids erupted into the shrillest screams you'd ever heard, as Susan fumbled frantically for the zip.

'Only us!' I giggled, reassuring them it was fine.

On the way home the kids would start singing: 'We've been to the seaside!' at the top of their voices as we turned the corner into the crescent.

Doug used to tell them to hush up, half-laughing. 'The neighbours must think: "There's that bloody Black family back again,"' he would say.

We've never been 'political' people although we were life-long Labour voters. Government was only something we took notice of if I managed to catch the *News at Ten*, half asleep on the sofa, or if a particular strike affected our day-to-day lives, like the bread strike. On the whole it didn't feel relevant or of interest to me in the slightest. After all, the grey suits in London were a universe away from my life collecting eggs or riddling potatoes!

But occasionally I'd see glimpses of what was to come.

On 4 May 1979, I was holding a basketful of eggs when one of the young lasses I worked with came running in.

'We've done it,' she squealed with intense excitement. 'We finally have the first female prime minister. Margaret Thatcher!'

Her words made me feel as if I'd been punched in the face. Not just because the Tories won, but because I'd seen this woman on TV and there was something about her I really didn't like.

'Are you bloody stupid?' I said. 'Just because she's a woman doesn't mean she's any better. It probably means she's a bloody good liar or has a heart of stone.' In the end I was correct on both counts.

The lass shrugged off my comments. 'Well, I think it's good news,' she said. 'A woman leader can only be good for women after all.'

Many of the young lasses had voted for her simply because she was a woman – nothing to do with her policies or beliefs. To me that was just plain ridiculous. It doesn't matter if you're a man, woman, a genius or a fool, it's what you stand for that counts. That was the extent of any political interest I had. Voting for someone because of their sex? Ridiculous!

Back home that night, both Doug and I felt rather low. It was common knowledge Ted Heath's Conservative government in 1974 blamed the unions for bringing them down, including the miners who had gone on strike then. We knew the Tories might seek revenge on the unions, most likely including the National Union of Miners.

'It'll be interesting to see what happens next,' I said to Doug.

'Interesting or worrying?' he laughed.

'Both!' I replied.

'People will still need coal,' Doug said. 'And there's hundreds of years' worth down there. If there's one thing I'd put money on, it's our jobs are safe.'

Thinking Doug's job would be safe at least was some comfort but news of accidents would still rock the crescent from time to time, and served as a stark reminder of what our men were up against. News of any injury spread like wildfire and sometimes they were so shocking, it almost felt unreal.

One afternoon, I popped over to Margaret's for a catch-up and she answered the door, pale as a ghost. She'd heard from Billy that a man had lost his leg in the mine that day.

'Whole thing came clean off, Cath,' Margaret shuddered. 'Human error, Billy called it. Oh, there but for the grace of God. It doesn't bear thinking about, does it?'

Only when I saw Doug back early did I realise he'd not been spared the sight of it happening.

When a miner witnesses an accident first-hand, he is allowed the rest of his shift off. They can return to the canteen for a drink of sweet tea and a smoke to calm their nerves before they're let off home.

This time the pit claimed a miner called George Robson as its victim. He was working near a steel chain that operated some of the machinery when it stopped. He went to see what the problem was. Doug had been on the coalface nearby when he heard a blood-curdling scream, audible even above the din of the rolling machinery. George had slipped and the chain tore off his leg clean from the socket.

Doug ran to the emergency tannoy, yelling for help, and within moments a deputy was by George's side, and the on-site nurse was on her way.

In an attempt to comfort him, Doug grabbed the man's hand as he started sweating profusely with the pain.

'Don't let me die,' George whispered.

Doug clasped his hand as if his life depended on it.

'I won't,' he cried.

The nurse arrived and packed the wound with padding to stop the flow of blood. The man was given an injection to try and get the blood to clot, and then they had to act fast. The main artery is in the thigh and you can bleed to death within three minutes. A stretcher arrived and they laid poor George on it, as he passed out. Then they set off on the six-mile journey back on the train. As they went the nurse stuck her hand in the man's thigh to physically keep the artery squeezed closed until they reached the surface.

I felt sick to my stomach as Doug recalled the events. In my mind those nurses deserved medals dealing with battleground-style injuries like that.

Doug thought many of the deputies were just paying lip service to first-aid duty, though, as many couldn't stand the sight of blood and 'bottled' it when faced with bad injuries. As he was upstairs in the canteen, a manager demanded to see Doug.

'Where's the deputy, Harry?' he asked.

Doug shrugged. 'Did he not come up with us?' he asked.

The manager sent a man down to find his errant deputy. After a quick search they found Harry huddled down by a pile of rocks, quivering like a jelly on a plate. He was suffering from deep shock from seeing all the bloody mess. It was all too much for him, even if he was a trained first aider.

Once again, I felt proud of my Doug for stepping in

when he had. Typical Doug. Never afraid of the muck and bullets.

The roots of our neighbourly friendships showed their strength when any of the men were injured. Doug always said the men were worse than the women for gossip and he was right. Within minutes, news would shoot around that so-and-so was injured and the wives and miners off shifts would rally to their front doors.

They'd check the wife had transport to her husband's side at the hospital or to see if she needed the kids babysitting. In the following days, folk would offer to do her grocery shopping or check she was getting the right sickness benefits. Whatever it was, people were desperate to help. After all, everyone was in this together. In the following days or weeks it could be their own family's turn.

Chapter Thirteen

Because I've always been an early bird, I started to become the unofficial alarm clock for some of the men on shift. Up at 5 a.m. usually anyway, I'd bang on the doors on the crescent to get the men up for work.

That's not to say our close living proximities didn't sometimes test the bonds with our neighbours in other ways. That autumn, I came home from work to find Pete standing outside my house, with the front window smashed in.

'Where are they?' I cried, thinking one of the kids had put a ball through it.

'It's not the kids,' said Pete, looking worried. 'It was me! But I've bought a new pane to replace it.'

Turned out Ann had asked Pete to move her TV aerial again. She was always changing her living room around, just like I did, as we both grew bored of having everything in the same place and it was easier than decorating it all again. But Pete was scared of heights and hated clambering around the roof to get a good reception. So he tied a brick to the aerial, and tried to throw it up there. However he missed and it went straight through our living room window.

I was flabbergasted but he said he'd fix it so I let it go. He came back a few hours later with a new pane.

Doug was back by now and it was his turn to stand and watch him. 'You need putty round the edges,' Doug suggested.

Pete pulled a face. 'I can do it perfectly well, thanks, Douglas. See, it fits perfectly.'

Standing back to admire his handiwork, Pete looked very pleased with himself. Until a few seconds later, the whole thing fell backwards, shattering on the front path. It needed putty to hold it in place.

Cursing, he went off to get a replacement piece of glass. But as he carried it out of his car, he slipped and the whole thing shattered again. It was a case of third time lucky as he got another one and managed to follow Doug's instructions this time.

There wasn't any bad feeling, though. Pete and Ann were good neighbours and thankfully they took the same view, even when it was inadvertently our fault a terrible mishap struck their family.

I had a cat at the time called Tober. A huge grey tabby,

he had an eye missing after someone had shot him with an air rifle. He didn't look pretty but I loved him to bits. Our neighbours, however, were less keen. To put it bluntly, he tended to terrorise everyone a little.

He'd chase after Ann and Pete's boxer dog, called Prince, without a moment's hesitation. We'd often hear Prince yapping wildly, running as fast as he could, with Tober hissing and chasing him from behind like a streak of lightning. A real hunter, he was always fearlessly going for the biggest bird in the garden, leaving me bloody feathery presents at the back door.

Ann and Pete had three kids, all older than ours, and one of their sons, Pete, kept a tawny owl in the shed. The bird lived off mice but was quite vicious by all accounts with its sharp talons.

Whenever I saw him over the fence, Pete Jr always warned me about the owl. 'Cath, I'm worried my bird will get your cat one day. It keeps sniffing around my shed.'

'Don't you worry,' I said. 'Tober is too fast for him. It's the bird that needs to worry.'

Pete Jr insisted his owl was always jumping to attack other cats and therefore Tober was at risk, but I told him he could look after himself.

Around that time, Ann knocked on my door in the morning after I'd done my jobs. She knew I was often around for a cup of tea after getting the washing and cleaning done, if I wasn't working that day.

'You OK, Ann?' I said. She looked a bit flustered.

'No,' she replied. 'Your cat is following me. He's giving me the creeps.'

I laughed. 'Really? How?'

She explained how Tober would sit and stare at her with his one green eye while she sat in the living room. Then when she went into the kitchen, he'd leap up on to the sill by the sink, making her jump. Then he'd sit and stare at her while she washed up. Even when she went to the bedroom he followed her in there!

I couldn't help laughing. 'That's my Tober all right,' I said.

'And what with her chasing Prince, too,' Ann sighed, 'I don't know what to do with your cat.'

I shook my head. 'Neither do I,' I admitted.

Tober might have made himself a nuisance to everyone else, but to me, he was the most loyal pussy you could imagine. He'd sit on the hedge, the same time every day, as I came home from work. As I walked past he'd leap up on to my shoulder, purring loudly.

A few weeks after Pete Jr's warning about his owl, Doug came home to an almighty racket in the back garden. He rushed outside to find Tober with a mouthful of feathers and a huge wing flapping furiously. Somehow he'd got into Pete Jr's shed and swiped the owl for himself and was now trying to sink his teeth into it.

Doug yelled at him: 'Tober! Drop it!' But instead the furious cat turned on Doug, scratching and hissing at him like a demon.

He was not going to let his prey go or let Doug go near him. After a ten-minute fight between Doug, Tober and the owl, the bird's wings fell flat. He was dead.

I went round to tell Ann, not knowing what to say. Her son loved that bird and it was such a shame. But Tober was untameable.

We all loved our pets on the crescent. Even the more unusual ones. Pete was always making us laugh with his crazy money-making schemes. One January we heard a honking noise. Doug looked out of the bedroom window to see a goose strutting about the Jacksons' back garden.

That afternoon we chatted to Pete and he explained his idea.

'This is our new goose, and we're going to fatten her up all year long and then eat her at Christmas.'

Sure enough, all the neighbours helped. I'd chuck all my vegetable peelings over there. The bird loved the tops of carrots. The kids loved going round to feed it and before long it grew so fat it was waddling as if pregnant. Of course, though, Ann and Pete's youngest, Julie, wasn't too thrilled about the original idea to turn the pet she'd grown to love over the past year into dinner. And when it came to the chop it turned out Pete and Ann weren't too keen on doing it either. In the end they had to take the goose to the butchers and let him 'take care' of their dinner.

Later on, Pete acquired a rabbit hutch. He'd managed to trap a couple of wild rabbits and was intent on breeding them as pets. Little did he think, though, how quickly they bred and before long his whole garden was teeming with them. People came from all over with their kids to buy them.

'What breed are they?' they'd asked.

Pete would just laugh. 'Not sure, but you can hand rear them now!' he'd say.

Over the years we had a variety of animals in and out of our own house. Little Douglas absolutely adored them and once turned up with a squirrel he'd managed to 'tame' on the way home, sitting in the hood of his parka coat.

'Look, Mum,' he said.

I looked to see it sticking its grey head inquisitively above the fur lining.

'It's nothing but a rat, though,' I said. 'And wild. You'll have to let it go.'

But he was right when he said this animal didn't want to leave and it went everywhere with him for a few days. It was a little swine, always jumping about the rooms, and when it sat on top of my wardrobe it ate through my suitcase. Douglas took it next door to Esther's house to show it to her, but it leapt out of his hands and started running around the house. Esther came out screaming. 'It's running up and down the curtains and everywhere!' she cried.

I sent Douglas back to get it, and quickly. He got it home and I told him enough was enough, so I rang up the local wildlife centre in Bellsthorpe, which agreed to take it in.

I had to put it in four Avon boxes and an old thick cardboard whisky box to get it in the car, but even then it ate through them all!

Meanwhile, in early 1981, a job came up at Bevercotes colliery, but this time for me – in the canteen, serving the miners. I'd done some cleaning shift work there before, but one of the cooks went off sick for ten weeks getting her varicose veins done and I jumped at the chance of a job. My new role was serving food to the miners before and after their shifts, cleaning up and a spot of cooking. The Coal Board laid on buses that picked up all workers to drive them to start the shifts. So one morning, after Doug got home from work, I set off to the colliery myself.

There were six staff in the canteen plus a manageress: Betty Lawson; Pauline Wilkinson; Carole and Barbara

McIntyre; Eva, the assistant cook; Grace, the cook; and Mary, the manager.

On my first day, I pulled on my overalls and arrived bright-eyed and bushy-tailed (well, as bright-eyed as possible with five bairns), with a real willingness to work hard, as I always did.

The day started at 5 a.m. and the first thing we'd do is set up the breakfast for the day, usually bacon and eggs. Before even then, at 4.30 a.m., the ambulance men were actually the first to help as they laid all the baking on the metal tray and put it in the oven for when we arrived, kind souls that they were.

Then us cooks and staff set to, making the breakfast for the miners coming back after the night shift or going down for the new day. If there was one thing I learned quickly – miners know how to eat! Such a heavy labouring job required many calories, and fatty, fried, stodgy foods were the order of the day.

After I arrived and started asking where things were kept and what my role was, I quickly realised the canteen staff were not as friendly as they had first seemed.

'Where is the spatula for the eggs?' I asked Pauline.

Without so much as looking at me, she waved her hand vaguely at a cupboard. 'Over there,' she said, unhelpfully. I gave her a funny look but she looked straight through me.

A bit later, I asked Barbara where the bin bags were. She didn't answer me at all. So I asked again, louder. This time she stopped what she was doing and sighed, like it was a huge inconvenience.

'Over there,' she snapped. Then in the next breath she chatted away to Pauline like they were best friends. I could see the pair of them looking me up and down, and felt my hackles rising. I'd tried to be as nice as pie up until this point, but I could see this group was like a clan – they'd worked together so long they didn't seem to want any newcomers joining them. I found out later I had replaced a colleague who had been there for years, so they obviously resented me coming in from the start. To say they were unfriendly was an understatement.

'Right,' I said to Barbara. 'Cut the bull! Answer me properly or I am going to find the manageress.'

She did a double take. 'Ooh,' she said. 'No need for that, is there? I just couldn't hear what you were saying.'

If I thought these staff were bad, I'd yet to meet Betty Lawson, the deputy manager. She came in a little later and the moment I laid eyes on her, just the sight of her sent a shiver down my spine.

Waddling in, she stood around 5'10" tall and was very overweight. Her eyes narrowed like a little pig's at the slightest thing and her nasally loud voice cut through you to the quick. Within a few short seconds of meeting her I knew she was a very nasty piece of work indeed. Everyone seemed to jump whenever she spoke and just her presence made the room feel like a black cloud had filled the canteen.

Not only did she treat her colleagues with contempt, she also treated the men we were supposed to be serving with the same ballsy attitude.

Along with food, we also sold other items like soap, and one afternoon a miner came in from his shift with a black face and asked Betty for a tablet.

With her nose wrinkled in disgust, Betty handed the poor guy a piece, taking the money from him like she could hardly bear to look at him.

'There. You. Go,' she snarled.

Not surprisingly she was deeply disliked. A real stickler for cleanliness, she placed this above anything. One morning she handed out a toothbrush to everyone. I stared in amazement as she walked around the canteen, pointing at the tiling, the ovens and even the skirting boards, all of which she wanted scrubbed with the wee brushes.

'I want it spick and span,' she spat. 'Do you hear?'

Her bosses loved her as the Coal Board had set up a competition between mining canteens to find the 'Canteen of the Year'. Thanks to Betty's merciless cleaning campaign, Bevercotes had won two years running. Her obsession came at a price to the poor men we were actually working for, though.

The queue for breakfast or tea could be a mile long and Betty wouldn't let us serve them.

'Finish that cleaning,' she'd growl.

I've never liked it when people didn't show respect to the miners, in whatever manner. To me they were heroes really, working as hard as they did, risking life and limb. They knew my husband was among them, so they showed me equal respect.

We served the men all day. First breakfast, which was bacon, sausage, eggs – fried, poached or scrambled – then sandwiches for snacks, with fillings like roast beef or cheese and onion. Lunch was different every day and usually consisted of old favourites like steak and kidney pie; sausage, egg and beans; curry; and always chips with something on Fridays. If the men didn't like it and the sales were down then it would vanish from the menu the next week.

Milk was the most popular drink. Sold for 12½p, the men loved it after their shift. Cold and thirst-quenching after sweating in the mine, it was just what they needed. The miners only had one water bottle to last them all shift. No drinks were provided down there.

Sometimes the men asked for more while you were dishing up, but we were under strict instructions: no extras. Sometimes I'd keep on side with the boys by giving them a little wink when I piled their plate with the usual amount, just so they'd think I was treating them. It worked every time, the daft lads!

Once a poor temporary server girl was caught giving an extra sausage to a miner who'd kept on at her for extra. Betty sacked her on the spot, not even giving the wee lass a chance. I could see what an unreasonable so-and-so she was after that.

Betty even intimidated the actual manageress, Mary, a little. Mary was a sweeter soul and just wanted us all to get on and work hard. She was very pleasant but would soon pull you up if your work wasn't up to standard.

Another canteen worker was Grace, a stout Irish lady in her late forties with dark hair. She was another one I had little time for at the beginning. To my face she was all sweetness and light, but I often heard her joining in the catty comments with the others. I felt she was easily led and at one point told her so.

Generally I just grinned and bore all the women though. I needed this job and knew if I started losing my cool my job would go with it. And that I couldn't afford.

Nevertheless, I sailed close to the wind occasionally. One morning, I was serving the men at the 'shop' part of the canteen, which sold socks, towels, soap, and even chewing tobacco and chewing gum. The latter two always sold well as the men had dry mouths down the mine with the dust and lack of water. The tobacco was a replacement for cigarettes, as of course it was a sackable offence to light up a fag down below.

On this particular morning as I stood, serving the men, a group of the big bosses came in. They strutted around the miners, who I see as the real workers, like little gods, pushing in, taking up seats. Without a moment's hesitation they shoved the general and coalface workers to the side and stood to the front of the queue, ignoring all the tired, blackened faces coming off shift. It was their lack of respect that got me. Barging up to my till, one of the bosses barked at me to get him a cup of tea.

'With extra milk,' he ordered.

'Piss off,' I snapped. I couldn't quite believe I'd said it, but my reaction was instinctive. How dare he speak to me like that? And especially after showing such disrespect to his men.

I carried on serving, ignoring his shocked face.

'You can't say that . . .' he spluttered. He was looking around him to see if anyone else had heard.

'Just did,' I replied, as I carried on serving.

He carried on staring at me, and I ignored him. There was a rush on, so there were many men to serve. I just hoped he'd go away.

A few minutes later, Mary tapped me on the shoulder.

'Yes?' I asked.

'I need a word,' she said.

'I'm busy,' I said, taking change from one of the men.

Mary waited until I'd finished with the next man and then pulled me gently aside.

Nervously pushing stray pieces of hair behind her ears, she stared at me. 'Mr Crowhurst says you told him to, er, "Piss off",' she said, blushing a bit.

'What?' I said, in mock astonishment. 'Never!'

We stood looking at each other as she waited for my explanation. Instead of apologising I started laughing.

'Oh,' I giggled. 'Well, he must have misheard me. What I'd actually said was "Pit socks". I was just asking him if he wanted any pit socks! Ha ha! Oh dear, he must've misheard. Fancy that.'

Mary nodded, giving me a wry smile. 'OK,' she said, looking anxiously over at Mr Crowhurst, who was watching our conversation. 'Are you sure?'

'Positive,' I said. 'I said, "Pit socks", not "Piss off".'

I looked at her, willing her to swallow it.

'OK,' she repeated. 'I'll explain this to 'im.'

Afterwards some of the men got wind of this story and for years afterwards people would laugh and call 'Pit socks!' at me, even when I was walking down the street. Everyone thought it was hilarious.

Chapter Fourteen

On the whole I liked most of the men. They were decent family men and hard workers, and the atmosphere in the canteen was generally a good one. They saw the canteen as a place for light relief, to make wisecracks and relax a little before they descended into the darkness again. We got to know some of them, having a laugh as we served them. Sometimes we'd crack up at their expense when we teased them.

I'd see Doug but only fleetingly. He'd give me a little wink and smile as I served him in the throng of men. He knew I kept my head down at work, and didn't have time to stop for a natter. But seeing him was nice all the same.

One miner – we'll call him Dave – was quite a loud-mouth. He was rather domineering and would often get into little tit-for-tat rows with the men. One day he told us all how he was treating his wife to 'dinner out' on the Friday.

'Yes, she deserves a wee treat,' he went on. 'Important to keep the little woman happy, like.'

I raised an eyebrow. I could imagine all the treats in the world wouldn't make me happy to be married to this particular man. He didn't seem to have much respect for women in my opinion.

Friday arrived and Dave was scheduled to do a late shift. As I served up for the men clocking on we watched in amazement as Dave turned up in the canteen with a bag of fish and chips, followed by his poor wife behind him. She sat down opposite him while he dished out the greasy fare as if they were dining in the Ritz, licking each finger as he did so.

'This is nice, innit?' he smiled through salt-covered lips.

We soon realised that Dave's idea of treating his wife consisted of bringing in a fish supper from the chip shop on the way to work on his shift.

All us girls noticed and everyone started laughing. If that was what he called a 'treat' we felt sorry for her, as he spoke for her even when she ordered something to drink.

As life had changed for me in my new role in the canteen, it seemed the children were growing up faster than ever. Susan, now sixteen, was having boyfriends and proved popular with them. One day she told me about a miner called Rob, who was about the same age as her. It turned out it was Grace from the canteen's son.

'Watch out, we could be mother-in-laws,' Grace joked. I gave her tight smile back. That wasn't a thought I relished at the time, I'll admit. After a few dates drinking Cokes in the pubs and going to the pictures though, Susan decided they were not suited, although they decided to remain friends.

Now I was working in the canteen, I felt closer than ever to the action at the pit.

Whenever I arrived for work, I always looked out for the stretcher propped up by the medical door. It meant a man had been lifted out of the mine overnight or was about to be carted off during the day. My stomach always felt heavy just looking at it. We'd bustle past with trays and plates of food, trying not to look. We knew that another man had copped it.

Shortly after I started my new job, it wasn't the stretcher that told me something terrible had happened. It was the look on the men's faces.

A few of the men came trickling in off the night shifts. We usually had thirty or forty at a time, and the atmosphere was normally noisy and jovial. But this time their faces were blank, and no one was looking anyone in the eye.

'Oh goodness,' I gasped. 'Grace, whatever has happened?'

'He were only a twenty-year-old,' she whispered. 'A pole went straight through him and he stood no chance.'

I felt my stomach turn over. This was the first time I'd heard of a miner's death at Bevercotes. And a lad so young. I felt shaken to the core.

As the men came up and quietly started talking, the story slowly emerged. The lad, Jimmy, was working on one of the conveyor belts from which the men had to pick up the poles of wood that were used to help hold up the roofs. These poles were the size of half a telegraph pole and all miners were trained on how to lift them with the minimum risk of injury. They had to pick them up in pairs, one end each, and time it carefully so they had a firm grip.

Tragically, this young lad went to grab it by himself. As it flew by, it flipped upwards and speared him straight through the chest, killing him in an instant.

He wasn't married but he had a girlfriend, we'd heard, and he'd only been working down the pit for a year or so.

'Such a waste,' I kept repeating. 'A wee lad, dying for coal. It's not right, is it?'

Later on, Doug came home, pale and tired but angry too.

'It was stupidity,' he kept saying. 'Pure unadulterated stupidity, that's what killed him. A young lad who never listened. I can always spot them a mile off.'

Doug never usually spoke ill of the dead, but as far as he was concerned, you didn't ever argue with safety rules. You stuck by them religiously. The result when you didn't follow them was usually catastrophic.

After such an incident, the lads were obviously devastated. Doug said how full of life this young lad had been, how senseless the whole thing was. The Coal Board didn't put on a memorial or give anyone the day off. You got let out for the funeral and that was it. The Board didn't want miners to contemplate their mortality and pit dangers for too long. It was a case of: 'What a shame, now let's crack on.'

It was around then our own son, Douglas, who had always taken a keen interest in his dad's job, announced he too wanted to be a miner.

'It's a good life, isn't it, Dad? A proper man's job,' he said.

I watched as predictably Doug's face grew serious. Neither of us had anything against our son joining the pit. But not working on the coalface. Doug always said it was a job for the toughest nut and there were so many easier roles to aim for, from electricians to managers.

'I don't think so, lad,' said Doug. 'You must promise me if you ever think about joining you only go for the top jobs. You get your exams and become a manager, a deputy, an electrician or something proper. Don't do what your dad did.'

Just as his own father wanted a better life for his son, so did my Doug.

The idea of a 'man's job' in the mine was a tempting one for Douglas though, as he was always trying to prove himself. Barely standing at 4'6", he got ribbed at school. The slightest thing would set him off into a fight. His lack of height really got to him. I'm only 5'1" and Doug is only 5'6", so his genes were against him on this one.

He was a cheeky one, too, and the one I had to watch the most. One day I popped into the local shop, whose owner Sally, knew me very well. We got chatting.

'Er, Cath,' she began. 'Did you send your Douglas to the shop to buy gas for lighters?'

'No, I most certainly didnae,' I said.

'Well, he came in here the other day with his wee friend to buy some . . .'

I thanked her for the information and waited until Douglas got home from school.

'Did you buy a gas lighter?' I asked, studying his face carefully. I knew my five inside out and there was no way they could lie to me.

Looking sheepish already, Douglas stuffed his hands in his trouser pockets.

'Yes,' he said, slowly. 'But it wasn't me; it was Peter who said we could . . .'

Within a few minutes I'd extracted everything I needed to know. Not only had Peter bought the lighters along with him, but the pair of them had been sniffing them to get high.

'This stops and it stops right now,' I said.

Grabbing my coat, I marched around to Peter's mum's house to tell her. She didn't look especially bothered, but that wasn't going to stop me from punishing Douglas.

'But Peter's mum doesn't mind,' he protested, as I grounded him for a month. 'He's not got told off.'

'I'm not Peter's mum,' I said. 'And if Peter asked you to jump out of a window I wouldn't expect you to do it either.'

Fear that my son would harm himself was at the bottom of my reaction. Thinking how I needed to nip this in the bud, I decided to take him down to the local police station too. I quietly explained the situation to the officer on duty as he nodded sagely.

'Come this way, young man,' he said to Douglas. Showing him the cells he explained how sniffing lighter fuel could lead to other drugs and if you ended up caught you'd be straight in the slammer.

By the end of the visit I thanked the kind officer and took Douglas by the hand. I didn't need to say another word and I knew he'd never touch the stuff again.

Although I admired Doug and the miners for the hard job they did, I was accused once or twice of not 'understanding' about how the mines worked by one of the bosses. He'd start to lecture someone about a machine in the mine while he was in the canteen and he would turn and give me a knowing wink.

'Of course you won't know what the blazes I'm talking about, will you?' he chuckled.

As a wife it was presumed I was ignorant to the ways of the mine. After all, few wives, if any, ventured down there. But every now and then the managers took a group of miners' families or people considering pit jobs down to tour the mine. One evening, I chatted about joining a tour with Ann and Margaret over one of our cuppas.

'You'll not get me down there. Not bloody likely,' said Margaret.

Ann physically shuddered. 'It scares the life out of me,' she said. 'Some jobs are men's work and should stay men's work. And think of all the filth.'

I agreed. I'd seen on the news recently a piece about the women's libbers. There had been a march with them shouting and screaming for equal rights. There had also been another piece about women joining men down the mines in America. But the fact is, men are bigger and stronger than women and able to cope with hard physical challenges better. Best to leave them to it. But then Doug was down there every single day – surely I should go at least once to experience it myself? Somehow it seemed like the right thing to do.

So I stuck my name on the list to join the next 'behind-the-scenes' tour of Bevercotes.

'You sure you wanna try it, lassie?' said Doug, after I announced my decision.

'Aye, well, I'll only be down there for a couple of hours,' I chuckled. 'I am sure I'll be able to cope with that.'

Doug looked impressed.

'Well, it is scorching down there, Cath, so you'll need nothing on but a boiler suit and your bra and knickers,' he said.

I couldn't believe I'd need so little. But when the day of the tour arrived, I pulled out the boiler suit I wore to do home decorating in, and set off with the group of twenty in the bus to be taken around by one of the bosses. Among the group was a young lad, Barry, who was considering becoming a miner. He was a twentysomething student but wanted to earn extra income in the holidays. He looked very keen, and asked lots of questions to the boss.

When we arrived, we were handed hard hats with lights on the top, then we were herded like sheep into a cage lift. A button was pressed and down we shot. My stomach lurched as it felt like we were plunging at quite a speed. It was a long, long way down.

As we sped downwards, the darkness quickly enveloped us all. Finally the lift stopped, the door was opened and the boss led us into a small cavern. Sounds of rumbling, clanking machinery and the occasional yell of a miner were the only noises we could hear. Already our group seemed to be in semi-shock. We were so far below the ground, it didn't seem real. The smell was over-powering;

the air dank, musty and sooty. Already I longed for the fresh air from the surface. It was suffocating and disorientating. The only light we had was provided by the pale beams from our helmets. We'd entered a twilight world, as if it belonged to another planet.

'Right, time to flick them off,' said the boss cheerfully. We all snapped our lights off and stood in utter, total darkness. You simply couldn't see a jot, even a hand an inch away from your face. I felt consumed, and swallowed down a rising feeling of panic.

'Ewww,' cried one of the other wives. 'This is what it must be like to be totally blind.' We all fumbled with slight panic to flick our lights on again.

'Ah-ha,' said the boss. 'Now that's a real blackout for you. Right now, come this way . . .'

Like an underground Willy Wonka showing us around his factory, he led us on a short walk, pointing to the water dripping off the coalface and the rocks containing fossils. I was surprised by just how uneven the ground was. It was jagged coal we were walking on. No proper pathways or roads. I didn't know what to expect but this seemed such a raw, basic environment. After five minutes of walking through a low cavern, we arrived at a little train.

'Here is what we call the panda cars,' he said, inviting us to hop in. We got seated in the wagons and slowly we creaked off on the rails, all in silence. It vaguely reminded me of a funfair ride on a ghost train, except this was a serious, dangerous version for grown-ups.

The coal roof was held up by scaffolding 'rings'. All were bolted into place with steel girders, the type Doug had described so vividly. The feat of engineering impressed me. How it held up all the coal above it, I didn't know. I thought of Doug describing how the most dreaded sound for a miner was the tinkle of coal dust falling down, heard just before a ceiling collapse, and I found myself gripping the train bar in front of me as we whizzed underneath. The thought of it crashing down was terrifying.

The size of the 'ceiling' varied hugely. Once we entered a high cavern filled with the most awesome stalactites and stalagmites. Like enormous spears they rose from the rock face like a giant's fork prongs, glinting and twinkling at us in our head beams of light.

The wives oohed and aahed as if they were fireworks setting off in the sky. 'Beautiful, aren't they?' beamed the manager. 'Millions of years old.'

I resisted the urge to reach out and touch them. I still felt afraid to touch anything in case it broke. The natural beauty took my breath away. It made me realise just how old the mine was. Coal, after all, is just squashed plantation that's millions of years old. Amazing! It was practically the only beautiful thing in the mine, though.

As we carried on our tour we were shown lots of baffling

machinery and the boss explained how it all worked, most of which went over my head. The coal cutter was the most incredible thing, though. The noise was eardrum-shattering as it plundered the coalface, slicing through it like a piece of wire over Edam. Plumes of soot rose from the rocks as they clattered to the ground. Just standing near it sent a shudder down my spine as I could feel the reverberations in my chest bone. It felt dangerous just to stand close to it, let alone try and operate it. Thinking of my Doug in charge of this awesome machine seemed incredible.

At one point in the tour, the walls of coal grew narrower and lower, until we had to literally crawl on our hands and knees. Luckily we had kneepads to save ourselves from the craggy floor, but even then I felt scraped and bruised. As my helmet grated on the 'roof' I felt a jolt of panic rise in my throat. It was impossible to ignore the intense feeling of claustrophobia. Having to deal with this day-in day-out was just unimaginable. I'd decided that instant I'd rather deal with Betty and her nasty looks any day!

Barry, the young lad, was crawling behind me. He'd grown more quiet as the tour wore on. The heat was insufferable, too. I moved my helmet slightly at one point and felt water dribble down my neck. I couldn't believe how much I was sweating.

Eventually we reached the feeder and loader gates. Doug

had told me about them and I felt the blast of fresh air and then the difference with the fetid hot air closing in again. It reeked terribly, like how I'd imagine rotten corpses would smell.

On this particular day a tank of some sort had burst, sending water pouring into the gate. As the pit had visitors they'd laid out pieces of chalk and timber for us to clamber over to keep dry. Ordinarily the miners would just get soaked.

Finally, after two hours of walking, crawling and sweating, it was time to go back to the surface. Again in silence we waited for the lift to glide us back up. Back to the fresh, cool air and freedom.

As the boss opened the doors for us, he smiled. 'Well, what did you all think?' he asked cheerfully.

'I don't know how they do it,' I said, shaking my head. 'What an experience.'

I glanced at Barry, who looked pale.

'And so, lad, do you think you'd like a job?' asked the boss, patting his back.

Barry pulled his hat off, his curly hair framing round his face, sopping with sweat.

'No,' he said, handing him the helmet. 'Never again.'

Chapter Fifteen

That night I looked at my husband again with renewed admiration. I already thought he was an incredible man, but to think he went down there every day for years just staggered me.

'I don't know how you do it,' I said, quietly.

He smiled. 'Ah, you get used to it,' he said.

Like everyone else, Doug did have bad days too. Especially on hot summer mornings, when the kids were laughing outside and the air from the fields blowing nearby smelled so sweet and fresh you could taste it. He'd bang about downstairs as he got together his lunch and packed his fruit. Having to descend to the bowels of the earth on days like these was painful.

'I'll see yous later,' he would growl, stomping off to the minibus as I hung out the washing to dry in the fresh breeze.

'Bye, love,' I said. My heart went out to him.

Over the years we heard of some men who didn't cope so well. Working in dangerous conditions day-in day-out, in darkness, doing heavy labour, wasn't any easier on the mind than it was on the body. One man, a lovely young Scottish lad, needed extra cash for his family so he started doing overtime. For months he did extra hours and double shifts, working days back to back with only four hours off in between. He began to look more and more tired and withdrawn, until his colleagues started suggesting he took a day off.

'Nah, I'll be OK,' he insisted, as he joined the lads in the lift. 'We need the money.'

We all understood that feeling. But working like a dog in those conditions meant he was at risk of paying a heavy price.

After several weeks of this lad working round the clock, Doug was working down the pit one day when he heard a terrible animal-like screaming. He ran over to find the young man looking distressed.

'There's a crocodile!' he yelled, pointing down below.

Doug looked down to see a pipe filled with gravel moving beneath.

'It's a snake!' the lad screamed, trying to clamber out.

A few of the men gently took his arms and led him fighting and shrieking like a child away from his nightmares. The poor man was signed off work sick and we never saw him again. The pit had claimed another victim and he'd entered a darkness from which there was no return.

After my trip down the mine, my daughters Susan, then sixteen, and Lorraine, fourteen, were keen to go and see what went on down below too. 'Can we Mam, can we?' Lorraine badgered. 'We just want to see what Daddy does.'

Lorraine was always in awe of her dad. A real tomboy, she was fascinated by the pit.

She relished dressing up as a miner for Halloween and was glued to the TV when the mining serials came on.

I looked at them both. 'Well, I can do it with you,' I warned. 'But you might not like it.'

They both swore they'd be brave and it was only for a couple of hours anyway.

This time we had a private tour, just the three of us, with Doug and a deputy. It meant we could visit the parts of the mine we liked and not get stuck like 'tail-end Charlies', like I did during my last visit.

To begin with the girls bubbled and giggled with excitement. They loved wearing the hats, flicking on the lights and shining the bulb in each other's eyes.

'Stop it,' I said. 'You'll blind one another.'

We trooped into the lift as if on a school trip. 'We're

going underground,' Lorraine sang, to the tune of Paul Weller's song. But as the darkness and the stuffy atmosphere quickly enveloped us all, her song petered out and we all grew silent.

'Ooh, that lift makes my stomach jump to my throat,' Susan groaned.

As we were taken on the railway, after only a few hundred yards in, Lorraine started complaining.

'It's so hot, Dad!' she cried.

'It's OK sweetheart,' he said. 'It's going to get even hotter the further we go in. We'll take it nice and slowly.'

The pair of them were fascinated by the 'endless rope' that pulled the wheels of the train. One man sat at one end and one sat at the other. 'What does that man do?' asked Lorraine.

'He pulls the train up and down,' joked Doug. Really a mechanical crane did this. The deputy looked at him like he was a nut. It'd take an army of men to swing such a system into use!

We carried on until we reached an area we had to crawl into. Although we were given kneepads it was hot and intense. Lorraine started breathing heavily, as we all focused on the effort of moving forward without scraping our knees too much.

'Maaaaaam,' said Lorraine, as I followed her feet

while we crawled in between the rock faces. 'I don't like this . . .'

I rubbed her ankle. 'Just head down and keep going, my love,' I soothed. 'We'll be out before you know it.'

I swallowed hard, tasting the musty air. I knew exactly how she felt. The place felt almost medieval. This part of the mine was unbelievably hot and some men just worked in their underpants and nothing else. Part of me couldn't believe working conditions existed like this in the 1980s. But then how else were they to get the job done? It was dirty, hard, heavy work. Machines had made mining easier but someone had to drive them. And it was only humans who could bring these machines down.

Doug took us all the way down to the coalface. Once there, Lorraine looked around, confused.

'But where is it, Dad? All I can see is a machine?' she said.

Doug peered down a gap into a nearby hole. 'Hey, lads,' he shouted. 'Is it OK to bring the girls down?'

We all looked on in wonder.

'Who you shouting at, Dad?' asked Susan. 'There's no one there.'

Finally a voice cried: 'OK, Doug!' and we squeezed into a tiny hole, before dropping down into a little cavern where two men sat. The now-suffocating heat was so intense, I had to gulp down a feeling of claustrophobic panic.

After a little look at the machine and a chat with the two brave souls who worked in such a tiny space, Doug gave the nod and we all clambered out. The coalface and the feeder gates were where most accidents happened. It was where gases and fresh oxygen came in and out, all highly flammable in the right conditions. In such confined spaces so far below you'd never stand a chance if a spark went off.

As we started to make our way back, everyone grew silent, lost in their own thoughts.

We were visiting on a Sunday when most of the machines stood idle, so it felt very quiet. The pit was nearly empty, with only a few faces coming out of the gloom. Quietly, Doug admitted even he found it eerie.

'You want to try walking down a tunnel on a rare quiet moment after a shift,' he laughed. 'It's enough to send you running, I can tell you!'

After our two-hour tour, during which we travelled two miles to the coalface, both girls' faces were covered in soot like their dad's and they looked a little more wide-eyed than when we arrived.

'I don't know how Dad does it,' whispered Susan, gazing up at the light at the end of the tunnel.

'Me neither,' said Lorraine, looking pale. 'Poor Daddy.'

As we emerged from the surface, our heads wet with sweat, coughing as we got rid of the soot in our throats, I thanked the manager for taking us down.

'Well, how was it second time around?' he asked.

'I am never going down there again,' I vowed. 'Twice is more than enough.'

Later on Doug laughed. 'I don't blame you, lassie,' he said.

There were enough dramas on the surface for me to be more than occupied without taking another tour down the pit. One of the main events of the year was the vegetable show. In Ollerton and the surrounding villages, this was one of the big competitions of the year and the miners took it as seriously as the Olympic Games.

The preparation would begin in March and April with many miners choosing to use their back gardens instead of allotments in case their prize crops were accessed and sabotaged. The competition was fiercest between the Geordies for some reason. Leeks and gladioli were big events, but all vegetables from tomatoes to marrows were popular.

One neighbour over the back of us, Ron Fox, the trainer, could barely make a cup of tea, but he announced one year he was going to take part. He planted a series of leeks in his garden, boasting to everyone how well he thought they'd do.

'My garden is on a slope,' he explained to Doug one day. 'So I am covering the top with fertiliser so it drains down slowly.'

Doug nodded, not entirely convinced Ron had what it takes. Like most of the men, Ron used an up-turned washing-up liquid bottle filled with top-notch fertiliser. The men used all sorts, always experimenting and trying out different combinations to try and out-fertilise the other miners.

Anyway, proud Ron was determined to win this year and we watched in awe as his leeks started to grow into mini monsters.

But a few weeks after he'd boasted of his new triumphs, I bumped into him in the street on the way to the shops, his face like thunder.

'What's up, Ron?' I asked, thinking someone might have died.

'My leeks,' he cried. 'Some bugger has poisoned them!'

Poor Ron had woken up one morning to find his green gems wrinkled and dying. Unable to work out what had happened, he didn't have to look far in the end. Picking up a washing-up liquid bottle, he had found his carefully concocted fertiliser had been replaced by bleach.

'Sabotage,' he snapped. 'That's what it is.'

It wasn't just Ron who was the victim of a jealous vegetable-growing rival. The biggest rivals were neighbours who lived at the back of our house: Arthur Marshall and a retired deputy called Maxwell, whom everyone called 'Old Geordie'. The pair of them fought like tyrants, always trying to outdo each other. First Arthur bought a greenhouse, then Maxwell bought two of them. We watched in amusement as however hard Arthur tried he could never keep up with Maxwell, who was now retired and had all day long to tend to his prized crops.

Doug tried to join in when he could, but thankfully he could never take it as seriously as the other two. Their vegetables became like the crown jewels to them, and they clearly saw them as a test of their manhood, much to all the wives' amusement.

I'd get free manure from the chicken factories, so when Doug dug a trench and planted loads of veg, we got off to a good start.

Our neighbours' rivalry reached a pinnacle when Old Geordie managed to grow a square-shaped tomato. As soon as Arthur spotted it over his fence, he set all out to create the same shape.

'Aye, you'll never do it,' said Old Geordie, grinning his toothy grin. 'It's a craft, that is.'

Strangely enough, Doug was also growing tomatoes around this time and bizarrely he also managed to grow a square one. But it was more by luck than judgement: he just happened to plant two seeds next to each other and they germinated together, merging to create a cuboid shape.

When Arthur saw Doug had managed it too, he was incensed. 'What's your trick?' he begged. 'Tell me!'

Doug went along with the joke and just laughed, tapping his nose. He found it very amusing to watch as Arthur went out and bought every outdoor tomato breed going in a bid to grow his own square fruit. As soon as he got in from work, he'd roll up his sleeves, potting and planting like a maniac. The look of steely determination on his face sent us both into fits.

After weeks of trying, his garden a sea of juicy red fruits, he gave up.

'OK, OK,' he conceded one day, over the fence to Old Geordie. 'Just put me out of my misery. How the hell did you grow a square-shaped tommy?'

Old Geordie threw his head back and laughed.

'Like I said, it's a craft,' he said. 'You know, like Kraft cheese slices. They come in squares. Well, these tomatoes are grown like they are, so they make a perfect fit for a cheese and tomato sandwich . . .'

Realising he was taking the mickey, Arthur's face turned a shade matching that of his very round tomatoes. Boiling with anger, he started shouting until Doug stepped in.

'It's all a big fluke,' Doug admitted, before explaining how the seeds germinate together.

The 'Kraft tomato' joke swept around the pit the next day like wildfire and did nothing to calm Arthur's ill temper. For weeks the miners ribbed him, waving their cheese sarnies under his nose.

When the day of the vegetable competition finally arrived, we'd go and marvel at the produce all laid out on display at the Miners' Welfare. Crowds would gather around leeks the size of a man's thigh and marrows the size of a pig. The vegetables looked like cartoon versions of themselves, almost science fictional. It was always a fun day out for us and the kids to see what the men had managed to create.

The winner was awarded a trophy and lauded for the day, and usually Old Geordie claimed first or second prize every year for most of the categories.

As far as I was concerned it was the wives who were the true winners during the competition season. The crescent would be awash with leek soup for weeks and we had more vegetables than we knew what to do with. We saved a fortune on food.

While veg competitions were entertaining, it wasn't long before another spate of accidents shattered the conviviality of our little community. One day Doug came home with news of yet another miner copping an injury.

'It was Craig,' said Doug, as he flopped on the sofa. 'Might have known it would be him . . .'

Craig had been working next to the heavy seven-inch thick cable that took the electricity to the coal cutter. It was Craig's job to watch it, and it was an easy job, but if it got caught on the coal surface you had to use a special stick to prise it up. A bit of a cocky character who was not one to take a telling about the right way of doing things, Craig didn't use the stick and stuck his hand underneath it instead. The cable twisted on the ground, trapping his hand and pulling it clean off.

Unfortunately for him, Doug was a witness to this accident too. He ran and hit the tannoy button connected to the emergency system, which is placed every five metres along the pit. 'Emergency, deputy needed! Bad injury!' he yelled.

A deputy soon arrived while Doug held the man's arm above his head as he sat mute with shock. The pain of these sorts of injuries always comes later.

Then the deputy picked up the severed hand, still in its glove, and as he held it aloft, Craig spotted sight of it and promptly fainted on the rough ground.

Doug had to drop the hand in a brown paper bag, as a nurse arrived to administer morphine and Craig was whisked to hospital, his hand following him in the bag. Incredibly, doctors managed to sew it back on.

As if this wasn't enough, shortly afterwards I was walking Allan and Carrie to school when I saw Agnes looking upset, coming out of a shop. We didn't get on and I didn't think much of her, but I am not one to walk past anyone in tears.

'What's happened, pet?' I asked.

'It's Ruby's husband . . .' she said, her plucked eyebrows knotted. 'He's had an accident. Lost an arm.'

I gasped.

'What a horrible thing,' I said, shuddering.

We fell silent for a moment. We didn't often speak, me and Agnes. She was a foolish lady in my opinion, but as we looked into each other's eyes we sensed an understanding.

'Do let Ruby know if there's anything I can do,' I said sincerely, before tailing off. 'Better go, getting the kids off.'

Carrie's eyes widened as we hurried along to school.

'Do lots of men lose their arms in the mine?' she asked.

'No, my darling,' I said. 'Only those who're not keeping an eye on them.'

Later on, Doug came home with yet another macabre story to tell, this time involving Ruby's husband Brian. He was working on a conveyor belt when he came a cropper. The belt was five feet wide and took coal and muck away from the face but sometimes flipped over when the build-up of dust grew too big. To keep the belt going, water had to be sluiced over the top to soften the mud so it could be scraped off.

When it got caught one time, Brian tried to sort it out himself by climbing over it. As he pushed his arm under it, the belt started back up and he flew over it like someone had given him a karate kick. It pulled his arm straight off. The men rushed over and made a tourniquet to cut off the blood flow so he didn't bleed to death. Later he was given a false arm and retired. Shortly afterwards, Ruby ran off with another man to America, taking Brian's kids with her. Tired of the mining life before the accident, she had little sympathy for her now-limbless husband. None of it surprised us, really. It always seemed to us that she thought living in a pit village was beneath her station.

Although we were shocked by this run of accidents, deep down we weren't surprised. In such a dangerous environment, accidents were inevitable. And in Doug's eyes it was no coincidence the characters he believed had more of a lax attitude to safety were the ones who ended up injured. But no miner was completely free of risk, however careful you might be.

Chapter Sixteen

With all the accidents happening around him, Doug was less than impressed when Paul, the arrogant lad who'd caused his knee accident, arrived at the coalface needing training up. Doug was assigned to teach him new techniques, but the cocky so-and-so still refused to listen and do what he was told, again putting them in danger. Doug refused to sign off his paperwork to say he could work in that field. And he told him so to his face.

Paul went crying to the managers claiming Doug was picking on him, and it was discrimination of one sort or another.

'I just don't want you killing anyone – you're a bloody danger,' Doug told him bluntly. 'And if you have a problem with that then I'm not sorry, either.'

Eventually Paul dropped the case and went to work in another part of the pit. His new work colleagues quickly learned his foolhardy ways, no doubt.

Generally speaking, though, Doug got on well with the men who worked alongside him. Maybe it was a result of their extraordinary jobs or even the dangers that went with it, but Doug loved the comradeship underground. He said there was nothing like it. The lads were always playing jokes on one another, taking every opportunity to have a laugh and a craic.

There was one deputy called Gail, who the men couldn't stand, as he was always shouting at them for no good reason, coining himself the nickname 'Stormy Gail'. He had a reputation for working people harder than anyone else, always criticising and chasing the younger lads.

One day he ordered Doug to get some of the men to move tonnes and tonnes of dust in bags a mile down the mine. It would have been back-breaking, fruitless work.

'No problem,' grinned Doug helpfully. 'You go and get your tea and we'll set to with this lot.'

After Gail left, the lads looked at Doug, completely baffled. 'Why did you tell him that?' they said. 'Moving this lot that far will take forever.'

'You just wait and see,' grinned Doug. 'We've got some building to do.'

With all their strength and laughing as they did it, the lads started building a commando-style bunker from the bags. It took a good hour and by the time Gail returned they'd finished and were hiding inside.

'Doug?' Gail yelled, his voice echoing. 'Where are yous all? Why's this pile not been moved? What's going on?'

Leaving him to wander around for a few minutes scratching his head, the men stifled laughter as they unscrewed their water bottle tops.

As Gail went through the alphabet of swear words, calling the men every name under the sun, the men got into position.

'One, two, three . . .' Doug whispered.

'Fire!' they yelled, throwing their water at the deputy.

'You total bastards!' Gail screamed, as they stuck their heads above the bags.

Doug called deputies like him 'brown noses' because he thought they worried more about getting onside with the management than they did about the men they were responsible for.

Some of the deputies presided over areas of the mine in their offices way above ground, keeping in touch by tannoy. Doug had a button he could hit at any time when he was in charge of some of the machinery. If this happened it was called 'lockdown', and automatically everything shut off, allowing the men time to find out what the problem was.

On this occasion Doug was operating the coalface machine when sparks started flying off it. He didn't hesitate to hit the button for lockdown, as he feared a fire starting, which would have endangered the lives of everyone.

Through the tannoy system, high above ground, the deputy started yelling.

'Get that machine back on. Time is money. What yous playing at?'

Doug ran to the answering machine. 'It's sparks, though,' he cried. 'It's too risky.'

'What kind of sparks?' asked the deputy. 'Electrical or mechanical?'

Doug pulled a face. He couldn't believe the stupidity of the question. 'I've no idea. Why don't you get off your backside, get down here and take a look yourself!'

Another time a deputy was talking to the lads about the machinery called 'ROLF', the one that cut the coalface remotely. After giving a quick run-through he smiled at the men.

'You could teach a monkey to do this job,' he added, patronisingly.

Doug glared at him. At only 5'6", he was much shorter than this deputy who stood at 6'4" and was literally looking down his nose at him. Doug resented his tone and intimidation. He wasn't going to let him get away with it.

When the men started going up to the surface, they switched their lights off for a minute, to rest their eyes so they could gradually open them when they got to the top again.

In the pitch dark, Doug positioned himself behind this deputy and kicked him in the back of the legs. As the lights went back on, Doug shuffled quickly to the side.

'Who kicked me?' growled the deputy, looking at all the men. They all shuffled their feet, as Doug stared straight at him.

'I'll have you, Black,' he snapped.

'Wasnae me,' Doug laughed. 'Must have been one of the monkeys jumping around the cage.'

Despite the odd barney with those in charge, Doug had built a reputation as a reliable, trustworthy hard worker. It was only a matter of time before he caught the attention of management and soon afterwards he was offered the chance to start training as a deputy.

Full of beans when he came home with the news, he picked me up and span me round the kitchen.

'My salary will rocket,' he beamed. 'This will change all our lives. We've made it, lassie.'

If I wanted to I could even afford to give up working. It was the best news we'd had since we'd arrived.

'Well done, Dougie,' I beamed, as he put me down again.

Best of all it meant Doug would be off the coalface, one of the most dangerous places to work. I would finally be able to breathe a slight sigh of relief. As a manager he'd be overseeing the safety and not in the firing line himself. It would still be dangerous, but possibly not as bad.

Things couldn't be better. But as John Lennon said: 'Life is what happens to you when you're busy making other plans . . .'

On 6 October 1982, the one thing I'd dreaded happening since Doug joined the mines, six years earlier, finally occurred. The night before I'd gone to bed as usual, after working all day and seeing to the kids. Doug was off doing the night shift. But I felt a sense of unease.

'I feel like something has happened,' I confided to Susan. 'I can't put my finger on it.'

'Mam,' she said. 'You're just over tired. If anything's happened to Dad you'd have had the phone call. And no one's rung, have they?'

'Yes, you're right,' I nodded, yawning. 'My imagination is just running on overtime. I must just be a little stressed.'

Life had been tough recently. I'd been diagnosed with fibroids and been in lots of pain, on and off. Women's troubles were the bane of my life. But as usual I just got on with it. And Grandad's health was deteriorating too: he'd been complaining about diarrhoea on the last visit and I was worried about him. What with one thing and another it was no wonder I was just waiting now for the next bad thing. So after having a cup of cocoa I switched off all the lights and took myself upstairs to bed. A good sleep was all I needed.

Before I went up, though, I found a poem little Allan had written at school that day about his dad being a miner.

Calling it 'The Pit' it read: 'At the pit, men are working on machines, / Machines are banging, / Men are working with spades, / Spades are clicking, / Men are underground digging, / Big boulders come crashing down . . .'

I smiled. What imaginations wee ones have, I thought. Little did I realise how prophetic it would turn out to be.

The next morning, I woke early as usual to get into the canteen. It was Douglas's fourteenth birthday and we'd had an excited morning, seeing what the postman had brought and singing 'Happy Birthday'.

While I bustled around I felt a wave of relief as I realised the phone obviously hadn't rung all night, which meant Doug must be fine. I was being silly after all.

Arriving at work, I pulled on my overalls, and then spotted the dreaded stretcher propped up by the medical room door. An ominous sign.

'Oh dear,' I thought. 'Some poor bugger has copped it.'

Setting to in the kitchen, I opened the fridge to start

making the porridge and get things going. A few minutes later I heard a frantic banging on the door. A miner's black face appeared at the glass.

'Go away,' Grace mouthed. 'You're too early.'

I turned and carried on, but his rat-a-tatting didn't stop. I span round again and realised he was pointing at me.

'I've just told you . . .' Grace began, as she unbolted the door.

'Cathy!' cried the miner, looking past Grace at me. 'It's Doug. He didn't want the sister to call you and wake you up, but he's in hospital. He's broken his back. A wall collapsed on him.'

I felt my knees turn to water as I dropped the rashers of bacon in my hands.

'I'm going,' I said, throwing down my overall.

A miner gave me a lift to Worksop hospital. My mind was racing. After all these years, I'd been so grateful Doug had escaped any serious injuries. Now this had happened, and to break his back could barely be worse. Images of the wall collapsing on him replayed like a newsreel in my imagination, along with visions of poor Doug in a wheel-chair. How would we cope now? I just didn't know what to expect, but whatever it was it didn't look good.

Running into the ward, feeling a sense of déjà vu after his knee injury, I scanned the beds and spotted a familiar form. Doug was laying on his back, wincing with evident pain.

'Oh, Doug,' I said, grabbing his hand. 'I'm here now.'

He clutched my hand for a few moments but we didn't speak. We both knew the worst had happened now, but he was still alive.

'What happened?' I cried.

'Oh, Cathy,' he said. 'A whole part of the ceiling collapsed on to me.'

'You've broken your back?' I gasped, tears starting to well up.

'Nah, love! Who told you that?' Doug said, looking angry.

'One of the miners – Jock, I think his name is,' I said.

'Well, he had no right to make such a wild guess. Oh, you must've been so worried. No, Cath, I am very lucky and it's just nerve damage.'

I wanted to sob with relief. The miner had made a mistake, which on the face of it was a terrible thing to get wrong. But thank God he had.

Doug went on to explain how he had been working at the coalface, standing on some scaffolding made with wooden slats, and tightening up the sides of the arches that hold up the ceiling.

'I'd shovelled up some stones in the bags and was packing them in to the sides for extra support,' he explained slowly.

'And I was thinking it looked good and quite strong. Then I heard a tiny tinkle, only a small one. It barely registered. You know, it's not like the films on TV, when there is a warning if there's drama like that. I just had a terrible feeling in my gut and then after a few bits of dust, the whole lot just went whoooomph!'

I fought back the tears as my husband described how he was pinned to the scaffolding with heaps of coal on top of him, flat on his back, out cold for a good forty seconds. The men dug him out as fast as possible and as he came round, the deputy was standing over him giving him a shot of the morphine he kept in a sachet on his belt.

His hard helmet had been split from front to back. Without it he'd have had his skull crushed. To say he was lucky was an understatement.

'I don't know why drug addicts like morphine so much,' Doug said wryly. 'It really didn't do much for me. I was so scared strapped to the stretcher on the journey back. I was aware of everything happening.'

Staring at the coal ceiling, Doug was strapped on his back with a sandbag dumped on his chest to try and keep him still in case he'd broken his back or neck – which the men presumed he had. It took six men to hump him along the two miles back to the train. He was then heaved on to the carriage and had to endure the six-mile journey back to the lift. By the time he got out, he was trembling all over with fear.

'My dad always used to say he'd break my back if I worked in a mine,' said Doug, a far-away look in his eye. 'I suppose he's looking down on me and saying: "I told you so, lad."'

His father had died just after our wedding. It was a sad time, but we hoped he'd finally found the peace he'd never had in his life.

Meanwhile, the doctors were running tests on Doug's back. He was in huge pain. Later on they told me he'd hurt many of his nerves but had been very fortunate not to break his back. Instead we were told he'd ripped most of his tendons from the nape of his neck to the end of his spine.

'Although bones can sometimes mend more easily than nerves,' added the consultant, 'in some ways he'd have been better off if he had broken something.'

As he had waited for me to arrive, Doug had been laying on the bed, still coated in soot, looking like a minstrel.

A doctor had come up from London to work at the hospital and when he spotted Doug he read his notes and gave him a funny look.

'Can you tell me, Mr Black,' he said, 'what on earth you were doing at two in the morning, under some scaffolding in a coal pit, wearing nothing but underpants and boots?'

Doug tried to laugh. 'Are you kidding me?' he said. 'I am a coal miner! That's what we wear as it's so hot! That's our job, doctor!'

The doctor looked incredulous. He had no experience of mining and no idea how they operated down there. Unbelievably he thought Doug had been messing in a mine for no particular reason. We had a chuckle about it afterwards. What mad man would choose to go and play in a mine for fun?

Doug was in hospital for a week and off work for nine months. I went back to work quickly, with Ann and Margaret helping out where they could. Susan and Lorraine were also a wonderful help with the younger ones. On my first shift back, the whole coalface team turned up *en masse* to tell me how sorry they were to hear about Dougie. I was stood standing for about ten minutes, listening to the men, all offering help or passing on their good wishes. I appreciated all the support even if it meant I could barely get any work done.

Then Geordie Maddox popped his head in.

'Hey Cath, are you going to do any work today or just chat to miners?' he joked, making me laugh out loud for the first time in a week.

Every evening I'd pop into the hospital to tend to Doug.

Once I turned up and found him twisting his head away from the portable TV, grimacing.

'What's the matter, Dougie?' I asked anxiously. 'Are you in pain?'

'No!' he cried. 'I am just sick to death of watching the news about the blessed *Mary Rose* ship being found. It's been on all day long and I can't reach the remote to change the bloody channel.'

I laughed. I had my Dougie back.

Chapter Seventeen

Such an injury meant Doug's recovery journey was to be slow and painful. The discs in Doug's neck needed to settle down and in the meantime they were agonising. He'd been offered an operation to fuse them, but he declined. Later on we were convinced it was the right decision as a fellow miner had this operation and ended up paralysed for life.

So Doug came home wearing a neck collar, which over the next couple of months was whipped on and off. It was a long, tough recovery, with frequent occasions when it felt as if he had taken two steps forward and one step back. The slightest thing could set him back again.

Once he was napping on the sofa when Carrie prodded his chest, thinking he was awake. He jolted to like the devil had woken him, and started yelling in pain. The sudden movement set his recovery back again a few weeks.

Doug was on the sick for nine months, so I went back to work, trying to make ends meet and be the breadwinner.

As the months flew by, the colliery started looking into alternative forms of work for Doug as it became clear that working back on the coalface wasn't an option for him. The uneven ground, the heavy lifting and stress on his joints were no longer things he could cope with. Eventually the colliery offered Doug a position on the surface working on the telephone exchange. The managers were good like that. They had a duty of care to the men who'd got lifelong injuries thanks to their hard graft beneath the surface. As much as Doug wanted to try and carry on, he was only going to hurt himself again by trying to keep up with the able-bodied men on the coalface.

His own GP had tough words to say to him. 'I don't want to treat you if you just simply go back on to that face,' he said bluntly. 'It will be a waste of time and you'll hurt yourself even more.'

So Doug started a new role on the surface in an office alongside two poor fellas who'd lost their legs in terrible accidents. There were always pit jobs to be found, thank goodness.

Doug's injury wasn't the only thing we had to cope with. Around this time, my sister Mary rang to tell me that Grandad had been diagnosed with prostate cancer. But the doctors had told him that old age would kill him before it did. I was devastated, as I couldn't imagine my poor Grandad not being with us. He was terrible when it came to visiting the doctor or dentist – in fact, he never went. He was a big man but a big coward too. He used to pull his own teeth out with cotton wool if he had toothache, until he had hardly any left. One day, he was cutting the corns off his feet when he slipped with the knife. Ignoring the pain, he wrapped cotton wool on it and carried on. Within days, his foot was black and agonising. It had turned gangrenous, and he lost two toes. After that he went to live with my Aunt Mary in Manchester and stayed between her house and mine.

Meantime, Mum had also fallen ill with her heart again. Doctors said they couldn't operate, as her valves were too weak. She was just ordered to rest up and take it easy. I felt so surrounded by the sick and ill, I didn't know if I was coming or going.

However, despite all the woes in my family, nothing topped what was to happen next to one of my colleagues in the canteen at this time. One morning, I breezed in to work as usual to find the girls all looking pinched and quiet. The atmosphere was incredible.

'What's happened?' I asked Betty. There was only one person missing from shift. Grace.

Even foul-mouthed Betty was extraordinarily quiet.

'She was called off to the manager's office,' she said. 'It's her son, Rob.'

I knew that Rob, the lad Susan had been on a couple of

244

dates with, had been having a hard time. He'd been sacked from his pit job for falling asleep at some machinery. My heart went out to the poor lad as he was on a boring job and it was easy enough to send anyone to sleep. But it was a sackable offence if you did drop off, so away he was sent.

For months he'd been out of work. For a lad of nineteen, it was a shock to the system. Poor Grace had tried everything to find him another job. On her days off she'd sit on the phone ringing round. But no one wanted to give him another chance.

'What's happened to him?' I asked. Betty shook her head slightly. With that I knew he'd died but I had no idea how. My heart ran icy cold. No mother should ever have to lose a son.

Only later, chatting to Susan, did I find out the full extent of the tragedy. Grace had finally found a job for Rob that morning. A pit in one of the other villages had agreed to give him another chance. She'd rung Rob at his dad's where he'd been staying that very morning with the exciting news. But she couldn't get hold of him. An hour later, a passerby found Rob's body hanging from a tree. Unable to shake off his depression caused by unemployment, the poor lad had killed himself.

I'd suffered on and off for years with bleeding and fibroids and finally doctors decided I needed a hysterectomy. It was a big operation of course but one I hoped would put a stop to my 'women's troubles' once and for all.

I went into Worksop hospital while Doug looked after the kids. Waking up after the operation, I felt like a bus had run over my stomach, but I was still alive and just grateful for that.

Doug came to visit but he looked tired and stressed. I could tell it wasn't just about my operation. 'What's eating at you, Doug?' I asked. 'Don't worry about me. I am still here.'

He didn't want to bother me at first but then admitted that the NUM, which we were members of automatically as we worked for the Coal Board, was talking about a strike.

'It looks like it's going to happen,' said Doug. 'Not exactly what we need right now but they're talking about shutting pits left, right and centre.'

Without even needing to say so, we both knew we'd support the union's decision. Otherwise what was the point of being a member? It was a scary prospect, the mine closing. In my mind, what choice did any miner have but to support a strike? After all, if they got their way and closed us, it'd be game over.

Nottingham was a funny area when it came to supporting such action. The strike was unballoted, presided over by Arthur Scargill, and some people in our neck of the woods said it was illegal. I believed people would dream up any excuse not to help out. The fact the ballot wasn't 'legal' was one of them.

In fact, Nottingham had the lowest number of people who supported the strike in the country. I think one of the reasons was because the mines in Nottingham employed lots of people from all parts of the country, so fewer people felt a sense of loyalty to the area. I couldn't understand their attitude, but it was just the way it was.

Some of the employees at our pit were members of what we called a 'scab' union, too. Scabs were people who didn't support the strike and in my eyes were the lowest of the low.

Anyway, my mind was soon taken off my aches and pains with this lot going on. As the strike kicked off, Doug explained how miners from Yorkshire were descending on Nottingham to 'tell' our miners to down tools and join them. As much as I supported the strike, I resented this. We didn't want or need people from another county telling us what to do, but I did just wish more Nottingham communities were joining in.

Mum's husband, Hugh, was one to go about that. He was working in Yorkshire Main now and he was on the phone to Doug telling us how Nottingham needed to step up to the plate and more people needed to join in.

I laughed. 'Trust Hughie to have his twopenn'th!' I said.

A few days after my operation, I still wasn't feeling any better and was thoroughly fed up with being in hospital. My wound had become infected, as the doctors had had to cut through old scar tissue to do my hysterectomy. Now I needed to wait on tests to see what sort of infection I had.

One afternoon, I was well enough to watch a bit of TV, so a nurse brought one into my room. The headlines caught my eye. I sat up a bit straighter to listen. The news was unbelievable.

The Tories had shut Cortonwood colliery, the one in the hometown of Arthur Scargill. I knew they'd already brought in an American businessman called Ian MacGregor as head of the Coal Board, and I had suspected that meant he'd be the grim reaper and start cutting back the industry. But no one had suspected Cortonwood would go. A cynical ploy if ever I saw one!

In the great miners' strikes of 1972 and 1974, miners had picketed power stations and coke depots to stop lorries getting through. This time, miners were threatening to picket other miners.

I also noted the time of year. It was springtime. Miners

always got more public sympathy during winter strikes. To me it all seemed like this was a set-up, that the government were deliberately provoking the miners to try and create an industrial dispute. The government had even been stock-piling coal near power stations in preparation. It all seemed terribly cynical, like open war had been declared on miners. Yet they were decent, hard-working people who just wanted to protect their jobs and communities.

The next day I overheard some ambulancemen talking. 'All hell has broken loose in Ollerton,' one said. 'Pickets and police everywhere. It's like proper carnage!'

I was itching to get home. Doug told me he was joining the picket now and I fretted and worried, helplessly watching the news and the growing violence on TV. I didn't want my Doug caught up in all of that. Even though I could do with a few more days' convalescence, the nurses came in and asked if I wanted to go home early.

'Yes, as soon as possible,' I said, although I could barely sit up with the pain. It felt like a war had started. Well actually it had, but as some politicians said later on, it was one without guns.

Doug came and picked me up in a taxi. I was still too weak to get dressed properly, so I pulled on a housecoat over my nightie and Doug wrapped a blanket around my shoulders. I shuffled out of the hospital into the car park, every step sending pain shooting across my tender stomach. Painfully, I slid into the taxi, as Doug put his arm round me.

'We'll soon have you home, pet,' he said.

The taxi sped its way towards our house, but as we passed Thoresby pit, the roads grew increasingly busy with cars parked up everywhere and miners milling around, some holding placards. We saw scores of police and panda cars.

'What the blazes?' I started, as our taxi ground to a halt. There was a sea of police uniforms everywhere. An officer rushed over and banged on the window. Our driver wound it down.

'Officer?' he began.

'What do you lot think you're doing then?' the officer snapped. 'Eh? Where you off to?'

I was shocked, really astounded, by the PC's rudeness. It was plain nasty.

'C'mon, where you going?' he demanded, looking at me.

'Home,' I said. 'I'm just out of hospital.'

'Oh yeah?' said the officer. 'Really? I am not sure if I believe you.'

My stitches pulled as I tried to sit up. 'Excuse me?' I cried, feeling my temper flare up. 'I'm covered in stitches and just want to get to bed. And really, officer, it's none of your bloody business where we're going!'

The officer leaned in, sweat glistened on his top lip. 'Shut your mouth,' he barked, 'or I'll have you arrested.'

I pulled my blanket closer, my face red with fury. 'What threat do I pose?' I cried. 'I am stitched up to hell and need me bed. What are you doing over-running our village, any road?'

Doug pulled me back, gave a quick apology to the policeman and luckily our taxi driver managed to put his foot down. I was staggered, shaking with anger. How dare he speak to us like that? Was that the police's attitude to the strike? They seemed to be acting more like a police force from a totalitarian state rather than village coppers. What on earth was happening?

I thought back to how much I'd respected the police previously. How they'd helped when my son Douglas had sniffed the gas. Could these be the same men? Was it the government putting them under pressure to squash the miners? None of it made sense to me.

Later that night, Grandad rang and said he was coming down. I told him about what was happening, but he seemed to have nothing to say on the matter. 'You old Tory git,' I joked. I could always be honest with him, but was a little surprised he didn't have much to say one way or another.

Doug and I had a proper chat that night. We both instantly decided we'd support any strike. We knew if we didn't we'd both be likely to lose our jobs anyway.

'If every single miner lays down tools,' mused Doug,

'we'll have a fighting chance of keeping the pits open. But it'll take every single person to do it.'

'They can't just strip whole communities of their livelihoods. We have no choice but to fight,' I agreed.

For the first time, I felt scared. Scared of losing all we had built up over the years. Scared of returning to the poverty and the instability of our life in Scotland. I'd do anything to avoid going back to that. None of it made sense either. There was up to a thousand years' worth of coal sat below our feet. Surely the government wouldn't be insane enough to just stop production and then start importing it from abroad?

Nottingham had a 'scab' union, the Union of Democratic Mineworkers (UDM), which didn't support the strike, that much we knew. It was unrealistic to think all of Notts would stop work, but we hoped people would see sense and join in. We sat and watched the TV as they said that the unions had been told that after Cortonwood, twenty pits were due to close, with 20,000 miners losing their jobs. There was no question we would support our unions on such an important matter.

There were practical considerations to deal with before we could join the battle. Doug was still on the sick and now so was I after my operation. But we wanted to be registered as 'strikers' so we immediately came off the sick and went 'on strike'. As strikers we knew we were eligible for £14 each from the union. That meant we had £28 to live off as a family, much less than if we'd claimed sickness benefits. But it was the principle that mattered now. Our joint wage was usually over £100 a week, so this was a huge cut. It wasn't much, but enough to survive on, just. We thought it would just be for a few weeks. Surely we could manage that.

As we chatted about our decision, Susan's then-boyfriend, Simon, turned up. Doug opened the door to him and the pair spoke in hushed tones.

'Let's not tell Cathy, she needs to rest,' I heard Doug saying.

'What's that?' I called out.

Simon came in, his face drained. He looked shattered. Doug spoke up.

'Simon's just come from the picket line outside Ollerton,' he said. 'A young lad called David Jones was killed there this afternoon.'

'Killed?' I gasped, struggling up from the sofa where I had been laying down. 'Oh my God.'

Two stories were going round: one that he'd been killed during a crowd surge and the other that he'd been hit by a brick. We flicked on the BBC news and the coverage was everywhere.

Miners were being portrayed as violent bullies, trying to ruin the country. Maggie called us 'the enemy within'.

It was just unbelievable. All we wanted was to save our jobs and our homes. We all had kids to feed. All we'd ever done was work bloody hard in a difficult job. What had we done to deserve such vilification?

Ollerton was one of the first picket lines in the area. Previous to this, the strike was mainly centred in Yorkshire. But Yorkshire miners were coming over and acting as flying pickets. Chaos was ensuing across the country now. Pit after pit was going on strike and no one knew what was going to happen next.

And neither did we.

I didn't need to tell the canteen my thoughts, as they knew I was striking when I didn't show up. I didn't know what the other canteen staff's plans were. We never talked about it. To be honest I was surprised Barbara didn't strike. She always seemed to have strong opinions on everything. I wasn't so shocked about the others. I'd never liked Betty and the others had always struck me as too lily-livered in my opinion to stand up for anything.

Suddenly people fell into two camps: strikers and scabs. There wasn't a middle ground. You either supported the strike or you didn't.

My neighbours Margaret and Billy didn't hesitate in striking. Esther was less sure. We had a chat one day as I hung the washing out.

'I do completely agree with it in principle,' she explained, pegs in her mouth as she hung the sheets out. 'But to actually strike like this and grind everything to a halt? I struggle with it. It might close the pits.'

'Oh Esther, we're more likely to lose all our jobs if we don't strike,' I said. 'We can't go down without a fight.'

I didn't try and change her mind. It wasn't my place. But Sean, her husband, was a union man through and through. In the end there was no question he'd strike, even if his wife didn't agree.

Ann and Pete decided to join the strike after a few days thinking on the matter. Initially Pete had been unsure. But one morning he got in his car to nip out and get some dog food, driving past Ollerton pit on the way. As he neared the pit gates, en route to the shops, police pulled him over, demanding to know who he was.

'What do you think you're doing?' they snapped.

'Buying dog food,' said Pete.

'Don't get lippy with us,' one spat. Within a few seconds Pete found himself hauled out of his car and arrested for breaching the peace. Five hours later, the dog food still not having been bought, Pete arrived home a free man but vowing to join the strike too.

The decision whether to support the strike or not had far-reaching effects. Neighbours who'd been friendly for years were suddenly pitted against each other, as feelings ran high over who was striking and who wasn't.

For us, the scabs in our street turned out to be the Boswells and the Knightons. I was stunned at their decision not to join in, but right from the start Linda announced she couldn't afford not to work.

'Well, what about the rest of us?' I said, agog. 'We've got five kids!' The men tried to talk to her husband about it, to tell him we were all in this together, but he wouldn't budge either. Once their decision had been made, the result was instantaneous. They were no longer part of our community. Linda knew this, and stayed out of the road. We rarely saw them and if I did pass her in the street I completely ignored her. She knew better than to say anything; everyone was feeling too emotional.

As I walked off, I thought of our times working together on the potatoes and how we'd have a giggle. But now a divide had taken place between us and there was no going back.

Chris Knighton's attitude, however, didn't surprise me. Not one bit. He'd always given the impression of being out for himself. His wife, Jackie, had no choice but to go along.

But whatever my feelings about my former friends, the split between the strikers and scabs was immediate and absolute. Once a scab, always a scab: they were not on our side and that was the end to it. You couldn't be friends, not with everything the strikers had to endure to stay on strike. It wouldn't be right.

A few days in though, I had a big surprise when someone told me Grace from the canteen had decided to strike. 'Goodness me,' I exclaimed. Straight away she went up in my estimations.

By 12 March, just a week after the strike was announced, half of Britain's 187,000 miners had downed tools. Tony Benn called it a 'civil war'. I'd never been interested in politics before, but you couldn't escape this. My family had been caught up in the biggest strike in the country's history and we had no idea what would happen next. While we all talked non-stop about the strike, I was still being treated for my blessed operation scar. The pain was excruciating, and the district nurse who came to clean my wound didn't have a shred of sympathy.

'It'll heal,' she kept saying, as I sweated with the pain. 'Don't be a baby.'

But the pains were so bad it felt like I was in labour.

'Even though I don't have a womb any longer,' I said, 'can you explain why I am still bleeding?'

Without saying a word she left the house. Half an hour later, a doctor arrived with his bag of tricks and an injection for me. Finally it was being taken seriously and I only narrowly avoided contracting peritonitis.

Now we were on strike, decisions about our next steps needed to be taken. Lots of women were demonstrating locally in support of the miners. But as a full member of the NUM I could officially join the picket line too. This was a very rare position for a woman to be in and if I was able to join in, I most certainly wanted to.

'Right, well, I want to join a picket line tomorrow,' I announced a few days later.

Doug laughed. 'Sorry, Cath, no way. You are most definitely not. For a start you might get hurt and for a finish you're not long out of hospital. No. You're not going.'

He thought that was the end of the matter but I had a chat with Susan and she wanted to join me.

We decided to get up very early and leave before Doug woke up. Two of the stairs in our house made a terribly loud creaking sound if you stood on them, so we carefully opened the bedroom window upstairs and climbed out.

'Come on, Susan,' I giggled, helping her through. 'Your father need never know.' After shinning down the drainpipe, we walked into the street, where we spotted other people coming down the road, including Ann and Margaret.

'We're off to find a demonstration,' they said. 'We can't just sit at home cooking and cleaning while all this is kicking off.'

Chapter Eighteen

Every day the lads chose different pits to picket for what they called a 'hit' but there were not enough people to go to every single pit. We got a lift from a neighbour down the road and joined the picket line at Bilsthorpe, the nearest one on this day. A mass of people were there. We needed to cross a bridge to get there but a copper was standing near it looking menacing.

'You're not to go any further,' he said, holding up both palms of his hands. 'Now move along.'

'Why not?' I asked. 'It's a free country.'

'Yes and I am saying you're not going,' he said.

'If you don't want a swim in the river I suggest you let us aside, officer,' I said.

And I meant it. Well, I don't know if I'd have actually been capable of chucking him in on my own, but I was sure a few of the lads would've helped out.

Once we were on the bridge I could see the crowd

more clearly. There were mainly men but a fair few women at the sides of the roads with banners, proclaiming slogans like 'Coal Not Dole', 'The Longer the Picket Line, the Shorter the Strike', 'Save Our Pits' and 'Women Against Pit Closures'. The atmosphere was electric. There was clearly an intense camaraderie but I felt a sense of sadness too. I knew people would rather just be going to work than becoming involved with all this palaver but what choice did we have?

We marched across the bridge as the officer stood aside. He was outnumbered by far anyway, as more people streamed across behind us. I slowed my walk a little after getting past him. My scar was hurting terribly, but adrenaline kept me going.

The picket line only met for a couple of hours a day while the scabs were filing into work. The men usually tried to stop them and talk to them if they would listen.

'We're going to lose our jobs anyway,' they'd plead. 'If we don't all of us strike it will be so much less effective.'

With heads bowed, many scabs pushed through. One face I recognised immediately. Dave, the man who'd treated his poor wife to fish and chips in our canteen instead of taking her out to dinner. I was surprised to see him as a scab.

Waving a thin piece of paper high above his head, he

grinned. 'I'm the only one here getting paid,' he said, waving his pay slip. 'Bet you're all missing this already. Lazy bastards.'

To shouting and jeering he quickly slipped into the crowd, ready to start his shift. I couldn't believe the gall of the man. To me it was sickening. To be a scab was bad enough but to shout about it? Especially when families would be suffering through a lack of wage. No, I couldn't understand it.

The morning slipped by quickly and it was time for us to get home before Doug realised we'd gone. I planned to tell him I'd just popped out shopping.

Later on I put the tea on as Doug talked about joining the picket. We were already cutting back, so I was turning to cheap old favourites like mince and tatties and shepherd's pie for dinners now. I needed to stretch the food as far as possible.

'I am going to go down there to join the picketers,' he said.

'Well, so am I,' I announced.

'Er, no, you're not,' he replied, shaking his head. 'I've already told you.'

'Go on,' I pleaded. 'I'll be OK.'

'No, you won't and you're not,' he kept saying. 'You don't know that.'

'Well I was OK when I went this morning!' I cried, unable to resist a grin.

Doug's mouth fell open. 'You never did!' he said.

I nodded. 'And look: I am still here in one piece.'

After that he couldn't stop me and didn't bother trying, although he always worried about me. I was the only 'official' woman picketer I knew about. I had my own Pit Tally number – mine was 2308 – and a badge. I'd show this to the police or the men to prove who I was.

The men were very good about letting me take part and were all supportive of my involvement. Most of the men knew me through Doug or from working in the canteen. I felt I had as much to give as they did, even if I was a wife and mother. The picket line wasn't a place for sexism. The men needed their wives' support to see this through.

The picket lines were effective and certainly seemed to capture the press attention. Armies of photographers and cameras started turning up to film. Sometimes it was almost like walking into a movie set. But they could be very frightening and dangerous places to be, too. The lines usually went right up to the colliery gates and a throng of police and horses would be at the front. I usually stood at the front, as there was less chance of being crushed. All the 'pushes' came from the back, as people surged towards the police. Often the police started this by running at the ones at the front, causing people to move back, and then a counter-surge forwards would happen.

As the only woman and a small one at that, the men always put me first. If a surge happened, I was plucked to a place of safety and out the road before I could catch my breath.

I often joined the picket line near Ollerton. I'll never forget the first time I did this. I was standing at the front as we watched the buses rumble up towards us. There, as plain as day in the window, sat my old colleagues: Barbara, Pauline, Mary, Carole and Betty, all steely-eyed and grim-mouthed.

'Scab!' I yelled, running to the window and pointing. 'Scab!'

The driver slowed down, turning to his passengers and obviously asking them whether he should stop or not. They all shook their heads and he sped through the gates.

This scene was to play out several times during the strike. As it wore on, I noticed Betty would sometimes turn and smile very slowly at me.

'Nasty piece of work,' I thought, wishing I could hurl other insults at her. I could see she was enjoying it.

With growing support for the miners across the country, people started sending in food parcels and local shops offered to donate perishables they were going to throw away anyway. On the basis that the need was so great, soup kitchens started popping up in mining communities.

Of course I wanted to be there to help. After all, thanks to Grandma, soup was one of my specialities!

The annexe of the Miners' Welfare hall was quickly transformed into a working kitchen. It was a group of women from the Welfare who started it, but when I stepped in to be cook, they let me take over. Then Grace turned up on the second day.

'What you doing here?' I asked.

'I'm off as well,' she said.

I reached out and touched her arm. I'd barely seen Grace since Rob had died so tragically, and I didn't know what to say. I saw a sadness in her eyes I'd never noticed before, but also a grim determination on her face. Although we'd never been the best of friends, that was sure, I wanted to help her.

Grace's partner was a miner and was striking, and although Grace had a mortgage and bills in her own name she'd decided to join him. I admired that. We were the only two from the canteen who went on strike. The other lot were a bunch of scabs and that was the end of it.

'Good,' I said. 'Grab a pinnie then. You can come and help.'

The following day Ann and Margaret also came to help and, me being the biggest bossy boots, I coordinated the work. We started by making breakfasts, then sandwiches for lunch, and then it grew to evening meals too. The need was relentless. Very quickly I decided to start my day at 4.30 a.m., just to get a head start on the breakfasts – usually porridge or bacon and eggs. We had no idea how many were turning up each day so we quickly learned to cook tasty meals en masse with whatever ingredients were to hand. I did cottage pies, casseroles, pies, chips – whatever we could lay our hands on. That kitchen had never seen so much action, before or since.

Every morning Grace and I would sit down and plan what we'd make that day. Some days she'd say: 'Oh gosh, not that again!', as we chose the same meal like mince and dumplings over and over, but I'd laugh and ask if she'd had any better ideas with our limited supplies.

The local butcher and grocery stores were generous in their support, making soups and stews eke out even further. We got all the cheap cuts and the almost out-of-date veg, but everything was very gratefully accepted. We didn't have pans big enough for the volumes of soup we made, so I just got an old tea urn and we turned that into a mini soup factory. It was a case of making do with what was around.

I got very good at making 'something out of nothing'. It's surprising what you can knock up when under pressure. One hot and tasty favourite of mine was a meat stew with a bit of everything in it. I'd chop up tinned meat, chuck in onions, carrots, and whatever veg I could rustle up, and then cover with gravy and simmer. It was very simple and cheap but filled up hungry bellies. And believe me, with no wages coming in now, there were plenty of them.

We often got donated cheap fishfingers for the kids too, but sometimes when we ran out of meat the men would have them.

We'd also make up food parcels. By now we were receiving packages from all over the world, according to some folk, although I never saw any as they went to the main office. This sounds like we were inundated with food, but there was never any spare. In each box we'd put a tin of meat, usually corned beef or ham, tea, coffee, sugar, and some fruit and whatever else was left over. Everyone got the same and the parcels were collected at the end of the week.

We fed everyone. Flying pickets came from across the country. The under-fives came with their mums while their siblings were at school. Then during the holidays we fed even more as the school-kids filled up the kitchen. We only had around thirty plates so we'd feed that many and as soon as they were finished the plate was whipped from under them to be washed and then re-filled for someone else. We never knew who or how many would show up. Sometimes at the drop of a hat a bus would pull up and ninety men would pour out, all tired and hungry but always welcome. People came from all the nearby villages – Thoresby, Bilsthorpe, Bevercotes and further afield. It wasn't long before our reputation grew and people started to look up the 'kitchen in Ollerton'.

Once, a union official arrived to tell me a coach was on its way. 'But they have some vegetarians,' he whispered. 'Can you manage that?'

I looked at him blankly. I'd no idea how to cook anything veggie, so I grabbed a recipe book from somewhere and quickly scanned the pages. I saw lentils and pulses in soups were OK, so I just rushed around, throwing them in along with any veg we had and using vegetable stock instead of meat.

Testing it myself with a spoon I pulled a face. 'Eugh, tasteless,' I thought. But it would have to do.

The bus pulled in and forty-odd people sat down, so we served up the lentil whatever-it-was I'd made. I watched as they silently ate it, cringing a little inside. They probably thought it was horrible. I wanted to hide in the back.

Afterwards we cleared the dishes and one of the officials came to find me.

'Did you make the soup yourself, Cath?' she asked.

'Yes,' I said, eyeing her cautiously.

'Ooh, it was delicious,' she smiled. 'Can I have the recipe please?'

I nearly died laughing. 'I'm sorry,' I said. 'I don't even know what the hell went in it!'

As the weeks wore on I just kept going, making more and more of everything each day. We even rustled up puddings, like sweet pies made with tinned fruit, and rice puddings. Grace and I worked well as a team. I was good at soups and the savoury stuff and she was a dab hand at knocking up pastries. As soon as we ran out of food, I'd quickly think of something else to knock up. By the end of each day, we ached all over, our hands like prunes from scrubbing pots.

But the need was so great we couldn't even think of stopping. Every day a miner or a wife or a child looked at me and thanked me from the bottom of their heart. 'I wouldn't have eaten anything today if it wasn't for the likes of you,' they all said, or similar. And we knew that. This Tory government could've quite happily have seen these men, women and children starve as far as I could see. Some quarters accused them of 'starving them back to work' and there was a real element of truth in that. Strikers were not eligible for any state help or intervention. It was a case of go back to work or go hungry, whoever you were.

As time went by we started to get some extra help in the kitchen. Some of the pickets had been arrested and banned from going back on the lines, so they started to turn up to help out, peeling vegetables or washing up. Any extra pairs of hands were gratefully received.

During this time I lived completely on my nerves, my

mind always whizzing with ideas or trying to come up with ways of feeding the latest lot. I used to get home from the kitchen at 3 p.m., usually with a food parcel myself, and then immediately I'd have to think about what I'd cook for my own kids. Then I'd have to do all the chores like the washing, ironing or cleaning, all the jobs I'd do during the day usually. By bedtime I was completely exhausted. A couple of times Mum popped down to see me. 'You're doing too much, Cath,' she said, as I flew by balancing four plates on my arm.

'Not now, Mum, I'm busy,' I said.

'I'm proud of you though, lass,' she said.

I smiled back. Now we were older our bond was returning. But right then I didn't have time to think on it.

During the holidays, Carrie and Allan, then aged eleven and nine, stopped with me in the kitchen. As I ran to and fro with steaming plates I kept an eye on them. Susan and Lorraine were older and could look after themselves, whereas our Douglas was busy with his three jobs, cleaning people's windows, helping out the milkman, and moving people's dustbins back for them. Whatever he made he always offered it to me, but I never took it.

'Treat your sisters and brother to some sweets,' I used to say.

The older three knew what was going on and supported

the strike, but Carrie and Allan were too young to understand and didn't know what to make of it. We just explained in simple terms why it was happening and we tried to keep things as normal as possible. But kids will be kids, and of course the playground is the place where they speak their minds. Very quickly the children from the scab families and those from the striking ones became enemies, mirroring their parents' opinions.

One day Carrie came home from school outraged at some other boy's comment to her. She was always the one with a fierce temper, just like mine, and was quick to put the world to rights and speak her mind.

'He said: "My dad says your dad is a lazy man for not going to work." But Dad's not lazy, is he, Mam?'

'No, he's certainly not,' I agreed.

Allan once came home with stories of the children of the scab parents being bullied, but I told him to try and stay out of any trouble.

'Just leave them be,' I said. 'Don't get involved. It's not the scab kids' fault their parents made that decision, is it? You have to just avoid them to avoid trouble.'

'*I'm* not,' said Carrie. 'Some of them are my friends.'

'Well, just don't get involved in any fighting,' I sighed.

Of course in a soup kitchen as busy as ours I was constantly aware of safety. We were racing around like bluebottles, cooking, serving and washing up like mad. With the kids diving in and out, the kitchen was an accident waiting to happen, so I constantly had to 'shoo' people away.

'Please can you go outside?' I pleaded with the mums as they stood in the doorway for a gossip. Our soup kitchen had quickly become a social area. With the din of the cutlery on plates and the clattering of the dishes it was sometimes impossible even for a voice as loud as mine to be heard. So one day, after losing my rag, I found a very effective way of immediately clearing the kitchen without having to open my mouth. Grabbing a few saucepans, I lifted them high above my head and chucked them with full force against a wall. As they bounced off, the racket they made was loud enough to wake the dead and everyone stopped in their tracks to see where it was coming from.

'Now, everyone clear out!' I bellowed, pointing like a schoolteacher to the door.

Mums snatched their toddlers and school-age kids sloped out, all without me having to repeat myself. I was a stickler for getting people out of the way as I could see me or Grace tripping over them and someone getting badly hurt.

One young lass used to come every day with her three wee 'uns, who were always under my feet. I wasn't very popular with her as I constantly chased them out. But then I'd be even less popular if I'd scalded her wee child with hot oil or boiling water. It was a dangerous place, not a playground or social club.

Afterwards, Grace looked at me in shock. 'I didn't know you were so forthright, Cath,' she said. 'You were much quieter in the canteen, weren't you?'

'That's because I needed that job,' I replied. 'I couldn't show the real me or I'd have lost my temper with the lot of you.'

We actually made a good duo, me and Grace. She was mild-mannered, let things go and kept calm. Just what I needed when I wanted to let off steam.

After we settled into our routine of making as much food as possible to feed everyone who needed it, I couldn't believe my ears when some of the female bosses from the Miners' Welfare came down to tell us off.

'You're giving out way too much food,' they complained. 'Too much good food like meat and puddings.'

I was incensed. 'And you think that's too good for our families and lads? You must be kidding,' I said. 'No way are our menus changing.'

Both Grace and I refused point-blank to serve substandard food. Decent nourishment was the least these people deserved in our eyes.

A husband and wife called Norman and Mary often turned up to help when they could, too. Mary used to see my Douglas on the way to school on the bus and she'd often give him something to eat. She had no idea he was my son until she saw him give me a hug one day.

'I have an apology to make,' she said. 'I used to feel so sorry for Douglas whenever I saw him about the village. He's such a scrawny, wee thing, all skin and bone, and I presumed he never got much to eat, so I'd give him an extra something from my handbag if I had it.'

Mary went on to say that one day she spotted Douglas pulling out his door-stopper sandwiches and how he ate the lot and then asked if anyone had anything spare. I couldn't help but laugh. We'd nicknamed Douglas 'the Human Dustbin' a long time ago. He was just like his dad, all skin and bone but could eat anything.

Not all our visitors received a warm welcome. Once we saw a couple of coppers approaching the kitchen. 'You're not allowed in here,' I said, eyeing them suspiciously. 'There's no trouble here, you'll find.'

One of the coppers smiled at me. 'No, no,' he said. 'We're not here for that.' He dipped into his pocket and pulled out a £20 note.

'I wanted to give you this,' he said, popping it into the tin. 'That was all.'

'Thank you, officer,' I said. I could hardly believe my eyes – but just as there are good and bad folk, it's the same with the police. A few weeks later the same thing happened with another copper. Others were very generous. One miner who'd long since retired turned up every week and put his entire pension in the tin. I'll never forget him either.

Fund-raising nights started up soon afterwards to raise money for the communities hit by the strike. It was a good idea and a rare chance for us all to get together and have a laugh. Of course none of us could afford any booze, so we'd sit with our orange juices and nurse them all night.

At the Miners' Welfare, bands came to play for people to dance and sing along to. It lightened the atmosphere and brought people together again. One night UB40 played. I wasn't a huge fan, but I knew what a popular band they were and the place was packed out. We all sang along to their hits like 'Red, Red Wine' and listened as they told us how full of love and support they were.

I thought it was great that people from all walks were getting involved. It was exactly what we needed and made me feel even more like we were doing the right thing. The miners also started to spread the word and travel abroad to whip up extra support. They visited all over, from Russia to Poland, as well as nearby places like Norwich. For some reason the folk in Norwich took our plight to their hearts and sent us huge food parcels every week without fail.

While all the camaraderie was strong among the strikers, the same couldn't be said for the scabs. I suppose they must've stuck together in some respects, but in many ways they were out on their own.

A few weeks into the strike, I spotted Linda Boswell, my neighbour, walking down the street. She was on my side of the road and for a split second we caught each other's eyes.

I don't know whether it was sadness or regret that passed across her face. Although we'd never been close, I knew our friendship was dead between us. I didn't want to speak to her and she'd never dare to ask anyone to lend her money for her meter or the like now. Just like I had done with Jackie months earlier, we both looked away and carried on walking.

A few days later, I was chatting away to Ann over the front gate, as Nancy arrived to collect that week's debts. Jackie often avoided her when she couldn't pay up. This time Nancy asked if we'd seen her.

'Yep, she's in!' said Ann. 'If you go round to her back door, you'll see her slipping out of it when she sees you at the front door.'

I laughed. It might have seemed mean, but we had no loyalty to Jackie now. She was letting us all down.

Chapter Nineteen

Now months had passed with very little money coming in, our family was starting to struggle badly. I'd already written to the electricity and gas boards to inform them that we couldn't pay our bills and luckily they allowed us to defer them, as they did for a lot of miners. We couldn't have a weekly shop any more. All I could afford to buy was dairy, bread and toiletries. For heating we couldn't afford any coal. Our electricity was on the meter. We made the 50p last a few days and never had lights on unless it was absolutely necessary.

For extra heat, we relied upon the men going into the woods, cutting down trees and sharing out wood equally. They had to get permission from the woodland owner otherwise the police would be after them. Douglas was always one for going out and collecting wood for me. He'd haul bag after bag of great big logs, bigger than him. He was such a good boy.

The desperation for fuel grew. Some neighbours pulled down their own fences for firewood, while others had their fences stolen. Suddenly wood was a precious commodity but quickly people started burning anything just to keep warm.

Our family relied on the food parcels like everyone else. With my 'something out of nothing' cooking skills, I made the same meals over and over again. A mince, corned beef and potato pie was a cheap and filling dinner. We were sick of eating it after a few months.

I was always running out of bread, a staple in any home, and with five kids it could be difficult. It was then my kind neighbours came into their own again, with Margaret or Ann always popping over if they had anything extra. Even a potato or a few slices of bread were gratefully received.

Along with food, people started donating clothes to the miners too. Every week we'd get masses of jumbled up clothing and shoes dumped on the table in the soup kitchen. As I was always out the back cooking or serving, I used to miss out on the best bits, along with the other girls who worked alongside me.

Sometimes I found it hard to watch as grown women would fight over a jumper or a dress. People were fed up of going without and the winter was so harsh. Now and again someone would put something to the side for us, but we got fed up never getting a look-in just because we were working. Once I got a jumper for Lorraine who always complained of the cold. It was a nice blue and red hand-knitted job but as I held it out for her to have a look at, she stared at me in astonishment.

'You've got to be joking, Mam!' she laughed. 'No way am I wearing that thing!'

Once I got hold of an old pair of leather shoes no one wanted and I actually used them to burn that night. It was so cold and we'd run out of wood. I felt a bit guilty as I shoved them on to the fire, as someone had donated them in good faith, but it was also a shame to waste them. When you're that cold you'd do anything for a bit of heat.

There was a hardship fund people could turn to in times of great need. It was based at the Miners' Union HQ in Berry Hill. Usually the men would turn up, plead their case and get cash in hand. Often they asked for shoes for their children or a new coat, something they really couldn't go without for their bairns.

But we soon realised this system was open to abuse by the very few, spoiling it for everyone. One lad, Jimmy, had five kids and on the occasion we had a gathering in the Social, we'd be sat there with an orange juice for sixpence while he was sinking pint after pint of ale.

'Didn't Jimmy get some money from the hardship fund?' someone whispered to me.

'Aye,' I replied. 'But he'll no' get it again.'

The next day I went straight to Berry Hill with Dennis, one of the Miners' Welfare workers, to explain we had seen men abusing the system. After a long chat it was decided that any man in our area who wanted something from Berry Hill had to come to me and Dennis first before asking for money. We were seen as 'trusted' members of the community, and knew who deserved an extra handout better than the officials did sat in their offices.

So sometimes I'd be in the kitchen when a man would come up to me.

'Cath, can I have a word?' he'd always begin. Then I'd call Dennis over for a meeting and we'd listen to the man's requests.

Only two times did we turn people down. One man I knew who was a big drinker was wanting extra money to heat his home. 'I'm afraid the fund is running low, so it's looking unlikely,' I said to fob him off. Another time Dennis simply told another known drinker: 'Sorry, you're out of luck.'

The other part of the strike I felt was most distasteful was when people turned violent against the scabs. Of course we felt let down by these people but there is no need for bully-boy tactics from either party. Once a miner threw a stone at a scab's door, smashing it to pieces. The man was sacked by the Coal Board straight away and he was ostracised by the other strikers. That was the correct decision in my book. There was simply no place for violence on either side.

Another time a man called Jonny, who'd been good friends with another miner and his father, was shocked when the father was caught going into a meeting with the scab union. A big vote was coming up about who was going to be in charge of this union for Nottingham, and Jonny couldn't believe his mate's dad was there. He caught him by the sleeve.

'Hey,' he said. 'Why are you doing this? Thought you were one of us?'

The father shook his head.

'Well,' said Jonny. 'In many years time when you're lying in your grave and you hear a strange sound, I'll tell you now what it is. It'll be me pissing on it.'

Even the police laughed at that one. Jonny's friend's father didn't, though. He shook his sleeve free and walked off.

Although I've never considered myself to be one of the women's lib lot, I had to admit that the women's role in the strike was a massive one. Later on the men admitted the strike couldn't have gone on for so long without their unstinting support (although equally if the wives stopped their support some of the men had to return to work). Many women's lives were changed for ever after gaining skills they never knew they had. Some of them realised they were a dab hand at cooking en masse or organising things, and some simply discovered that they were able to feel passionately about a cause. It changed the way they viewed themselves and their lives at home suddenly seemed boring in comparison.

We may have been allowed to join the picket lines, but we were still seen as ladies. The men remained protective of us. As the strike wore on, the picket lines grew more menacing. Miners were hungry and feeling desperate now. Some were tempted back to work so they could feed their families, although I never bought this excuse. There was plenty of help if you went looking for it and we lived in the type of communities where someone, somewhere, would help if you were desperate.

One picket in Rainworth turned especially nasty. Grace and I were at the front to begin with and watched as a young lad was set upon by the police. They hauled him out with his bare back on display as his T-shirt rode up around his neck. Grace had brought her camera on this occasion. She wanted to get evidence of police brutality and here it was. She pulled it out and took a few snaps. The picket line was enormous, with thousands of people, and the atmosphere highly charged as police started pushing with their horses. Like always, Grace and I were pushed out of the way by the men before things grew too nasty and we stayed well out of the trouble. I spotted an elderly lady in a wheelchair who'd come out to support the miners in a road just around the corner, so we went over to her and we started chatting.

As we spoke a group of police from Thames Valley came to 'move us on'.

'We're not doing any harm here, officer,' I protested. 'This is a quiet road.'

He insisted they needed the room to move cars or something, although I couldn't see any.

'Just shift yourselves,' one said. 'Go home. Back to being mothers to your children.'

'No,' I replied, my stubborn streak rising. 'We're not harming anyone; it's supposed to still be a free country. I am stopping here.'

At that moment, voices and yells nearby began growing loud. I looked across the policeman's shoulder. The throng of men had noticed my altercation.

'You get away from her!' one yelled. 'Leave her be.'

'You touch her and you're for it,' yelled another.

Oh my goodness, I thought. If these police so much as breathe on me there'll be a massacre.

Instinctively I backed away from the officer. 'You don't want that lot starting on you . . .' I said.

The policeman turned and I could see him doing a double-take. The lads were now hot-footing their way over, with faces like thunder. All eyes were on the copper, who I could see was starting to sweat a little.

'No,' I yelled to the lads. 'It's OK. I am going home anyway.'

I pushed past the officers. 'I am doing this to save those lads' skins, not yours. I couldn't give a hoot about yours.'

On the whole I became very popular with the men and they would argue over whose van or car I'd arrive in to a picket. They knew having a woman onboard invariably meant I'd get let through any police blockades. The police tended to be wary of me and leave me alone; they knew if they ill-treated a woman it could turn into a riot. Plus they assumed there would be less trouble if a woman was onboard.

On some pickets, though, the police were very rude to me about being a woman.

'What kind of mother are you? Standing here rather than being with your kids?' they'd taunt. 'You should be where you belong. Back in the kitchen.'

I made up a whole list of my own insults myself, squashed at the front as usual, right under their noses.

'You need to try a different toothpaste,' I'd say. 'Your breath stinks.'

Or I'd laugh and say they smelled of BO. Anything to wind them up as they hurled insults at me. I could give as good as I got, that was for sure.

My neighbours Ann and Margaret joined in with demonstrations whenever they could. We'd get together beforehand, pull out a loaf of bread and make as many ham or cheese sandwiches as we could to give to the men. We wanted to help and support them in any way we were able. Often we went along with Doug and Margaret's husband Billy too. We would turn up on the minibus, trying to work out where the police had blocked off before we arrived and then trying a different angle or approach.

On this occasion we parked the car and then put Billy as 'lookout' on a nearby hill while we thought about following a railway track to reach the picket line. As we waited to see which way the police were going, we shouted up to Billy: 'Any sign of the police yet, Billy?'

'Nope!' he shouted back. So we decided to march over the hill. But as we got to the top, straight away we all noticed a command post set up by police.

'Billy!' we all cried. 'You said, "I see no ship", but look at that lot.'

We had no idea how he'd missed the police presence. For years afterwards we laughed about it, calling him 'I-see-no-ship Billy'.

Later on Grace got the pictures she had taken printed

and we went together to a solicitor in Mansfield to show him and make a statement against the police, although it didn't come to anything in the end. On the way back we passed Thoresby collicry where a picket was taking place.

'Shall we go and join in?' I suggested. Grace nodded. We thought we might as well seeing as it was on our way back home.

There were three coppers standing by. It was very quiet, with only a few men showing up. One or two muttered 'Scab' as the workers began turning up.

'Tsk,' I said to the officer, looking as innocent as possible. 'You don't shout "Scab" like that!'

The policeman nodded. 'Nope, it's no way to behave,' he agreed, rocking on his heels.

'No,' I said. 'You shout "Scab" like this!' And filling my lungs to the maximum, I screamed 'SCAB!' at the top of my voice, really giving it some welly. We could be cheeky, that was for sure.

When the picket lines moved to the power station in Cottam, near Markham, we went with them. The power station pickets were tough as they were held during the evenings and sometimes went long into the night. The point of these lines was for miners to stop the lorries turning up with the coal, although the police always made sure they got through. If anyone tried to stand in front of the lorries or lie in the road, they were quickly trussed up and put in a van.

The London Met police had the worst reputation for being belligerent bullies, even among other forces. The Wiltshire force were openly distrustful towards the Met officers, to the point where they would leave their men near their own panda cars to guard in case the Met officers pinched anything off their cars. Unbelievable!

We weren't troublemakers and with the Wiltshire police for once we had a force who believed us. The Wiltshire would leave us alone and let us just get on with shouting or holding banners. Once we heard them tell the Met to leave us be – they'd turned up to deal with some Yorkshire miners who'd set fire to bales of hay in the road nearby, and had started on us. 'These lot are OK,' a Wiltshire officer said, nodding at my group.

Some of the men wore badges proclaiming 'I've met the Met', meaning they knew how tough and unfair they could be. They were the bully-boys, the mafia of the police, that was for sure.

As a woman I could sometimes have a laugh with the police, too. Once I turned up and stood next to one as the picket started. I pulled out two paracetamols, handing the officer one.

'What do I need this for?' he asked, puzzled. 'I haven't got a headache.'

'No,' I giggled. 'But you will do.' A few minutes later, as the coaches arrived to bring the workers in, I started screaming 'Scab!' at the top of my lungs, as the officer put his fingers in his ears.

Even though I just shouted 'Scab' most of the time, a lot of the men tried to reason with the miners still insisting on working. Many of them had excuses, totally reasonable ones, but they were all the same as ours.

'I have a mortgage to pay, I have debts, I have kids to feed . . .'

'And so do we,' we'd argue. 'We have kids and homes and nothing you haven't got, except for one thing . . . GUTS!'

One excuse I heard over and over again was: 'My wife will leave me if I don't go to work.' Like I said, women were a powerful force in this strike and men needed their support to stay off work.

I was threatened with arrest many times but it never happened. Officers didn't like it when I shouted 'Scab'. So sometimes I changed it to 'Tube!' It's a terrible insult in Scotland, meaning someone who is hollow. I got away with this for ages, until a fellow Scot overheard me. 'I know what "tube" means,' he laughed. 'But the police don't seem to.'

Occasionally the men in the cars and vans coming to work would stop, turn around and go home. This was seen as a huge victory and the crowd would erupt into cheers. At the end of the day we believed completely that if every single miner went on strike then we could win this fight. That was what we needed.

As the strike wore on so did the TV coverage. It was just enormous. But I never saw any of it because I was rushing home most evenings to do all the washing, ironing and cleaning that I'd missed out on during the day. I had no time for watching TV or seeing what was happening. I wasn't interested either.

Often political rallies were held nearby, with union officials and politicians arriving and saying their bit and then leaving. We had them all up here, including Scargill, but I never took time to listen. I wasn't interested. It was a black and white position for me. We were standing by the unions, wanted to keep our jobs and the pit open, and that was it. I was too busy to think or consider any further issues or the politics of it all.

Chapter Twenty

Working in the soup kitchen meant TV crews were especially interested in us, to get what they called 'human
interest' stories. We had crews from Germany, Russia,
France, everywhere. As soon as they turned up I used to
busy myself in the kitchen, along with Margaret, who
also hated them. Whenever one of the reporters asked
to speak to me they got a resounding: 'No!' I'd heard
most of the coverage was skewed against the miners and
I didn't want my words twisted. One interview I did
catch involved a reporter asking a mum standing with
her kids about how threatened she felt with all the fighting
on the picket lines, but she never got a chance to respond
properly.

I got really cross sometimes when the camera crews
turned up, shoving cameras in people's faces as they tried
to eat. Sometimes I just walked out completely when they
bugged me too much. Other times, when word got out

that a news crew was on its way down, we'd suddenly have an influx of new 'helpers' all wanting to get their faces on TV. Personally, I couldn't think of anything worse: I hate having my picture taken at the best of times, let alone when I'm working. Plus I didn't want to be part of this media 'portrayal' – or 'betrayal' as I saw it.

We were often shown as being greedy, or troublemakers, although we weren't fighting for pay rises or better conditions. We were fighting to save our livelihoods and communities.

One day a smart, highly groomed lady turned up with a serious-looking cameraman and a big microphone.

'Are you Cath?' she asked.

'Yes,' I said cautiously, eyeing her microphone.

She introduced herself, thrusting her hand out to be shaken.

I wiped my wet hands on my apron and gave it a limp shake on purpose.

'Yes?' I repeated.

'As one of the very few official female picketers, would you consider giving me an interview?' she said, flashing me a set of perfect teeth. 'It would make an incredible exclusive.'

'Nah, thank you. I'm not interested,' I said.

'But this is to get your point of view across,' she replied.

'No, you won't put mine across, just your own,' I retorted.

I turned to leave. Nearby, Sid, a young lad who was very active in the union, had been listening to our conversation. He piped up.

'I'll do it instead,' he said. 'I'm Sid.'

I rolled my eyes. He always fancied himself in front of an audience. I stood quietly by as I watched him being interviewed. As it started I had a cheeky idea of my own . . .

After five minutes, I drifted off back to work and an hour later the pair of them were still rabbiting, with Sid doing his best to look intelligent, bless him.

Afterwards the TV lady thanked everyone and melted away. Her hours of film were safely in her possession. She'd got what she wanted. Or so she thought.

Sid looked so pleased with himself. 'You can all see me on telly tonight,' he said, proudly. 'It's on at six o'clock.'

'Well done, Sid,' said one or two of the men.

'I don't think they will use it,' I grinned. 'You've wasted your breath, Sid.'

'Of course they'll use it,' insisted Sid. 'Why wouldn't they?'

'Because I pulled out the plug,' I laughed. 'Just before it started I spotted the jack plug and whipped it out. None of you noticed.'

The whole room erupted into laughter, but I made Sid a cup of tea to make up for it. It was nothing against him – I just didn't like the TV crews. I'd have loved to have seen the reporter's face when she got back to her studio and realised what had happened.

By the summer, the strike was starting to grind down morale. We had lots of support still, but everyone was feeling the pinch in their pockets. Things like holidays or 'normal' life for the kids were hard. Then someone donated some tents, which gave us the idea we could take a big group of children camping. So Doug and I and a few others took a group of fourteen kids to Stonehenge for a little holiday. Every day we took them on different activities, like going to the pictures, visiting castles, and of course exploring the ancient site itself. They loved it. It wasn't a holiday for us, mind – we were run ragged by the end of it – but it felt good to get the kids out.

For our own family, we managed to slip away for the week to Sutton-on-Sea, to stay at the site we always went to. As we arrived the site owner came to greet us and offered us a free pitch, seeing as we were strikers.

'No, thank you,' I said. 'It's very kind of you, but no.'

I didn't want charity, as it wasn't his fight. In the end my mum paid for it for us.

Back at school, the children were now eligible for free

school meals, as all the other striking parents' kids were. One afternoon Allan and Carrie came home with bees in their bonnets.

'Aw Mam, you wouldn't believe what they did,' Carrie complained. 'Mr Watson told us to sit in the classroom while we had our dinners.'

'You what?' I said. 'Why?'

'It was the same with all the striking dads' kids,' said Allan. 'They put us all in there.'

I felt my temper rise. There was no question I'd be taking an hour off the soup kitchen in the morning to find out what the blazes this teacher was playing at.

The next day, I went with the kids down to school. When I got there, I found a couple of the other mums from striking families were already there, all with faces as grim as mine.

'Where is Mr Watson?' we all asked.

He came out to see us.

'Yes?' he said, as bold as brass.

'Why are you segregating the striking kids?' I asked.

He half smirked as if he was baffled.

'I don't know what you're talking about, Mrs Black,' he said.

'Oh, come off it,' I said. 'All the kids have their dinners in the school hall – why aren't our lot?'

He tried to smile again.

'I don't know what you are talking about, really,' he insisted.

'Stop giving me this bullshit,' I said loudly. 'We're not daft and neither are our kids. You're picking on the striking families' children and we'll report you to the education authorities unless you pack it in.'

He sucked in his teeth. I'd rattled him, I could tell. The next day the kids were back in the school hall sitting with everyone else.

I knew life hadn't been easy for the kids. In the same way that scab families were sometimes picked on by strikers, it also happened the other way round.

Once Carrie came home, indignant as usual, upset about her treatment at the hands of the Boswells. She often played with their kids before the strike. Now it was less frequent, but she still went over there sometimes. Apparently everything was fine and they were all playing dollies in the garden, until Mr Boswell came home from work.

'He came home and snatched the doll I was playing with off me and said: "Tell your mum and dad to get back to work and then they can afford a doll like that."'

Carrie didn't stand for it and explained how she'd thrown her vanity case, where she kept all the knitted outfits I made for her dollies, at him.

'I said: "I don't need the doll anyway as my mam can make things." I don't know why he was so mean, Mam.'

I sighed. Poor Carrie didn't really understand what was happening. Not in any detail. But with her mother's tongue she knew how to stick up for herself.

Another scab family, the Carters, were up the road from our crescent and the kids often went to play with their kids as they had a big garden. Every time Carrie came home from there she told us how when Mr Carter got home from work, his kids were put into new shoes and given ice cream, purposefully it seemed, in front of the striking families' children.

'We can afford things like this,' Mr Carter told Carrie. 'Your dad can't.'

Angered again, Carrie knocked the top off his son's ice cream before she left.

'And don't start crying about it,' she cried. 'Your dad can afford another one, can't he?'

During the strike, Grandad still came down for his frequent visits. He wasn't well, but soldiered on. He always laid the money on my kitchen table for his keep during every visit and now we were on strike nothing changed. But he never gave us a penny extra.

I never talked openly to Grandad about what we were doing as it was unsaid between us that he didn't agree with our actions. I had to respect his ideals. Also I feared that if I ever did start a proper discussion with him about the strike we'd have a terrible row. So we just carried on with our routine as usual. I'd use his money to make his dinners and we'd sit and eat something else.

Thankfully the children ate separately to him anyway, which helped to avoid any awkwardness about Grandad having more to eat or a greater variety of food compared to them. They had their meals at school and in the soup kitchen and anything at home was eaten in the kitchen, whereas Grandad ate at a small table in the living room.

I always did his meals the way he liked, as he was very particular. He had to have a cup of tea at midday with a digestive biscuit and he liked his fish to be fresh and skinned and boned. But now I was so busy with the soup kitchen I didn't have time, so I had to buy him one already dressed. He gave a loud 'tut' when I served it but didn't say anything.

None of the kids had said anything about Grandad's food; they knew he wasn't well by now and in any case, most of the time they didn't notice it. But once, the youngest, Allan, piped up about the unfairness of it all.

'Why's Grandad getting fish when I am eating porridge?' he complained. Funnily enough Allan didn't even like fish and never had, but the lack of variety was getting to him.

'Grandad needs it because he's not very well,' I said, hushing him up. I didn't want the strike to cause a rift in our family so I thought it better not to make an issue of it.

This wasn't the only time the strike threatened to create trouble within our family. By now my Susan was nineteen and she'd met a boy who I suspected she was serious about. All the furtive phone calls and the dolled-up dates to see him made me suspect so. I always encouraged my girls to talk about their boyfriends. I used to tease them and ask: 'Have you kissed him yet?' Lorraine, quiet and unassuming as she was, hated such talk.

'Ew, Mam, you make me sick,' she'd say, rushing from the room. But Susan took it with the humour that was intended.

I insisted they bring their boyfriends to the house if they'd been on more than two dates. I wanted to get the measure of them. But little did I know that Susan was hiding her next one – the man she'd go on to marry.

Susan quietly sat down next to me one evening. 'Mam, I've met someone and I really like him,' she said softly.

'Oh aye?' I replied. 'Who is he?'

Instead of smiling, Susan's face fell. She looked up at me under her fringe, biting her lip. Something told me she knew I wouldn't approve, whoever he was.

'Who is he?' I repeated.

'Mam, he's a scab,' she said, staring at the floor.

I won't lie, her words made me feel a little winded. My wee girl falling for a scab was not something I'd ever envisaged happening. Susan's brown eyes, the same colour as Doug's, gazed at me intently, wanting to know my reaction.

I wanted to be angry. She knew scabs were scum in our house. But this was different. This was Susan. And my girl seemed to be in love.

'OK,' I sighed. 'OK. Who is he?'

She explained he was the son of a scab I'd served in the canteen. Phil also went off to work, getting driven by security across the picket line. He worked at Bevercotes pit and I'd often been picketing outside that one.

Then a thought occurred to me. I'd gone on the bus when it arrived, shouting at the workers and asking them to join our fight. But I'd not seen Phil. He was a big lad as well – a good 6'4".

'But Susan, I didn't see Phil on the bus,' I said. 'I often jumped onboard and he was never there.'

Susan sighed. 'Aw Mam, you didn't see him because he saw you first and he ducked behind the seats.'

I let out a hollow laugh. 'Well, he knows what he's doing is wrong then, doesn't he?' I said.

Then and there, for our Susan's sake, Doug and I vowed to leave the scab issue alone with Phil. After all, he was under pressure from his father to go to work, plus we didn't want to make his life a misery if he was making our daughter happy.

The same couldn't be said for his father, though. At

every opportunity he bumped into me, he couldn't help starting up some political debate, something I wasn't interested in having. He couldn't justify his actions to me or anyone else as far as I was concerned. And for the young couple's sake, we didn't want to go into it.

Lorraine, now seventeen herself, had also fallen for a young miner. Anthony was an apprentice. As such he wasn't coerced into striking as it was viewed as disruptive to his education. But he did end up coming off work too.

During the strike our minibus had never seen so much action. Originally bought for going on holiday with the kids, we never imagined that one day it'd be invaluable for running miners to and from pickets. How much our lives had changed within the space of a year! Doug didn't mind. He was happy to help in any way.

The police grew to recognise our van and decided to give it a 'number', so they logged our registration plate and blacklisted us.

One evening when we were driving the short journey to drop Grandad back with my Aunt Mary, we found ourselves constantly being flagged down by police and stopped about thirty times. As soon as we set off again and turned a corner, another copper would flag us down.

They were as rude and disrespectful as you like. I sat,

desperately biting my lip, as I knew Doug would be cross if I lost my temper. I kept watching for Grandad's reaction. I knew he didn't agree with us striking, although he never uttered a word about it. But this scenario, played out in front of him, would surely make him realise how terribly we strikers were being treated? As we slowly made our way north-west, Grandad just sat humming, staring out of the window as another police officer stopped us, but he acted like nothing was happening.

By the time we'd reached Aunt Mary's, I so badly wanted to ask him what he thought. Surely he could feel some sympathy now? But he didn't say a thing. Nothing. I gave him a hug goodbye although inside I felt crushed. I knew we'd risk an enormous argument if I breathed a word of how I felt inside. I was so close to him I just couldn't risk ever falling out like that.

Only once did he allude to the strike. He knew I wasn't spending much time with the kids, as I ran to and fro between the kitchen and the picket lines, and he said: 'Don't you think you should see to the kids? Never mind the outsiders?'

I just grunted, and left it. Grandad didn't see things the way I did. I was determined not to get cross.

Despite the fact I'd never been bothered by politics before, now it was affecting every single aspect of my life.

My Aunt Mary was the same. She vocally didn't approve.

She never sent us any money or food for help. She just acted like it wasn't happening and then occasionally would make a comment.

'I saw you on the TV last night,' she snapped once on the phone. Unbeknownst to me, I'd been caught on camera a few times, however much I tried to avoid them. And she didn't mean it in a positive way. To see her niece, someone she looked upon as a younger sister, demonstrating and 'carrying on' was not something that made her proud.

I barely saw my sister Mary during the strike either. The man she'd married, Robert, was also on strike, but I didn't get on with him any better over the years. He was a lazy man, and sat at home doing nothing during the strike. Mary had always been more of a thinker than a doer so she didn't do much either. She worried about me, though.

'Mum and I think you're doing too much,' she'd say, on a visit. 'You're so tired. You need to slow down a bit.'

True, I was. But I couldn't stop. There was just too much to do and I've always been one to live off my nerves.

As time wore on the unions grew increasingly vocal, taking the demonstrations to the heart of London. They laid on buses and a few times I went down to join them. The rallies were long and exhausting, but now I'd helped get this far I wanted to carry on.

This particular one had been organised after the very unfair treatment of a seventeen-year-old lad. He'd been leafleting cars with the sign 'Coal Not Dole', when police arrested him. He was taken to one police station and then quickly moved several times. This was a tactic used by police to make it difficult for the person arrested to get proper legal representation. By moving them so frequently, their solicitor couldn't work out which station they were held at and couldn't help.

The news of the latest injustice got out and so we went to London to protest.

I went down with Susan and we marched down to Parliament Square, near Big Ben, waving banners and shouting loudly. While we were there some fool advised us if the police came at you with a horse, all you had to do was simply crouch down, as the horses would stop.

At one point the crowd stopped in the middle of the road as the police ring-fenced us, making it very difficult to move. I could never understand why they did this as it caused so much panic in the crowd, and it seemed especially unnecessary as there wasn't any violence or trouble actually happening.

Susan and I were standing with our backs against a brick wall, about four people into the edge of the crowd as the horses came galloping towards us. We both let out little screams. The man next to Susan pulled her out of the way and she grabbed my arm and pulled me. As she did so, an enormous dark brown stallion leapt at me, his leg catching my shoulder.

'Ouuuch!' I screamed. I started gasping for air as we all collapsed in a heap by the wall. Holding my aching shoulder, I struggled to my feet, as I faced the policeman on the horse.

'Where do you want us to go?' I screamed. 'We're right up against a brick wall!'

And sometimes that's what it felt like we were talking to.

Doug joined me on several rallies, and we never knew where we'd end up staying for the night. Sometimes it was a house belonging to a solicitor, an author or another activist – anyone who supported the miners' strike and wanted to help. Sometimes, I got annoyed as it felt like every organisation that wanted attention was jumping on our bandwagon.

I have no problem with women's lib or gay or lesbian rights but I don't want it preached in my face, thank you. One evening, we ended up staying at some house in London – even then I wasn't sure of the exact location – and as we opened the door, I soon realised we were in the minority. A woman with a short haircut, dungarees and bovver boots opened the door.

'Come in,' she grinned to me, Ann and Margaret. 'You're more than welcome.'

We sat down on the sofa and more women dressed like her came in. They were very friendly to us, but Margaret raised an eyebrow and kept looking at me as if to say: 'Who *are* these people?'

Doug thought the whole thing was hilarious. He was the only man in the house. And after a few hours didn't he know it. Our hostess happily chatted about marches, campaigning and all sorts to me, Ann and Margaret, but every time Doug tried to get his two penn'th in, she cut him dead. Or if he did manage to say something, she'd talk down to him in response.

While she popped out to make more tea, Margaret whispered to me: 'She's a right man-hater!' I nodded. 'You can say that again.'

Doug wasn't laughing now; he was fuming!

As the strike wore on we got to meet all sorts, even people we had previously only seen on the telly. Arthur Scargill often walked among us all, shouting into his microphone, whipping the crowds into a frenzy. Some people thought if he turned up then a big announcement must be imminent. Others were shocked that he seemed nicer and more down-to-earth than his TV persona suggested. I wasn't bothered one way or another about meeting him. Neither was Doug, really. Scargill seemed polite, normal, and said 'Hello'. But he was a divisive character. Some of the men couldn't stand him and later even said he was harming the campaign.

Once I stood and watched him speak passionately about the mining industry and how we had to 'win the war' and I found myself thinking: 'You're just like another little Hitler.' He was so over the top, I wondered what good he was doing. But he was the man the union had voted in so he was the one they stood behind. And everything he said, one way or another, came true. The closure of the pits, the end of the mining industry – it all happened, just as he'd predicted. He may have spat fire and brimstone but he talked sense. You had to give him that.

After a while, the army was brought in. Incredibly, someone had the bright idea of dressing soldiers up as police officers, although I never understood the reasoning behind it. At that time, it felt we were entering a new era, a police state.

My stepdad Hugh first discovered this when he was watching TV with his friend one day. This friend had spotted his son, an army officer, in the crowd, dressed as a copper.

One day on the picket line, standing at the front as usual, I was almost nose to chest with one of the officers. But his jacket sleeves were up by his wrists and his trousers flapped way above his ankles. In short, he looked completely out of place wearing a police uniform that didn't fit.

'Hey,' I shouted. 'This man looks like his mummy has washed his uniform too hot in Daz!'

The men looked around and this poor lad started to go red with embarrassment. He was soon taken off duty, I noticed.

From being someone who had never previously been a political person, I'd found myself becoming known as an activist. But I didn't see it like that. I was just a mum and a miner's wife, who wanted to help keep her husband's job. We were just ordinary folk forced to do something extraordinary.

Then someone from Norwich contacted the Miners' Welfare to ask for our support in a local campaign of their own. To thank them for all their help supplying food parcels over the past several months, a group of us including Margaret, Ann and I all went along for the afternoon.

The aim was to lobby a council meeting about the planned closure of a local hospital. We agreed to go, not knowing what to expect, but thinking we could boost numbers if nothing else.

As we turned up, a few of the nurses were there, standing around quietly, not knowing quite what to do. In small groups we were allowed into the town hall, but as we waited outside it was all too quiet for my liking.

'You don't do it like this,' I said. 'You do it like *this*.'

And at the top of my lungs I started chanting: 'Maggie Out! Maggie Out!'

Soon everyone was at it and the meeting was cancelled due to the noise and the heckling.

As we left that day, a man came up to me and took off a red star he was wearing on his lapel. I knew it meant something to do with socialism but beyond that I hadn't a clue.

'I want to thank you and give you this,' he said. 'You deserve it.'

I accepted it politely. To be honest it meant nothing to me, and I just put it in my drawer back home. It's still there today, but I've kept it because it meant something to him.

A few weeks later we heard our protest had called the council meeting to a halt and the campaign had helped save the hospital.

Chapter Twenty-One

The winter was approaching and the strike really was biting deeply into every area of people's lives now. It was a harsh winter from November onwards and finding fuel, again, was a big worry for everyone.

We had coal central heating, but carried on using wood when we could find it. We could only heat up the house between the hours of 5 and 6 p.m. and that was it. We had two fires, one in the living room and one in the kitchen. We were freezing. The kids seemed to be quite resilient, as they were always running around playing, but we all wore lots of jumpers. Lorraine was the one to feel the cold the most.

Once I came home to find her huddled with her back right up against the fire in the kitchen.

'What are you doing, Lorraine?' I cried.

'Aw Mam, I am so, so cold,' she shuddered.

'Get yourself out of there, you're taking all the heat,' I said.

As she stood up I started laughing. She'd been so close to the fire she'd burned part of her trousers. 'You're like a real-life Cinders!' I laughed.

And so her nickname stuck; Lorraine was 'Cinders' for years afterwards.

Doug and I felt the cold down to our very bones. Sometimes I'd arrive home so exhausted, feeling so low, all I wanted in the world was a hot bath – the one thing I couldn't have. I'd go to bed shivering but I'd soon drop off. I was working so very hard, either picketing or in the soup kitchens, I was bone tired. Every morning we'd wake up and find ice on the inside of the windows and the water in the sink frozen solid.

As the end of the year approached, more and more TV crews started turning up on the doorsteps, trying to get an interview, asking if we were going to stop striking before Christmas. I'd always avoided the cameras, but a union man told me of a crew from Scandinavia who were looking for an ordinary family to film to show the world how hard things were, but also how normal we were too.

'What do you mean?' I asked the official. After all, the last thing I wanted to do was chat on camera.

'People think if you're on strike you live in squalor or

are right scruffs,' he said. 'This is to prove you're just a family living through terrible times.'

'Well, if they film inside our kitchen cupboards they could see that all right,' I laughed.

And so I agreed. A group of blonde-haired men turned up wielding a camera and a microphone so I let them in.

They asked us questions about our roles in the strike and then filmed in our kitchen. Just as I'd joked, they asked if I minded them filming my kitchen cupboards and we all stood in silence as we peered in. Inside was one lone tin of Spam and another of baked beans. It felt like a very long time since the cupboards were full. They also spotted the empty coal burner, swept and cleaned months ago.

Outside Allan was playing, hitting a spade on the frozen pond. The pond, along with the goldfish, we had in our garden had long been neglected as we were so busy rushing from soup kitchen to picket line, then back home to see to the kids. Nothing extra had been done in the house for months.

The crew turned their cameras on to Allan. I wondered what they were going to say and how they were going to portray us, but I'd never see the finished product anyway, so decided not to worry about it.

As we approached Christmas more miners started dribbling back to work. Some miners who'd wholeheartedly joined in every step of the way were almost in tears as they confessed they were returning. A couple of Doug's friends, Derek and Jackie, went back too. We were staggered.

'They feel they have to,' Doug said. 'Both of their wives have given ultimatums. If they don't go they are leaving them.'

We found it hard to condemn men like that. Those who had given body and soul to the campaign, but felt compelled at the eleventh hour to return. They'd suffered hugely but the cost was too great. At the same time there was no way Doug or I were going to cross that picket line. It just couldn't happen.

As we all struggled to keep warm again, spirits in the soup kitchen sagged. The only way of keeping it up was to try and joke your way through. I'd laugh and then laugh some more, and keep up the wisecracks until I got a smile out of one of the others.

We all got depressed at some point, though. It was impossible not to. Margaret's way was to take out her temper on the nearest person and Ann's way was to go very quiet.

One night in the crescent we all heard a terrible row going off in the Knightons' house. The strike had split that family straight down the middle: the son, Kevin, had become a strike manager for his colliery, whereas his dad

Chris was a scab. I was lying in bed when we heard voices screaming and shouting from their house.

'I will kill you,' screamed Kevin. 'Do you hear?'

We sat up in bed, listening. 'Gosh, Doug,' I said. 'It's all kicking off now.' We knew tensions must have been high. A scab and a striker living under the same roof was untenable. After a few more bangs, crashes and yells, Kevin slammed the door and stormed off into the crescent. The boil had been lanced. It would be a long time before they made up that barney.

More and more of the men started to trickle back to work. This was a tough one as we were all suffering. One miner I knew who'd supported the strike all the way through, along with his wife, suddenly announced his wife had gone back to Scotland with their three kids.

'Why?' I asked. They'd always seemed so happy together.

'Because I am on strike,' he said. 'And now I have to scab. She's making me a scab.'

My heart went out to him. What a terribly difficult position to be in. This poor fella ended up scabbing for nothing too, as his wife never returned from Scotland.

Sometimes I'd hear the wives talk about their husbands in such a terrible way in the soup kitchen I'd presume they'd been scabs too. Then I'd end up serving them soup in the kitchen and realise they were decent men, trying to fight to keep the mines open like the rest of us. It was painful seeing the strains placed on people's previously happy marriages.

A couple of the men had wives who worked all along, which we only discovered after months of serving them in the kitchen. They were entitled to the food parcels, same as everyone, because they were strikers, but it was for their consciences if they received extra help when they also had at least one family income. It wasn't my place to play God.

Many women had simply had enough. I think some of them used the strike as an excuse to end failing, unhappy marriages. Some I knew became 'women's libbers' and broke away from the home, on the pretext they were out campaigning for the mines and the like, but a couple had affairs. One ended up marrying a man who turned into a wife beater, so it didn't do her any good. I couldn't stand the women's libbers' attitude that women can do whatever men can. Common sense tells me they cannot. Not many women have the physical strength and stamina to work down a mine, for example, not at that depth with some of the drops they had to deal with. It was a man's work and no woman should go down there. I know some do in America, but I am sure they do a different job. Some work is for men only and women should leave well alone. Let them get on with it.

That New Year's Eve we didn't bother staying up to celebrate seeing in 1985. It was just too much. Both Doug and I fell into bed around 10 p.m., looking at each other and saying: 'I wonder what this year will bring.' I dreaded to think. Already the men in the soup kitchen were starting to whisper about 'losing the fight'.

It wasn't something I ever wanted to dwell on. I shut it out of my mind. We couldn't lose. We just couldn't. What would the alternative be? There wasn't one. But we knew it was looking worse as more people were going back to work and the unions were just not getting anywhere. A sense of despondency was setting in. We were working so hard, picketing, keeping the soup kitchen going, on top of our day-to-day lives. The thought it might not lead to anything was unthinkable.

So we closed our eyes to the New Year, and just hoped somehow we'd find the strength to see in whatever was going to happen next.

By the February, we'd been on strike for nearly a year and we still couldn't see an end to this. We carried on the fight, though, working hard at the soup kitchen and picket lines. Around this time Grace and I were at a rally and almost everyone saw us on the news, as the cameras had honed in on our faces.

I never saw it, as the six o'clock news was never on in my house, but people told me it hadn't escaped anyone's notice. And that included the management, so it seemed. A day or so later a letter landed on my doormat telling me in no uncertain terms that unless I went back to work I faced the sack.

'Good,' I said to Doug. 'I hope they do sack me.'

I only half meant it, as we needed the money more than ever, but then again the thought of going back to work with the scabs was untenable too.

I grabbed the letter, shoved it in a drawer and went off to the soup kitchen as usual. Later on, Grace arrived, looking incredibly sombre.

'What's wrong, Grace?' I asked.

Instead of grabbing her pinnie and cracking on, she sat down. Her arms folded around herself like a hug.

I pulled up a chair. 'What is it?' I said.

'I have to go back,' she whispered.

'Go back? Where?' I asked.

'To work,' she said, not looking me in the eye.

I gasped. 'Grace! Why?' I said. Although I knew why. I knew she had a mortgage and bills in her own name. The red letters were piled on her doormat. She faced eviction, the loss of her home and also her pension.

'I can't do this any longer,' she said sadly, finally looking at my face. 'It's different for you, Cath, you're married. You're younger than me and will get another job. If I don't go back to the canteen who knows when I'll work again?'

I nodded. My heart went out to her, it really did.

Neither of us could understand why we'd received letters

like this. We knew of other women who'd gone off on strike in Ollerton but they'd not been threatened with the sack. We wondered if it was because of our TV appearance. Maybe we'd caught the attention of management a little too much.

The next day, Grace didn't turn up at the soup kitchen. I knew she'd gone back to work. I also knew the reception she'd get from the scabbers who'd worked throughout the strike wouldn't be pleasant. I wondered how she'd get on.

As usual, there wasn't too much time to think about it, as the kitchen soon filled up. I got on with serving, but as I did so, word spread that Grace had gone back.

'What a traitor,' one man raged.

'A true scab,' another said.

I threw my washing-up cloth at their table. 'No, no,' I cried. 'Stop it. Grace did what she could. She tried her best. Yes, she is a scab now, but she gave everything to this strike and had to go back. Things were bad for her.'

The men fell silent and carried on supping on their spoons.

I wasn't going to have Grace badmouthed in my kitchen. Not after all she'd done.

Two days later I bumped into her. Her arm was in a cast and she looked terrible.

'My goodness, what's happened to you?' I asked. She told me how she'd returned to work to find everyone had turned against her. No one spoke to her all day and the atmosphere was awful.

I nodded. I imagined Betty was in her element, nasty piece of work that she was.

'I couldn't take it,' cried Grace.

'So what happened to your arm?' I asked.

Grace had gone out that night to have a few drinks to take her mind off her terrible day when she slipped and fell, breaking her wrist. It meant she was put on the sick.

I felt sorry for her. Grace's temperament meant she couldn't handle the abuse. She wasn't tough like me.

The anniversary of the strike was approaching and the NUM were trying to negotiate a return to work. The whisperings about the strike being over increased. People's tempers were flaring, and the stress in the soup kitchen was palpable. Behind closed doors, decisions about the pit and our future were being thrashed out. And it wasn't looking like the result we wanted. So many miners had gone back to work, or had been imprisoned for breaches of the peace or any other offence the police could get them on, or were simply sick of living in poverty. The morale was at rock-bottom. But still this was unthinkable.

Then on 3 March 1985, I was in the soup kitchen, washing up, when a miner ran inside.

'That's it,' he cried. 'That's it. We're going back to work on Monday.'

I stopped dead. All the clattering of the pots and pans stopped, the women fell silent, and the whole world seemed to pause on its axis.

I slowly turned around, away from the pots I was washing, and looked at the lad who came with the news.

'Say again?' I said.

'Monday,' he replied, sitting down. 'We're back on shift. It's over.'

I cannot possibly put into words the feeling of how crushed we were. Ann and Margaret came over to me, in tears.

'I can't believe it,' whispered Ann.

Margaret welled up, pressing her hand on her mouth. 'It can't be,' was all she said, over and over.

The atmosphere was terrible; we all felt sick to our stomachs. I felt my knees wobble as I sat myself down. My insides were churning. It was Wednesday and we were all back to work on Monday. Back to serving with the scabs. Like nothing, nothing in the past year had ever happened. I just couldn't believe it either.

I closed the soup kitchen and went home. Doug was already there. We stood in the hallway, holding on to each other for support. Then the tears came.

On his shoulder I wept, my rage and anger now overwhelming.

'How. Can. This. Happen?' I screamed. 'How?'

'I don't know, I don't know,' said Doug. We staggered into the kitchen, like two people with shellshock. Doug slumped by the table, a broken man. Clutching his hand, I felt tears of bitterness and exhaustion dripping off my chin.

'What has it all been for?' I sobbed. 'What was the point?'

Our kitchen was freezing. The coal fire was empty. The cupboards were still bare of any food. Time had stood still as we'd fought for our jobs and our lives.

'We've lost money,' I raged. 'All the unpaid hours in the soup kitchen. Our kids have gone without. All for what? *What?*'

Doug sniffed, wiping away tears. I had never seen him cry before.

'We had to do what we did, Cath,' he said. 'Remember that.'

And I did. We believed in our principles and – despite the hardship, the loss of money, the hunger and the struggle – we'd stood by them, which is more than can be said of the scabs. And if we had stood together, every single one of us, then we'd have had a fighting chance of keeping those pits open. I knew who to blame for all this.

Maggie and the scabs. They were the ones who'd closed our mines. Not us.

That night we watched the news and it was full of the facts and figures about the 'cost of the strike'. We heard how the NUM had voted and won only by a tiny margin to return to work without any new agreement with the management, but they did so to save the union. In the conference that ended the strike, Kent apparently voted to carry it on but no one else did. Several other counties, including Nottingham, didn't even bother showing up. Basically everyone had lost hope.

Our guts churning, we left dinner uneaten that night and went up to our beds with hearts as heavy as stone. It felt like a terrible ache inside and nothing would alleviate it. I lay awake for a while, staring at the ceiling and thinking, always thinking of the injustice, the fall-out and how I now had to face the challenge of working with the canteen scabs. But then I quietened my mind with another thought. We'd tried and we'd failed, yes. But at least we'd tried . . .

Chapter Twenty-Two

A day or two later we saw on the news the Yorkshire miners going back. With flags waving and colliery bands playing, they marched through the gates triumphantly. I didn't know how to feel about it. I could see they wanted to go back with their heads held high, as we were going to. But I fought tears watching it.

I popped outside to get some fresh air, and knocked on Margaret's door.

'Stick the kettle on,' I said. Ann was already there at her kitchen table.

We all just sat there, looking at each other. We didn't need to say anything, as we all knew exactly how each other felt.

Ann shook her head. 'You know, it's going to be hard going back to being a mam, staying at home.'

Margaret, who'd never worked before the soup kitchen, nodded. 'Getting out and meeting all those people and being busy from morning till night. What will I do with myself now? I never knew I had it in me to help so much.'

'Well, I know what's in store for me,' I said, cradling my tea. 'Back to working for the scabs.'

Before any of this, we had to set to work for one last time, this time to close down the soup kitchen. We had to leave it in exactly the same condition as we had found it. We took all the pots and donated them to local charities. Then we started putting all the tables and chairs away. Downstairs we had to tackle the enormous pile of donated clothes. Bagging them up, we took them to charity shops or out to people who needed them. We were all almost silent during this. The reality of losing the fight was sinking in as each hour went by.

As we packed up the tea urn, I felt myself running my hand over its smooth edges. It had served us so well, helping us fill so many hungry bellies and giving people a bit of hope when we had none.

Tears in our eyes, we had a last look around, to make sure everything was clean and just so.

'C'mon then,' I said to Ann and Margaret, who both had their tissues out. 'We did a good job.'

To make matters even worse, on Sunday night I found out I'd been put on the afternoon shift in the canteen. The one Betty knew I hated, as it was such a late finish.

'That nasty git,' I said to Doug.

Doug went back in the morning to work on the

telephone exchange, so after packing the kids off to school, I was left wandering round my house, feeling like a lost soul. I didn't want to go back, not a bone in my body did. But now I had to and I had to do it with pride.

I got on the coal bus for the first time in a year. As I hopped on, the driver smiled at me. 'Have you forgotten what this looks like?' he laughed.

'Your comment is not even worth an answer,' I shot back.

I sat at the back in silence, as the bus wound its way to the colliery. All the camps and picket posters and banners had been taken down. It was as if none of the struggle had ever happened.

I walked up to the canteen door, hearing the voices of Barbara and Pauline inside. I drew the deepest breath I could, opened the door and walked in.

The pair of them stopped talking and stared at me. Both giggled loudly, exchanging glances.

Completely ignoring them, I pulled on my overalls and went and stood behind the counter, ready for the men to come in. All day long, no one said a word to me. And it wasn't just the women who were determined to give me a hard time. Some of the men refused to be served by me. I could see in their faces as they approached who was going to make a point, so immediately I looked to the next one. Eventually the queue was so long for those waiting for Pauline, they gave up and let me serve them.

For the entire week no one said a single solitary word to me. You could have cut the atmosphere with a knife and served it up with the chips. But I just stuck it out. Every break time, when we had to sit together, I simply pulled out a book I'd brought and buried my nose in it. After a few days of doing this, I actually felt rather amused. As I sat quietly reading I could tell the other four were struggling to make conversation. Then I realised they felt more uncomfortable than I did!

Despite their silences, though, if Betty wanted me to know something she'd speak loudly to one of the others.

'I miss having the policemen in here,' she said loudly. 'We served so many of them during the strike. They didn't pay for a bean either. They were so helpful.'

I glared at her. Nasty woman. And to discover that they gave free food to the police made me sick. But then again the Coal Board would be happy about it. The police were doing a good job for them, making sure their men could get to work, carrying on earning the money while the pits stayed open. Traitors.

After a few weeks of being in Coventry, I got a message to go and see the management.

'Here we go,' I thought.

I went and stood in Mr Crowhurst's office. He looked at me seriously from behind his desk.

'I need to speak with you,' he said.

'Well, here I am,' I replied.

'It's about the canteen. The manager is sick of the atmosphere, as are all the ladies.'

'Yes?' I said, staring at him. I was wondering what on earth he expected me to do.

'No one is talking,' he said. 'You must talk.'

'I am here to work, Mr Crowhurst,' I said. 'Not talk. You can sack me if you like for not talking.'

'Er, so I want you to come in and start saying hello to everyone,' he suggested.

'Right,' I said. 'Will do.'

After leaving the office, I took aside Joan, the manageress who'd taken over from Mary before the strike.

'When I come in,' I said, 'I will walk through that door and when you're in your office I'll look in and I'll say: "Hello, Joan." And then I'll get on to my work,' I said, clearly.

She looked at me, completely baffled. 'Yes, yes, OK,' she agreed, embarrassed, and off she shot.

Just a couple of weeks later, a highly regarded union man was sacked for putting up a poster telling folk when the next NUM meeting was. We had a meeting at lunchtime and after a show of hands, voted to strike for one day.

We were incensed the management felt they could bully us like this. So after just a couple of weeks back at work, I walked out again for twenty-four hours.

That morning, I stood on the picket line near the canteen, finding myself shouting 'Scab' once again. Then the next day I was back at work. I had no idea what reaction I could expect. After all, the feelings had barely thawed anyway.

Once again I made sure my shoulders were square and my head held high, before opening the door after a deep breath. To my amazement, Pauline and Barbara looked up from what they were doing and both said, 'Hello!'

I half smiled, and said a cautious 'Hi' back. Then I got my head down and into my work.

As we waited for the men to arrive, Pauline started making small talk. 'So, you doing anything at the weekend?' she said.

I looked at her. Whatever had brought this on? 'I don't know, Pauline, what are you doing?' I asked.

She nattered on about picnics or some such nonsense. I wasn't really listening. The fact she was talking to me at all was just unreal. By the end of the day, as they all cried: 'Bye, Cathy!' I took off my pinnie and went home feeling more baffled than ever. Then the penny dropped. Maybe they actually admired me for my principles. After all, they had none of their own. And it was hardly surprising that they couldn't ride out the bad atmosphere, given their spinelessness.

The next day the management sent for me again. 'Oh

God, here we go again,' I thought. I truly expected to be sacked now. My mind was racing with thoughts of what to say, what my parting shot would be . . .

Another deep breath. I walked in, hoping to look as bold as brass.

'You sent for me?' I said.

'Hello,' said Mr Crowhurst. 'Sit down.'

He scribbled a bit on some papers as I waited. His office clock was ticking loudly. The noise of his pen scrawling on the paper seemed to make my skin itch. I just wanted him to hurry up and get on with it. If I was going to be sacked at least I could get home in time to put the kids' tea on.

'Right,' he said, finally looking up. 'Cathy.'

'Yes, Mr Crowhurst,' I sighed.

'How do you feel about taking on the cook's job?'

I opened my mouth to speak but momentarily nothing came out. What on earth was he on about? I was all prepared to be booted out, not asked to step up to cook!

'We need someone to fill in and I know how good you are with soup,' he smiled.

I fidgeted on my chair, trying to gather my thoughts.

'Yes,' I said. 'OK. It means I get to do the early shifts and those suit me just fine. So go on then.'

I left the room, almost wanting to laugh. That was a turn-up for the books.

That night, on the sofa next to Doug, I snuggled up to him. It was a rare moment when the kids were in bed, the telly was on quiet and it was just the two of us.

His job was going well in the telephone exchange, and he enjoyed it.

'In a funny way, though, I miss being underground,' he said, 'with all the miners. Despite the muck and bullets, you don't have as much of a laugh sat behind a desk.'

He patted my hand.

'I am glad we're all back to normal though, Cathy,' he said. 'We survived it.'

I leaned my head against his shoulder. Neither of us knew what the future of the pit held. The mining industry had been irreversibly rocked. Mines were still closing all around us. Our jobs and everything we stood for were at risk of closure. We'd tried to save it and now it felt like it was in the lap of the gods what would happen next. Who'd have thought we'd end up in such a melee when Doug first signed up? The strike would go down in the pages of history and somehow my ordinary little family had been caught up in a few chapters. But right here, right now, we tried to leave our pit worries where they belonged – thousands of feet below us. We had enough coal in the fire to keep us warm and for that we were truly thankful.

Epilogue

A year after the strike ended, Doug came into the canteen. 'They've told me they no longer have a job on the surface for any of the former strikers . . .' he began.

I was stunned, but not surprised. The managers were always looking for ways to punish the strikers. Now he'd turned up for work in the morning to be suddenly told his job no longer existed. We both knew Doug couldn't go back underground. It meant constant risk of injuries to his back, and his own GP had said it would be a death wish to go back. By taking away the telephone exchange job Doug was forced to accept early retirement on the grounds of sickness, aged forty.

'In that case, I am finished here too,' I said, firmly. If Doug went on the sick, something he had no option but to do, I would lose most of my pay.

That day I handed in my notice.

Two days later, Mr Crowhurst, my boss, came to see me. 'I hear you're leaving, Cathy,' he said.

I laughed. 'You can raise a flag now, can't you, Mr Crowhurst? Although believe me the one I am raising on my last day will be higher!'

His face darkened. 'No need to be like that, you cheeky madam,' he snapped.

'Isn't there?' I replied.

He gave me the filthiest of looks and stalked off. In his eyes I was a striker, 'one of them', in the same way as I saw him as the personification of the bad side of management. The following day he came to my till.

'Coffee,' he barked, slamming some coins down on the counter.

This was an opportunity too good to resist. As he turned to chat to his colleague, I sank to my knees under the counter. Quick as lightning I filled a polystyrene cup with gravy salts, added a dash of water and mixed it.

Handing Mr Crowhurst his 'coffee' I gave him the sweetest of smiles.

Without so much as a thank you, he took it and sloped off to sit with the other bosses.

I watched intently as he blew the top of the drink and then took a sip. Quickly looking away, I caught him wiping his lip and half choking. He glanced at me, and then put the drink down. He never dared say a word to me.

I had to go out the back to wipe away my tears of laughter. Yes, it was a little childish, but in my eyes he deserved every mouthful.

On my last day, I said a polite goodbye to all the girls and grabbed my coat. I couldn't be so two-faced as to appear that sorry. Although I suspected they'd found some sort of respect for me in the end, I wasn't going to miss them and I dare say the feeling was mutual. We'd all been through too much in the strike for there to be any love lost between us.

Pulling my bag over my shoulder, I walked past the girls to say a final 'Cheerio' when I realised they'd all gathered together.

Betty was holding a wrapped box with a bow. Barbara was holding a bouquet.

'Right, I'm off . . .' I started, unable to believe it was anything to do with me. But Betty stepped forward.

'Before you go, Cath,' said Betty, 'this is from everyone in the canteen.'

I could hardly believe my ears. I sank down on to one of the tables, as the girls all gathered around.

'Wow,' I spluttered. 'Wasn't expecting this, I must say.'

I unwrapped the box to find a brass kettle. It was a thoughtful present, as they knew I collected brass nick-nacks.

331

Catherine Paton Black

Suddenly I missed Grace. I thought of her and the way they'd treated her when she'd left.

'Thank you,' I said quietly. 'Although I remember you never got Grace anything.'

'That's because she came back,' said Betty. 'She never stuck to her principles. We've not always agreed with yours, Cath. But we admire how you have them.'

I blinked away a tear. Even now I didn't feel comfortable enough to let them see me cry.

'Thank you again,' I said, putting the box in my bag. 'Take care of yourselves.'

Without a backward glance, I walked out to the minibus.

Losing our jobs wasn't the only fallout from the strike. Doug got a last payment from the Coal Board, the princely sum of £180.60, which we needed to try and settle our mounting bills and mortgage payments. After a year of no money, we had debts. We took it straight to our bank, TSB, to ask for the £80 immediately just to tax our minibus.

The cashier behind the counter shook her head when she spotted the Coal Board signature.

'It's our policy not to cash cheques so fast,' she said. 'Not for you.'

Doug stared at her in disbelief. 'I want to see the manager.'

He was equally rude. We'd heard TSB were not very

sympathetic to striking miners and this seemed all the proof we needed. We'd also heard NatWest were more supportive so we closed our accounts and took our cheque there, where they cashed it immediately. It amazed me how the political fall-out of industrial action had even filtered down to the high street banks.

The rest of the money went into paying the arrears on our mortgage. The relief of paying it again was immense. Many other families were not so lucky. I ran into a few sad cases at the Miners' HQ. Grown men were crying as they couldn't keep up with repayments and faced losing the family home. One family I knew cut their losses and sold their belongings and moved with their kids into a tiny caravan to try and get themselves back into the black. Some folk never recovered from that year of austerity.

But financial hardships were just part of the communities' struggles. The deep divisions between strikers and scabs, formerly good neighbours, didn't evaporate overnight.

Bevercotes was still open, but its future lay in doubt. Scabs blamed the strikers and vice versa. No one knew when or if the axe would fall.

Neither Ann, Margaret nor I had anything to do with Jackie and Linda, our two closest scab neighbours. Shortly afterwards both their marriages broke down, and they moved anyway. The local divorce rate shot up across the board during the post-strike years. Some women had found their own 'place' in society and learned new skills outside the home during the strike. They weren't happy to go back to being merely wives after finding a voice in the campaign. Some of them retrained and started whole new careers. Some used the excuse to end marriages they'd felt trapped in long before the strike. However, I noted that many of the wives who'd stood by their men during the strike had the marriages that lasted.

For some though, divisions were such that some families just couldn't move past them. Even my own didn't escape.

In September 1986, Susan came to me, looking sad and on the verge of tears. She'd been seeing her boyfriend Phil for a couple of years now, and I knew they were close. He seemed like a nice-enough lad. But I never imagined what she was about to say.

'Mam, I'm sorry,' she sobbed. 'I've just married Phil.'

I suspected something was up. She'd been on the phone and having lots of hushed conversations for weeks. Now she was confessing she'd got married to him in a quick registry office do without anyone there. It felt like a blow to my guts to know I'd missed my eldest daughter's wedding. It wasn't right.

'Oh Susan,' I sighed. She came and gave me a cuddle.

'We had to, Mam,' she whispered. 'It would've been too much for us.'

I knew she was right. Phil's scabbing family was dead against us for our support for the strike. A proper wedding with all the families together could only have ended in disaster. There was no way round it. Susan had done the right thing, but the pain of missing out on her big day stung. Somehow the grip of this terrible strike had reached right into the heart of our family.

'I'll not hold it against you,' I soothed.

After Doug 'retired', we talked about what to do next and luckily we managed to find a job running a sweet and paper shop in Mablethorpe, so we moved there. This was hard work of a different kind, with long hours and low pay. But it was a job and for that we were grateful.

One by one we heard how our neighbours fared after the strike ended. For everyone life would never be the same.

Margaret's Billy went back to work in the mine post-strike, and tried to carry on as normal. But he said the morale was very low and it never fully recovered. He stayed until Bevercotes itself fell under the government's axe in 1993. Afterwards, Billy did what many miners did. He found himself a job – any job – just to make ends meet. He became a care worker.

Time and again I heard stories of burly miners turning their strong hands to 'caring' roles in old people's homes or with the disabled. Jobs they probably never saw themselves doing or were at all suited to, but that was all that was left. Even though it paid peanuts.

Sean was another casualty. He and Esther carried on living in the crescent, and he became a caretaker in the local school after the closure. Another promising young man's career snuffed out.

Meanwhile Ann's Pete retired and they got a pensioner's bungalow just before the pit closed.

A few times, I bumped into former miners, some of them scabs, doing menial jobs like picking up litter in the streets or clearing up the graveyard.

I wondered to myself: 'Do you regret not joining in with the strike now?'

I didn't dare ask, but I still wondered.

As well as the loss of the pit, I faced a spate of losses of loved ones as the generation before me entered its twilight years. I said goodbye to my lovely Grandad in August 1985. He finally succumbed to cancer just before I left the canteen. Even then, Betty wouldn't give me compassionate leave to go and be by his side, so I took it as unpaid holiday. I only took his tobacco pouch when I cleared out his house. I didn't need anything else. The smell alone was enough to evoke strong memories of him. The rest are locked away in my heart.

Mum's heart finished her off suddenly in the end, bless her. Hugh woke up to find her dead in bed, on 16 May, Lorraine's birthday, in 1994. It was a terrible shock for us all. Hugh was devastated. He'd been devoted to Mum and his own health worsened afterwards. After a forty-year career in the mines he struggled with his breathing. Admitted to hospital with angina, tests revealed scar tissue that doctors said showed he'd had a heart attack twenty years previously. Hugh swears he remembers suffering terrible chest pains in the mine one shift. In all likelihood he'd suffered an attack on the coalface.

Over the years Hugh had been examined by many Coal Board doctors who all declared his chest completely clear. But he never believed them.

'Cath, I want you to do an autopsy when I'm dead,' he begged me. 'I want it proven it was the mine that's killing me. You can have the compensation after I'm gone.'

I shook my head. 'No, Hugh,' I said gently. 'That's not the kind of money I want. And it'll be no use to you either then.'

Hugh died in his seventies, in 1999, five years after Mum.

My sister Mary died in her fifties around this time. It was cancer. I sat by her bedside morning and night. In those last few days we'd grown closer than any sisters could ever be.

All she wanted was to have me there. The day before she passed on, she pulled me close.

'Whisper,' she kept saying. 'Whisper.'

I couldn't make head nor tail what it was she wanted. 'What do you want to whisper about, Mary?' I kept asking. Then it occurred to me. She'd always loved chocolate. Although she'd barely eaten for days, I wondered if this was something I could do for her.

'Do you want a Wispa bar?' I asked. 'I can get you one!'

But she shook her head and smiled. The next day, she pulled me close again and repeated the same request.

'Whisper,' she muttered.

This time, I bent down so I could hear better, putting my cheek next to hers. As I did so she turned her face and kissed me gently.

Mary died a few hours later. It wasn't a whisper she wanted, it was a last kiss.

Shortly after Susan married, Lorraine married her miner boyfriend, Anthony. Both had three children in the end and both divorced. Susan remarried and had another child. She works with disabled kids while Lorraine runs a hot food stall by herself. Carrie is a stay-at-home mum, also married twice. Allan lives with his girlfriend and decided marriage wasn't for him.

I have twelve grandchildren now and I can honestly

say they are the apples of our eyes. Every step of the way I encourage their schooling and I hope they will all go off to college or university. Doug and I have talked to them about the mine, about our struggles and hardships. We want a better life for all of them.

I still speak to my ex-son-in-law Anthony and he works at Wellbeck mine, one of the few left, as a ventilation officer. He's been in the pit since school, and like my Doug's father, he doesn't want his son Alex to follow in his footsteps. Alex has just started at university, much to our pride.

As you get older you expect to lose people of the generation before you and maybe your contemporaries. But never did I expect to experience what happened next.

Having discovered narrow boating a few years earlier I was recovering after my latest bout of heart problems on a little holiday with Doug. Gazing from our deck chairs on the roof, a slight breeze on our faces, I was contemplating whether to make a pot of tea and Doug was doing some DIY on the boat, when we got a phone call.

It was Douglas's girlfriend. Our Douglas had been living with her for a while after getting a good job working with computers. He'd grown into a fine man, hard-working if a little sensitive. Doug took the call and the look on his face as he came to see me was something I will never forget.

The light from those chocolate-brown eyes had gone and had been replaced by a depth of anguish I'd never seen before.

'Oh God, what's happened?' I began.

Doug took my hands, barely able to contain the sobs rising from his chest. 'Our Douglas. He's dead.'

Like automatons we raced to the hospital, to find our son, our lovely boy, always full of beans, who once dreamed of being a miner, who loved his animals and was always the first one to lend a hand, dead on a mortuary slab. He'd hanged himself.

Our family was never to be the same. When someone commits suicide you are left with so many questions but never any answers. Never any direction. We all drifted from shock to despair to disbelief like leaves in a whirl-wind. One small consolation was the doctor giving us the option to allow his organs to be donated.

'Would you mind giving consent?' a doctor asked.

Without hesitation both Doug and I said a resounding: 'Yes.'

So my boy's organs were taken and we hoped they'd be put to good use.

In desperation, I looked back over every conversation I'd had with my boy, to find out if there was any inkling of why he'd chosen this path. Maybe it was because life hadn't worked out the way he wanted. I know he wanted children and a family, something he'd longed for over many years and watched his sisters achieve. But that happiness always eluded him. Maybe it was just because he'd always been the sensitive kind and too sensitive for this world. I didn't know and now I never will.

Shortly afterwards I was out to pick something up from the shop when Grace spotted me. Unlike so many others who turned their heads, unable to know what to say, she hurried across the road to reach me.

She looked deep into my eyes, and for a split second I saw nothing but a mother's grief to reflect my own. In that moment we were just two mothers who'd lost their sons, trying to carry on, trying to make sense of it all.

'I know what happened,' she said quietly. 'And if you ever need me, Cathy, I am here for you.'

Grace had blamed the mine for claiming her son. When he lost his job he lost his mind. I still didn't know what had driven Douglas to his death. All I know was during his very quick birth I'd said afterwards to the midwife: 'He's brought himself into this world.' And now I tell folk: 'He's taken himself out of it, too.'

Around this time the hospital donation unit got in touch with us and told us Douglas's heart valves had been used to save the lives of two women with heart problems. This brought us small comfort. It was a tiny shard of light in an otherwise very bleak, dark period.

'That's my boy,' I thought. 'Always helping someone else.'

Today our family is still healing. I've learned to live with the pain – although as any mother can imagine, it will never go away. What I can say is that the mining community, the one lost to the cuts and the closures, still has an underbelly, a core of folk who are still there, and they've been as big a support as ever. Sometimes it takes me two hours to get to the local shop and back as I spy neighbours and friends from yesteryear, still here, still wanting a natter. I see wives I used to share baking tips with, whose children are all grown up now and bringing their own kids for visits. I pass former miners on their disability scooters, oxygen tanks on their backs to help their soot-filled lungs keep going. My immediate neighbour is an eighty-five-year-old who lost her husband in a mining accident years ago, but she never talks about pit life with anything other than pride.

Gradually though, everyone is slowing down and our friends' long hard lives are ending. Sometimes when we visit the shops we realise we haven't seen so-and-so for a while, so we ask around to find out what they're up to. Sadly, it often means they've gone into hospital or passed away. Only the other day we joked about how we only see some folk at funerals these days!

Our memories are never far away, though. The recent tragedies hitting the news brought them all back. The four men who died in a flooded colliery in South Wales and the man who died in the rock fall at Kellingley colliery in North Yorkshire within a fortnight of each other last summer were heartbreaking to hear about. Doug said those sorts of accidents wouldn't have happened in his day. Along with the unions, safety standards have gone out of the window.

Although there are far fewer working mines today, coal still supplies about one third of the heat and energy we use. Much of it is imported – something that still staggers us. Now UK Coal is the biggest producer of coal in the country. They have just four deep mines and three surface ones left, but with rising importing costs they're looking to maybe open more. How incredible would that be? But we know there is plenty of the black stuff down there, so I believe it's only a matter of time. Some people estimate the Tory government spent £12 billion of the nation's money on trying to defeat the NUM. Sometimes we still wonder what that was for.

The colliery fell silent nearly twenty years ago now and the Bevercotes site is a nature reserve managed by the Forestry Commission. It's known as Bevercotes Pit Wood.

Apparently it's rarely visited by the public as it's not well signposted, but it attracts all kinds of birds and wildlife now. Someone told me it's a great place to spot dragonflies! I don't go up there any more as I can't get around like I used to. But sometimes we drive past and in the distance you can see birds circling over it and bluebells in the spring. The industrial side may have fallen silent but it will never be forgotten. Not by me, Doug, nor any of the villagers. Echoes of its legacy live on. We'll bear both the scars and the memories forever.